Library of
Davidson College

The Barrow Family
and the Barataria and
Lafourche Canal

Thomas A. Becnel

The Barrow Family and the Barataria and Lafourche Canal

The Transportation Revolution in Louisiana, 1829–1925

LOUISIANA STATE UNIVERSITY PRESS   *Baton Rouge and London*

Copyright © 1989 by Louisiana State University Press
All rights reserved
Manufactured in the United States of America
First printing
98 97 96 95 94 93 92 91 90 89   5 4 3 2 1
   Designer: Patricia Douglas Crowder
   Typeface: Linotron 202 Aster
   Typesetter: The Composing Room of Michigan, Inc.
   Printer: Thomson-Shore, Inc.
   Binder: John H. Dekker & Sons, Inc.

LIBRARY OF CONGRESS CATALOGING-IN-PUBLICATION DATA

Becnel, Thomas, 1934–
    The Barrow family and the Barataria and Lafourche Canal : the transportation revolution in Louisiana, 1829–1925 / Thomas A. Becnel.
        p.   cm.
    Bibliography: p.
    Includes index.
    ISBN 0-8071-1437-5 (alk. paper)
    1. Barataria and Lafourche Canal (La.)—History.   2. Barrow family.   I. Title.
HE396.B28B43   1989
386'.48'0976338—dc19   88-34070
                                                                    CIP

All photographs except that of the Company Canal locks ruins (1978) are in the Robert Ruffin Barrow, Jr., Papers and are reproduced here with the kind permission of the Division of Archives, Nicholls State University Library, Thibodaux, Louisiana.

The paper in this book meets the guidelines for permanence and durability of the Committee on Production Guidelines for Book Longevity of the Council on Library Resources. ∞

for Dixie

Contents

Chronology xi

Prologue 1
Part I Robert Ruffin Barrow and the B and L, 1829 to 1875
  1. Early Settlers in Bayou Country 11
  2. The Barataria and Lafourche Canal 41
  3. The B and L No. 2 Through the Civil War and
     Reconstruction 66
*Part II Robert Ruffin Barrow, Jr., and the B and L No. 2,
       1875 to 1925*
  4. Robert Barrow, Jr.: Carrying on the Family Tradition 101
  5. Uncle Sam Buys the Company Canal 132
  6. The End of the Barrow Era 160
  Epilogue: The Intracoastal Canal System Today 182

Bibliographical Essay 190
Index 197

Illustrations

Following page 98

Ruins of the Company Canal locks in Lockport, 1978
Robert Barrow's home at Residence plantation
Robert Barrow, Jr., and family
Robert Barrow, Jr.'s home in New Orleans
Robert Barrow, Jr.'s motor launch
The *Ohio* in the Company Canal
Unloading sugarcane on the Company Canal
Unloading produce on the Company Canal
The *Phyllis* entering Bayou Terrebonne
The *Houma* in the Company Canal, 1913
Entering the Company Canal at Lockport
Repair work on the Company Canal locks
The Company Canal locks at Westwego, 1918

Maps

Louisiana's Sugar Country: The Mississippi to Bayou Teche 21

Early Canals: New Orleans to Barataria Bay and Attakapas District 29

The Barataria and Lafourche Canal 44

Chronology

1798	Robert Ruffin Barrow is born in Halifax County, North Carolina.
1820	The Barrows move to Louisiana.
1828	Robert Barrow comes to Terrebonne.
1829	The Barataria and Lafourche Canal Company (B & L) and the Lafourche and Terrebonne Navigation Company are chartered.
1833	The B & L receives tax-exempt status. William Field gives land in Lockport to the B & L.
1850	The B & L receives a lucrative state contract. Robert Barrow marries Volumnia Washington Hunley.
1853	The locks at Lockport are completed.
1854	Roberta Barrow is born.
1858	The state of Louisiana ends ties with the B & L. Robert Ruffin Barrow, Jr., is born.
1859	Robert Barrow becomes the sole owner of the B & L No. 2.
1860	Robert Barrow owns more than seven hundred slaves and many plantations.
1861	Robert Barrow writes a tract opposing secession.
1862	Robert Barrow buys canal property just as Yankee forces reach New Orleans.
1866	Volumnia Barrow files for legal separation.

1867 or 1868	Bayou Plaquemine is dammed.
1868	Volumnia Barrow dies, and Robert Barrow is appointed executor of the estate and guardian of the children.
1871	The Barrow children run away from their father. Roberta Barrow marries William J. Slatter. Robert Barrow leases the B & L No. 2 to the Louisiana Canal and Land Improvement Company.
1873	Robert Barrow is declared destitute.
1875	Robert Jr. is emancipated from his father and placed in possession of one-half of his mother's estate. Robert Barrow dies of cholera.
1876	The Barrow children acquire their inheritance; Robert Jr. becomes executor of his father's estate.
1880	Robert Jr. marries Jennie L. Tennent.
1881	The first of the six Barrow children is born.
1887	Robert Jr. becomes the owner of the B & L No. 2.
1890	Robert Jr. moves to New Orleans.
1903	Bayou Lafourche is dammed. The B & L makes money, as does Myrtle Grove plantation. Robert Jr. tries to sell the B & L No. 2.
1909	The Plaquemine locks open.
1910	Plans for an intracoastal canal are discussed at a national convention in New Orleans.
1914	Agriculture thrives during World War I.
1919	Manager Henry Clay Duplantis of Myrtle Grove dies.
1921	Robert Jr. negotiates with the U.S. Corps of Engineers for the sale of the B & L No. 2.
1922	The sugar industry suffers economic disaster.
1924	The U.S. government buys the Harvey Canal for $500,000.
1925	The U.S. government buys the B & L No. 2 for $84,000. Stella Leathers enters Robert Jr.'s life. Jennie Barrow becomes president of R. R. Barrow, Inc. Robert Jr. and Jennie are legally separated. Robert Jr. writes a confusing will.
1926	Robert R. Barrow, Jr., dies.

The Barrow Family
and the Barataria and
Lafourche Canal

Prologue: Louisiana and the Transportation Revolution

Louisiana's colonial population stayed close to the numerous streams that traversed the region. Giant swamps and huge virgin forests of cypress, oak, and other hardwoods covered the land. The early white settlers, like the Indians who inhabited the area before Europeans arrived, lived close to nature, hunting, fishing, trapping, and farming. Epidemics, storms, floods, and periodic Indian attacks kept the population from growing rapidly.

Virtually all the early settlements fronted streams that provided transportation and many of the resources on which the people depended. Additionally, in coastal south Louisiana the high land invariably lay along the banks of alluvial streams. Even before the French established their capital on the Mississippi at New Orleans, they sent young Louis Juchereau de Saint-Denis to a strategic spot on the Red River to build a fort at Natchitoches. Other settlements—all along streams—followed in short order: Baton Rouge, Natchez, Manchac, and Arkansas.

The French sent slaves to clear the land and till the soil long before cotton and sugarcane became Louisiana's main crops. Even though colonial agriculture was geared more toward subsistence than commerce, indigo and tobacco became fairly well-established cash crops. In a limited sense, the remote settlements were a part of the commercial intercourse between the Mississippi Valley and the Missouri-Ohio system to the north.

Although the cotton gin had been invented and sugar had been successfully granulated before the Louisiana Purchase in 1803, Louisiana's population did not expand rapidly until after it became a state in 1812. By the time the smoke and fog cleared from the Battle of New Orleans in 1815, the transportation revolution had begun. Mechanized cotton gins devoured all the available raw cotton, quickly separating the seeds from the fiber, the step that had been the bottleneck of production in the cotton textile industry. Textile mills greedily consumed cotton thread as fast as it was spun from the fiber. Adventurous settlers transformed huge tracts of virgin land into cotton plantations that, in some cases, earned great fortunes in just a few seasons. South Louisiana produced cotton and another crop, sugarcane, that brought even greater profits than cotton.

Antebellum planters suffered from an east-to-west transportation problem created by bayous running inexorably in a southerly direction. To achieve lateral movement, early planters dug small canals connecting streams and lakes. In 1829 prominent growers chartered the Barataria and Lafourche Canal (the B & L), an ambitious waterway designed to stretch from one end of the sugar country to the other—from the Mississippi River across the Terrebonne and Lafourche country to the Attakapas country of Bayou Teche.

Long before railroads and steamboats were available, water transportation was important to early settlers. In fact, it determined settlement patterns before 1830. A subsistence farmer could survive just about anywhere on Louisiana's rich soil, but a commercial planting operation had to be near a navigable stream or canal to succeed. Canals connecting natural waterways were costly to build but cheap to operate. One animal could pull as much cargo on a canal as fifty animals could pull by wagon. Even after railroads came into wide use, canals remained an efficient way to transport high-bulk cargoes over long distances.[1]

Economic history often deals with routine events of life that people faced every day. The economic realities in the cotton and sugar king-

---

1. Susan P. Lee and Peter Passell, *A New Economic View of American History* (New York, 1979), 63, 72, 78–79.

doms of Louisiana included floods, droughts, freezes, and the problem of transporting produce to market. Even recent work in economic history, with its emphasis on counterfactual hypotheses, sophisticated use of numbers, and models, often concentrates on these practicalities. These everyday events took up more of the time and energy of early settlers than did Mardi Gras, dueling under the oaks, and the opera season in New Orleans. Overcoming these problems meant profit and solvency; a failure to adjust meant deficits and bankruptcy.

There is little room for the largely mythical moonlight-and-magnolias setting in this study. Legends of plantation mansions, octoroon mistresses, and other trappings of wealth add little to our knowledge of antebellum Louisiana. The popular image, often encrusted with myth, usually clouds the picture instead of illuminating it. Yet slavery did play a significant part in this story. The builders of the B & L were big sugar and cotton planters who owned slaves, and slave labor constructed the canal. The planter Robert Ruffin Barrow, of Terrebonne, was for a long time the owner of the canal. This canal tycoon and planter also owned over seven hundred slaves.

Two generations of Barrows—Robert Ruffin and his son, Robert Ruffin Jr.—grappled with economic realities over a one-hundred-year period, growing cotton and sugarcane and operating a toll canal. They struggled with the price of land and slaves, the difficulty of clearing land, the price of cotton and sugar, and the problems of getting produce to market. Their story is not unique; all farmers faced similar problems. But their story is complex, for in their canal-building ventures they grappled with the geography of the region and with state and federal government systems that provided subsidies and regulations. That they survived so long under difficult circumstances is a tribute to their perseverance and understanding of how the political economy of Louisiana and the United States functioned.

Several significant studies in American history provide a paradigm against which to assess the role of the Barrows in their canal-building activities. George Taylor's *Transportation Revolution, 1815–1860*, and Robert Wiebe's *The Search For Order, 1877–1920*, and *Opening of American Society from the Adoption of the Constitution to the Eve of Disunion* all deal with the sweeping changes in American life brought on, in part, by improvements in our national transportation system. The observations and conclusions of both authors apply to Louisiana and to the two generations of Barrows.[2]

In several ways Taylor's views fit the career of Robert Ruffin Barrow, the wealthy planter and canal tycoon who is featured in the first half of this study. Like many other Americans from the Atlantic seaboard, Barrow drifted to the virgin lands of the Southwest to make his fortune. He was not a typical rugged individualist pulling himself up by his own bootstraps to amass a great fortune through determination and hard work alone. He arrived riding a fine horse and carrying money from his father to buy land in Terrebonne Parish, Louisiana. Likewise, after he became a wealthy planter, he did not advocate a policy of laissez-faire, for he relied on subsidies from the state of Louisiana to complete his pet project, the Barataria and Lafourche Canal. As a sugar grower and a Whig, he looked to the federal government for tariff protection.

During the years of the transportation revolution—from 1815 to about 1860—American industrial technology improved transportation across a vast continent rich in untapped resources. In the years before the Civil War, a large percentage of American capital and energy went into building steamboats, canals, and railroads. This initial industrial surge made the United States the fourth-ranking manufacturing nation in the world on the eve of the Civil War. The industrial revolution of the 1880s and 1890s brought the U.S. into prominence as the leading industrial nation in the world before the turn of the century. Even then, most Americans were farmers.

Another significant economic study is Carter Goodrich's *Government Promotion of American Canals and Railroads, 1800–1890.* Goodrich's broad observations about government subsidies to internal improvements nationwide can be used to evaluate the activities of the Barrows and the canal company.[3] At first glance the B & L

---

2. George Taylor, *The Transportation Revolution, 1815–1860* (New York, 1962); Robert Wiebe, *The Search for Order, 1877–1920* (New York, 1967); Robert Wiebe, *The Opening of American Society from the Adoption of the Constitution to the Eve of Disunion* (New York, 1984).

3. Carter Goodrich, *Government Promotion of American Canals and Railroads, 1800–1890* (New York, 1960).

seemed different, even unique; but in many ways it matched a pattern followed in other sections of the country. Louisiana, like other states, contributed to the construction of public transportation by water and rail. What is different about the Barrows and the B & L is timing—the Barrows continued their canal operations long after canals had succumbed to railroad efficiency in other sections of the country. Louisiana geography and Barrow stubbornness explain the local phenomenon.

Goodrich's observations are perceptive. Local governments in nearly every state aided turnpikes, canals, or railroads; the federal government from time to time provided funds. That the government provided aid in the nineteenth century, when America was considered laissez-faire, is not surprising or paradoxical; government funds also built railroads in Latin America and in Russia. In the United States, where there were many sparse settlements to link together, the likelihood of success was not as great as in Europe, where public transportation linked larger population centers. In some cases there were joint ventures involving the federal government, a state government, several municipalities, and private interests. The Chesapeake and Ohio Canal Company was such a venture.

The role of the national government in internal improvements was important, although sporadic. Treasury Secretary Albert Gallatin's report in 1808 was an ambitious and prophetic outline of projects that would tie the young American nation to markets across the Appalachian barrier. Gallatin's report on roads and canals presented to the U.S. Senate called for an appropriation of $16.6 million. Many of his ideas, including the Erie Canal route, ultimately led to significant avenues of commerce. Other leaders, such as John C. Calhoun (as secretary of war in 1819) and John Quincy Adams (both as president and as a member of Congress), envisioned a national program, the American System.

President Andrew Jackson's 1830 veto of the Maysville Road Bill, because it would have used federal funds to build a road entirely in Kentucky, symbolized a change in policy and speeded up the drift away from the American System. No longer would the national government take a leading role in planning and funding internal improvements. Southern politicians, who feared that high tariffs would be needed to finance improvements, led the opposition. Jackson's Whig opponents actively supported internal improvements.

The end of federal aid did not mean the end of support for comprehensive public works. The Erie Canal—which cost $7 million, provided mostly by the state of New York—was a tremendous economic success, collecting over $1 million in tolls before it was even completed. Soon its tonnage rivaled that of the entire Mississippi River system. Not only did the Erie Canal help New York to become the nation's leading port; it also helped Michigan, northern Ohio, and Indiana grow at a much faster rate than other, less fortunate areas.

Many communities hoped to emulate the success of the Erie Canal. The states facing the Appalachian barrier had the most energetic programs; New England spent far less. Ohio, Pennsylvania, Kentucky, and Tennessee all had ambitious plans. New Jersey, Rhode Island, Delaware, and Connecticut did not spend much on canals or railroad construction.

Many state projects were doomed to fail because of poor planning, inefficient management, or fraud; default and foreclosures soon followed. Tennessee and Louisiana both had early aid that gave way to laws limiting or prohibiting state subscriptions or loans to railroads or canal companies. Unsuccessful ventures nearly bankrupted some states. Pennsylvania, Maryland, Indiana, and Illinois were all in default on obligations before the Civil War. Eight states in the South defaulted on projects during Reconstruction. Not surprisingly, many programs were abandoned. Because some programs were viewed as general benefits to the community at large, they continued to receive subsidies from local governments even after suffering losses. Private investors could not afford to sustain such losses; only those projects that could succeed and turn a profit without aid were privately owned and operated.

Goodrich concluded that the transportation system of the United States before the Civil War would have been far less extensive without government aid. No major canal or railroad was built without some public monies. Thus mixed enterprises, those featuring public and private ownership, flourished before the Civil War. Such ventures tended to leave management in private hands. Where there was unanimity of opinion about a project, state aid usually was forthcoming. Railroad construction in Georgia and the Erie Canal in New York, for instance, succeeded in part because they were supported by large segments of the populations of the two states. In contrast, rival projects that vied for public support often became mired in political stalemates and controversies and were not funded.

In such a fluid political state, it was not surprising that Robert R. Barrow became a Whig for economic reasons. He and his neighbors wanted tariff protection for the sugar industry and federal monies for internal improvements such as rivers and harbors. Pretending that their privately owned canal was a joint venture of local farmers eager to improve ways of getting their produce to market, they turned to the Louisiana legislature for help in completing the B & L. Barrow stick-to-itiveness and the quirks of Louisiana geography permitted the canal era in Louisiana to continue long after it had declined in other sections of the country.

In *The Opening of American Society,* Wiebe describes the sweeping changes that Robert R. Barrow lived through. By the time he was an adult ready to move to Louisiana to make his fortune early in the nineteenth century, the hierarchical structure of eighteenth-century America had given way to a more open political and economic system where any man could make his fortune. There was room for all; a man's energy and ability alone determined how far he would go. Barrow capitalized on the times and made good use of his opportunities. Yet after he accumulated property, he took on airs and postured like a gentleman. He seemed oblivious to the rise of the common man and unaware of the expanding role of political and religious institutions in the democratization of American society.

Wiebe's observations in *The Search for Order* more closely coincide with the career of Barrow's son, Robert Jr., who inherited some of his father's property and much of his determination to complete the Barataria and Lafourche Canal. Robert Jr. is featured in the second part of this study. *The Search for Order* does not concentrate primarily on changes in the American system of transportation, but it nonetheless notes the development of national, and even international, markets in certain commodities with the advent of the transcontinental railroad, the expansion in world trade, and the greater sense of community in the United States. The island communities of the elder Barrow's days no longer existed.

Robert Barrow, Jr., a forceful entrepreneur like his father, came to understand what Wiebe observed: The hand of the federal government reached many Americans directly and indirectly, especially in the years after World War I. Like other Americans, Robert Jr. griped about paying federal income taxes, but he received bounties on his sugar crop and relied on the U.S. Corps of Engineers to keep rivers and bayous navigable. And finally, when he was on the verge of bankruptcy in the mid-1920s, he turned to the U.S. government to buy a portion of his canal and make it a part of the Gulf Intracoastal Waterway. Robert Jr. used political influence in the name of the public good, and he received a substantial sum from the Corps of Engineers, even though the United States did not really need the canal route for its inland waterway network.

Albert Fishlow's study of internal transportation calls the period from 1860 to 1910 the "Reign of the Railroad." Large land grants and the efficiency brought on by new technology account for railroad ascendancy but do not explain Louisiana's late-blooming success with canals, even after the turn of the century. Fishlow sheds light on the demise of toll canals as surfaced highways fanned out across the land during the height of the automobile era in the 1920s.[4]

Clearly the Barataria and Lafourche Canal was different from most other canal systems in at least three ways: in its time span, in its geographic uniqueness, and in its long association with the Barrow family. The canal-building activities of the Barrows extended long past the end of the canal-building era, for this family lived with unique geographic conditions that made canals practical in marshy south Louisiana. Taylor's classic study explained the decline of canals by the 1850s, when railroads became the rage; in Louisiana, canals continued to be a viable means of transportation even in the twentieth century. The Barrows realized this geographic phenomenon and took advantage of it. In that sense they were capitalists ahead of their time, noting an economic opportunity to exploit.

4. Albert Fishlow, "Internal Transportation," in Lance Davis et al., American Economic Growth: An Economist's History of the United States (New York, 1972), 468–547.

PART I

Robert Ruffin Barrow and the B and L, 1829 to 1875

1

Early Settlers in Bayou Country

The rapid movement of cotton and sugarcane planters into Louisiana during the 1820s and 1830s stressed the need for internal improvements such as roads, canals, bridges, and port facilities. Eli Whitney's cotton gin, invented in 1793, revolutionized the textile industry and created a clamorous demand for raw cotton. New plantations proliferated; soon cotton became a leading cash crop. South Louisiana's warm climate, abundant rainfall, and alluvial soil permitted growth of another crop that was even more profitable—sugarcane. Technological advances in granulating sugar, like the invention of the cotton gin, came in the last decade of the eighteenth century, but the big influx of sugarcane planters did not occur until the 1820s.

Sugar plantations sprang up in south Louisiana from the Mississippi River westward to Bayou Teche. To the north they extended to a point just south of Alexandria, where the winter climate created a natural boundary. Originally plantations lined both banks of the Mississippi; later, planters cleared land on Bayou Teche, Bayou Lafourche, Bayou Terrebonne, Bayou Black, Bayou Grand Caillou, Bayou Petit Caillou, and Bayou du Large and placed it under cultivation as well.

Planters flocked to the virgin lands of Alabama, Arkansas, Texas, Mississippi, and Louisiana when cotton became king; others bought coastal lands and turned to sugar production. Some wealthy planters owned both cotton and sugar plantations, in different counties or even different states. Those leaving the eastern seaboard usually sold their land but not their slaves, who were needed to clear and cultivate the lands of the Southwest. Sometimes they bought uncleared lands and carved plantations from a wilderness; often they bought out the small holdings of early settlers and enlarged the operations with additional land purchases. This "American" invasion of settlers brought significant change to the Acadian countryside of south Louisiana. The newcomers spoke English rather than French, and they were Protestant, unlike the French and Spanish settlers, who were Roman Catholic.[1]

New settlers came from a variety of places. William Minor came from Natchez, Mississippi, and bought Southdown plantation in Houma. Sometimes newcomers joined a company already doing business in Louisiana. The new Louisiana planters sought experienced people to run new operations. Robert R. Barrow's nephew John Pittman came from North Carolina to manage one of Barrow's plantations. Benjamin Barker, a native of New York, settled in 1838 in Lockport on Bayou Lafourche, where he served as collecting and shipping agent for the Barataria and Lafourche Canal.[2]

Early French settlers gave the name Terrebonne, which means "good earth," to the region built by alluvial soil in the vicinity of what is now Bayou Terrebonne. The newcomers came in large numbers; in 1822 Terrebonne Parish became a separate political entity from Lafourche Interior Parish. Even though planters had settled the upper reaches of the parish, lower Terrebonne was largely an undeveloped frontier area during the first third of the nineteenth century. In 1825 the police jury offered a bounty of $5 for each "tiger" killed. (The "tigers" were probably panthers and, in some cases, jaguars.) Michel Theriot established the first plantation on Bayou du Large shortly after he arrived there in 1839, "when the country was a

---

1. George Taylor, *The Transportation Revolution, 1815–1860* (New York, 1962); Roy Robbins, *Our Landed Heritage* (Princeton, N.J., 1942); Frederick Merk, *History of the Western Movement* (New York, 1978); J. Carlyle Sitterson, *Sugar Country: The Cane Sugar Industry in the South, 1753–1950* (Lexington, Ky., 1953); and Joe G. Taylor, *Negro Slavery in Louisiana* (Baton Rouge, 1963), document the movement of Americans to the bayou country in the 1820s and 1830s.

2. *Biographical and Historical Memoirs of Louisiana* (2 vols.; Chicago, 1892), I, 261–62.

perfect canebreak and wilderness." As late as 1841, when Joseph Robichaux's family settled on Bayou Terrebonne near Montegut, the "country was a complete wilderness . . . and nearly all kinds of wild animals abounded, deer, bear, etc. Houma consisted at that time of three or four little houses."[3]

A number of settlers in the sugar country became wealthy and prominent. These included the Pughs, Barrows, Bislands, Mc-Collams, McBrides, Minors, Bonds, and Shaffers. Not only those of Anglo-Saxon descent prospered; the Ellenders, Wurzlows, Sulakowskis, Thibodauxs, Champagnes, Goodes, Krumbhaars, and Vigueries were also important families.

A most prominent Terrebonne family during the antebellum period was that of Robert Ruffin Barrow. One of the largest planters in the South, Robert Ruffin owned plantations in several Louisiana parishes and in Texas; by 1860 he had over seven hundred slaves to work his land. According to one family story, Robert Ruffin arrived in Terrebonne in 1828 riding a fine horse named Tom Bennett and carrying with him $1,800 with which to purchase land. Not surprisingly, the legendary figure was tall and handsome. He became the richest of all the Barrows. In 1860, in Terrebonne Parish alone, he owned 21,256 acres valued at $1,062,000, as well as 399 slaves.

Robert Ruffin Barrow was the oldest son of Bartholomew ("Batt") Barrow and Ascension Slatter Barrow. He was born in Halifax County, North Carolina, in 1798. In 1820 Batt moved his family to Louisiana, where he settled on his estate, Afton Villa, in West Feliciana Parish. Robert's two brothers, David Bennett and William Bennett, also became planters. David became the owner of Afton Villa after the death of his father in 1852. William, who never married, lived with Robert until his death in 1842. In the 1830s Robert increased his landholdings at a rapid rate.

On February 7, 1850, Robert married Volumnia Washington Hunley, from Smith County, Tennessee, whom he had met in New Orleans. Her father had business interests in the city and eventually settled his family there. The Reverend Edmund Neville, of Christ Church Cathedral on Canal Street at the corner of Dauphine, per-

3. *Ibid.*, II, 342, 418; Randolph A. Bazet, "Houma—An Historical Sketch," in *Centennial Celebration, Houma, Louisiana, May 10–13, 1934* (Morgan City, La., 1934), 9.

formed the Episcopal ceremony. Robert was fifty-two years old; Volumnia was twenty-five. John Burnside, who owned Valcour Aime plantation, was best man at Barrow's wedding; Hallette Hatch, the maid of honor, was accompanied by Horace L. Hunley, the bride's brother. James B. Conner, stepfather of the bride and a wealthy cotton and sugar factor, gave a reception for Robert and Volumnia at his home in the French Quarter on Ursulines Street, between Chartres and Royal streets.

Robert and Volumnia had two children: Volumnia Roberta, born in 1854, and Robert Ruffin Jr., born in 1858. Volumnia Roberta, who was usually called Roberta, married William Slatter and lived in Winchester, Tennessee. Robert Jr. grew up in Terrebonne, following in his father's footsteps. Robert's business partner John Pittman claimed that plantation bells chimed when Robert Jr. was born. Episcopal bishop Leonidas Polk, a personal family friend, was Robert Jr.'s godfather. The Barrows lived in a large two-story house below Houma at Residence, one of Robert's plantations on Bayou Terrebonne.[4]

Even though Robert was sixty years old in 1858, when Robert Jr. was born, he and Volumnia displayed characteristics typical of doting parents. The birth of a son seemed to take on greater significance than that of another daughter would have, and the parents gloried in the congratulations. Sarah Dawson, an old family friend from West Feliciana Parish, wrote, "I hope your son may be as promising as Roberta." When Robert was away from home, he always mentioned the children in his letters to Volumnia. "Kiss Roberta & little Bob for me," he wrote in 1859. The next year Robert learned from Volumnia's brother, Horace Hunley, who was on vacation with Volumnia and the children, that Robert Jr. hunted frogs, played in the water, and did the things expected of a two-year-old. The concerned parents became upset when all was not well with the children. "Our little Ruffin is sick I know not whether from fatigue or heat traveling or from cutting

---

4. Sheri Coats, Houma *Daily Courier*, October 8, 1972; William Barrow Floyd, *The Barrow Family of Old Louisiana* (Lexington, Ky., 1963), 24–25, 101; Newspaper clippings from New Orleans *Daily Picayune* in box 19, folder 4, Robert R. Barrow Family Papers, Manuscript Section, Howard-Tilton Memorial Library, Tulane University, hereinafter cited as BFP; Joseph K. Menn, *The Large Slaveholders of Louisiana, 1860* (New Orleans, 1964), 103–105, 262.

teeth and cold," Volumnia wrote from Virginia in 1859. She hated to be away from Robert during these trying circumstances; everything seemed to go wrong. When Robert Jr.'s nurse, Valey, sat him on a box at a railroad station to feed him, a terrible odor came from the crate. When it was later discovered that the box had somehow become the coffin of a man who had died of a mysterious and possibly contagious disease, Volumnia, of course, feared that the child would contract it.[5] Her fears proved to be unfounded, however.

By the 1850s Robert Barrow was indeed a wealthy man. He owned several plantations in partnerships with others, as well as some outright. In Terrebonne he owned Residence, Caillou Grove, Honduras, Myrtle Grove, Crescent Farm, and Point Farm. In Lafourche Parish he owned Oak Grove; in Assumption, Locust Grove; in Ascension, D'ville. Records indicate that his sugar production in the 1850s was impressive. By 1859–60, for example, he produced 175 hogsheads at Residence, 100 at Myrtle Grove, 202 at Caillou Grove, and over 200 at Oak Grove. Barrow also produced impressive amounts with various partners. In the same year, he and John McDonald produced 220 hogsheads; he and Joshua and Howard Bond, another 400. With other partners he produced at least 853 additional hogsheads.[6]

Barrow's wealth impressed people, but it did not make him popular. His abrasive manner often offended acquaintances. G. W. Pierce, writing for *De Bow's Review* in 1851, made a number of prophetic observations about him. Predicting that Barrow would be one of the richest men in the state, Pierce noted qualities of foresight, prudence, and sound management. He said that Barrow lived in a beautiful home surrounded by fruit and shade trees. But he closed with an observation that others would often make, especially during Robert's declining years after the Civil War. "He is hospitable, but unpopular with all," Pierce noted, "from what cause I am unable, or rather unwilling to say."[7] These sentiments would be shared, unfortunately,

5. Sarah Dawson to Dear Friend, May 29, 1858, Volumnia Barrow to Robert Barrow, November 5, 1859, Robert Barrow to Volumnia Barrow, November 8, 1859, all in box 3, folder 7, BFP; Horace L. Hunley to Robert Barrow, August 9, 1860, in box 4, folder 1, BFP; Volumnia Barrow to Robert Barrow, July 18, 1859, in box 3, folder 8, BFP.
6. Menn, *The Large Slaveholders of Louisiana*, 103–105, 262; P. A. Champomier, *Statement of the Sugar Crop Made in Louisiana* (New Orleans, 1844–62), *passim*.
7. G. W. Pierce, "Historical and Statistical Collection of Louisiana—Terrebonne," *De Bow's Review*, XI (July, 1851–January, 1852), 606.

even by the planter's own children; family friction lingered even after Barrow's death in suits over the disposition of his estate.

The Civil War, which brought disruption of southern agriculture and an end to slavery, is usually blamed for the decline of wealthy planters like Robert Ruffin Barrow, but an examination of financial dealings long before the war suggests problems unrelated to it. Big purchases reveal the fragile foundation of plantation wealth. Barrow speculated in Texas lands, but often his titles were not clear. Ephrain Knowlton, his agent, and Horace Hunley, his brother-in-law, served as contacts with F. W. Latham, Barrow's representative in Texas. Latham informed Hunley in 1858 that some land Barrow bought had been sold several times.[8] Barrow sued to reclaim title.

Barrow's financial dealings in purchasing a plantation in Lafourche Parish reveal his modus operandi. When Robert bought Oak Grove plantation in 1836, he paid $100,000 for a tract of land with a 20-arpent front, sixty-six slaves, and farm animals and equipment. He paid only $25,000 in cash; the sellers held a mortgage for the balance due. In order to raise the $25,000, Robert borrowed $8,750 from his brother William. In other words, he managed to make a $100,000 purchase with only $16,250 in cash. Three months later he sold the plantation to William, who agreed to pay off the mortgage. Later he reacquired Oak Grove from William. But in 1851 he mortgaged it to his other brother, David, "for money advanced and loaned to him, in the full sum of forty thousand dollars." In 1855 Robert gave his nephew John Pittman a half-interest in Oak Grove. Pittman thanked Barrow for his kindness: "Your family will never be in want or distress of any kind." He was to prove true to his word; he came to the aid of the two Barrow children under trying circumstances after the Civil War when their father, then an old man, had lost much of his fortune. Eventually Pittman became sole owner of the plantation. Robert Barrow and John Pittman also owned a number of other tracts purchased at sheriffs' sales.[9]

Frequently Barrow became involved in imbroglios that could be

8. Horace L. Hunley to F. W. Latham, March 21, 1858, Latham to Hunley, April 3, 1858, both in box 3, folder 7, BFP.
9. Lafourche Parish Conveyance Book, Thibodaux, La. (hereinafter cited as LCB), "L," fol. 332, 402; LCB 3, fol. 248; LCB "CC," fol. 427; John Pittman to Robert Barrow, May 15, 1855, in box 3, folder 5, BFP.

settled only in court. In 1836 he sold to Thomas R. Shields a sugar plantation on Bayou Terrebonne and a cotton plantation on Bayou Petit Caillou with seventy-five slaves for $227,000. Shields gave him sixteen promissory notes endorsed by William Bisland that were due to mature on different dates. For some years Shields paid off his notes, but in 1842 he could no longer meet his commitments, and he still owed Barrow $119,965. Then he and Barrow reached an agreement whereby Barrow would get his plantations and slaves back and Shields would pay him $32,000, secured by notes from six different people. Eventually Barrow became disenchanted with the six noteholders and sued. Sixteen years later the Louisiana Supreme Court ruled in Barrow's favor.

Barrow did not always win in court, even when he thought he had a strong case. In 1850 his agricultural partner John McDonald killed a slave named Prince at Point Farm, the plantation owned by the partners. McDonald acknowledged killing Prince, and in the presence of witnesses William and John Bisland, he agreed to reimburse Barrow for the loss. However, McDonald left Terrebonne without fulfilling his promise, and Barrow sued in the district court, asking $1,500 from McDonald, who "wantonly, maliciously and without any cause or excuse killed a negro belonging to said partnership." In the same action Barrow attempted to attach McDonald's property and collect $6,500 for other plantation accounts. Both the district court and the state supreme court on appeal ruled against Barrow, who had not provided specific values on properties he referred to. This case was a civil action involving money; at no time did the court consider the morality of killing a slave. No criminal law had been violated.[10]

Obviously Barrow was quick to sue for a redress of grievances, but court records in Terrebonne Parish indicate that he was as often the defendant in suits as he was the plaintiff. He disputed with his neighbors over land, slaves, boundaries, notes, wages, and other matters. Often the police jury of Terrebonne Parish brought action against him for failing to maintain roads fronting his property. Occasionally people threatened to shoot him if he set foot on their property.

10. *R. R. Barrow v. Shields et al.* (1858), 13 La Ann 57; Suit No. 1556, vol. 87, Suit No. 1650, vol. 90, 5th Judicial District Court, Terrebonne Parish, March 20, 1856; *R. R. Barrow v. John McDonald* (1857), 12 La Ann 110.

In 1843 Barrow's father made poignant observations about his bachelor son's financial dealings that further explain Robert's unpopularity: "I am security for you to Allin for 44000 thousand Dollars all on demand how are you going to pay that sum these times. You are counted a rich man if so why not pay your debts, you have no one to give it to. You cant carry it to another world." Others, too, complained that Barrow did not pay his debts. In 1852 Andrew O'Connor requested payment that Barrow had promised but not sent. O'Connor claimed he was pressed for funds and needed his money.[11]

When people owed Barrow money, however, he was quick to demand payment. If payment was not forthcoming, he often sued. Barrow's attorney complained in 1852 that he could not proceed with a suit against the Bislands unless Barrow provided some needed family information. Barrow did not reply to queries from his attorney, whose services the obstreperous Barrow nonetheless often required. In 1857 Barrow tried to collect for sugar lost when the barge *Lodi* sank. His business associates told him insurance companies required more than just his word of what had happened to the vessel. They told Barrow he needed eyewitnesses, detailed descriptions of cargo, and full particulars about the accident.[12]

Argumentative and proud, Barrow sometimes published legal materials to publicly justify his position and protect his reputation. At other times he did not seem to care what people thought of him. In 1856 he published a brief prepared by F. S. Goode, the Terrebonne Parish attorney who represented him in civil action against John McDonald, who killed the slave Prince. The brief, however, did not provide details of how or why McDonald killed the man. The year before, Barrow had printed a long-winded and repetitious account of his land dispute with Thomas R. Shields. Barrow apparently printed the book-length account to prove that he was right.[13]

Louisiana's bayou country, a vast region covering much of the south-central part of the state, is the setting for this history of canal build-

11. Batt Barrow to Dear Son Robert, July 20, 1843, in box 2, folder 2, BFP; Andrew O'Connor to Robert Barrow, July 11, 1852, in box 3, folder 3, BFP.
12. L. Janis to Robert Barrow, August 6, November 13, 1852, both in box 3, folder 3, BFP; John Tarleton to Robert Barrow, April 30, 1857, in box 3, folder 2, BFP.
13. See box 26, folders 1, 4, BFP.

ing and agricultural empire building over a one-hundred-year period. Geologically speaking, coastal south Louisiana is quite young, a part of the Mississippi River delta system built by alluvial silt deposited over the past five thousand years. The great river created the entire coastal region as it overflowed its banks and deposited rich layers of soil in fan-shaped patterns, or deltas. Repetition of the process over the centuries built the delta system that covers coastal south Louisiana. During this time Louisiana's bayou country underwent a building and shifting pattern. Distributary bayous of the Mississippi, like the great river itself, overflowed their banks during high water and built up deltas that were higher than the surrounding countryside. During low water some of the channels silted up, thereby reducing their ability to carry floodwaters. Then, perhaps years later during high water, the mighty river shifted its course, finding a shorter, steeper path to the Gulf of Mexico through the valleys between the deltas. Over the years the shifting Mississippi created seven separate delta systems stretching from the Chandeleur Islands east of New Orleans to Vermilion Bay south of Lafayette on the west.

About one thousand years ago, the delta system became stable and stopped creating new outlets. There is clear evidence that the main channel of what is now the Mississippi River coursed through the lower reaches of a number of other streams. At different times both Bayou Lafourche and Bayou Teche served as the main outlets of North America's greatest river. Today the Mississippi remains locked in its channel by man-made devices: levees, spillways, and other barriers to prevent the river from meandering. What remained from earlier outlets were the delta systems built up over the years as the river meandered from east to west in south central Louisiana.

In recent times the river has had four distributaries: Bayou Manchac, the Atchafalaya River, Bayou Plaquemine, and Bayou Lafourche. Only Bayou Manchac discharges on the east, or left descending, bank of the river. It never carried a great volume of water, and its navigational qualities have been marred by shallow water, sandbars, and snags. All distributaries on the opposite bank became significant. Both Bayou Lafourche and Bayou Plaquemine have been important transportation links, but both in time were dammed at their sources on the Mississippi. The Atchafalaya, the first and greatest of the distributaries, today is restrained by artificial devices from capturing the main channel of the Mississippi and carrying its waters through a shorter, steeper route to the Gulf of Mexico.

Louisiana's sugar country, part of the land mass created by these streams, is all delta lands. The area can be divided into four distinct agricultural regions: the banks of the Mississippi itself, the Lafourche country, Terrebonne, and the Attakapas country.

The biggest delta was along both banks of the Mississippi itself. The first settlers clung to the riverbanks, where the land was high and fertile and the river provided the main means of transportation. Small rural agricultural communities developed between New Orleans and Baton Rouge. Above New Orleans were Edgard, Reserve, Vacherie, Donaldsonville, and Plaquemine. Steamboats made regular stops at plantation landings located on both banks of the river. As the population grew, settlers drifted farther into the bayou country, seeking cheap virgin lands to convert into cotton, rice, indigo, or sugar plantations.

Bayou Teche is the center of the Attakapas District, the rich agricultural region that was named after the Indians who lived in the area. Today the district is often called Acadiana after the Acadians who settled there starting in 1765. The Attakapas District includes the present parishes of St. Mary, St. Martin, Iberia, Vermilion, and Lafayette and was formed about 2,500 or 3,500 years ago, when the Mississippi swerved westward from its banks and followed the course of Bayou Teche. The Red River also flowed into the Teche until about the first century A.D., when it returned to its ancient outlet to the sea—the Mississippi. Before shifting to a more easterly route to form the land mass in and around New Orleans, the Mississippi built the alluvial cone that forms the outer fringe of Vermilion Bay. The Teche is lined with sugarcane in its southern section and with cotton in its upper reaches. The modern Teche rises near Bayou Courtableau, flows in a southeasterly direction for 125 miles, and empties into the Atchafalaya about 10 miles above Morgan City. It has no tributaries.

Towns along the Teche from Morgan City northward include Patterson, Centerville, Franklin, Baldwin, Jeanerette, New Iberia, St. Martinville, Breaux Bridge, Cecelia, Arnaudville, Leonville, and

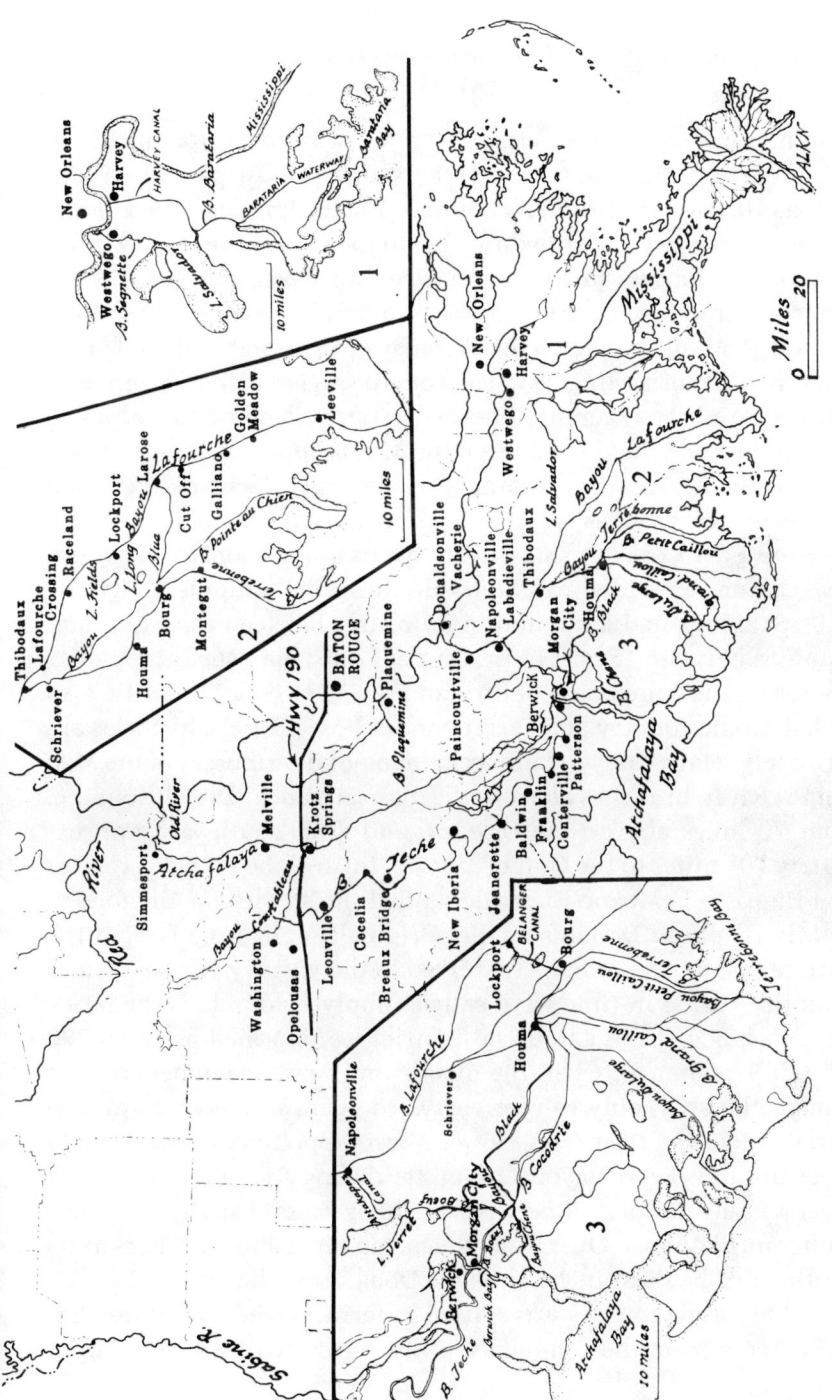

Louisiana's Sugar Country: The Mississippi River to Bayou Teche

Washington. Sugarcane generally gives way to cotton north of Breaux Bridge. St. Mary Parish, the southernmost part of the Attakapas District, traditionally has been the leading sugar-producing parish in the state. Northwest of Leonville, approximately 8 miles away, is Opelousas, in St. Landry Parish; Opelousas became an important trading center for the surrounding prairies. Early settlers shipped goods up and down the Teche by pirogue, flatboat, and other watercraft. Transporting produce from the region to markets in New Orleans taxed the ingenuity of early settlers, who had to traverse a difficult obstacle that lay between the Mississippi and the Attakapas District: the Atchafalaya Swamp. Consequently, Teche planters had few ties to New Orleans merchants; often they arranged with factors from the East Coast to ship sugar by coastal schooners. However, New Orleans provided essential supplies and equipment. By the 1850s St. Mary had a population of nearly fourteen thousand and produced between 15 and 18 percent of Louisiana's sugar crop.

Between the Attakapas country and the Mississippi River lie also the Lafourche country and Terrebonne, whose geologic histories are intimately related. Bayou Lafourche, a major distributary of the Mississippi River, branches off from the main stream at Donaldsonville, about 70 miles above New Orleans, and flows southward approximately 105 miles to the Gulf of Mexico. In 1699 the French explorer Jean-Baptiste LeMoyne Bienville named the stream for the fork in the Mississippi at Donaldsonville. Originally called the Fork of the Chitimacha, for the Indians that lived in the vicinity, the bayou and the entire region in time were called simply Lafourche, "the fork." The rich lands of the Lafourche District were formed between 700 and 1,500 years ago, when the Mississippi's main channel coursed through the area, only to veer eastward again in modern times to form the deltas of the present lower Mississippi. Small vessels could travel up and down Bayou Lafourche during the entire year, but larger vessels performed best during high water, usually from December until August. Over time, the bayou tended to form bars at its mouth, and shoals at its head below Donaldsonville.

The Lafourche country was settled by farmers who moved steadily downstream from the confluence of the bayou with the Mississippi and by fishermen who ascended from the settlements along the Gulf of Mexico near Grand Isle. The French-sounding names of some of the small towns that sprang up along the entire length of Bayou Lafourche hint at the predominant group that came to settle in the Acadian country. Starting just below Donaldsonville, towns include Paincourtville, Napoleonville, Labadieville, Thibodaux, Lafourche Crossing, Raceland, and Lockport.

Bayou Lafourche itself branched off into several significant waterways that formed the Terrebonne land mass. At Thibodaux the Lafourche formed Bayou Terrebonne, whose banks were fertile like those of its parent stream, but whose delta was narrower than that of the Lafourche. Bayou Terrebonne, too, branched off into several distributaries. These included Bayous Black, Blue, Pointe au Chien, and Petit Caillou. Bayou LaCarpe, a small stream, flowed through Houma midway between Bayous Black and Terrebonne. Houma, the largest town on Bayou Terrebonne, became a thriving community, an agricultural and fishing center. Further downstream were Bourg and Montegut. Along the distributary bayous, settlements were remote and small.

Bayou Black became one of the most important of the distributaries of Bayou Terrebonne, because it flowed westward into the mouth of the Atchafalaya, making it a connecting link to the bayous that ran inexorably north to south. Certainly its size did not make it the important waterway that it eventually became. The Black originated 4 miles below Thibodaux at Schriever, where it left Bayou Terrebonne and flowed southward parallel to Bayou Terrebonne for 13 miles until it reached Houma. There the Black veered sharply westward, ultimately reaching one of its branches, Bayou Boeuf, 30 miles away. Bayou Boeuf is wide and deep and flows into the Atchafalaya River. Another deep, wide branch of Bayou Black flows into the lower Atchafalaya and is usually called Bayou Chêne. Bayou Black connected the waterways of the Attakapas District to Houma, less than a mile away from Bayou Terrebonne.

Smaller distributaries of Bayou Terrebonne—the Blue, Petit Caillou, and Pointe au Chien—were important for their agricultural and seafood products. Still other bayous rose below Houma. Bayous

Grand Caillou and du Large began just south of Houma. The latter branched off from Bayou Black at the southern end of the severe bend that Bayou Black formed in Houma.

The Mississippi River's distributaries did not all form significant deltas. The Atchafalaya River is the first and greatest of the distributaries. Its growth has been both aided and thwarted by man in recent years. Man's efforts originally helped the Atchafalaya become an important outlet; then, when it threatened to take over the main channel of the lower Mississippi, man's efforts prevented it from doing so.

The Atchafalaya River is an outlet for both the Red and Mississippi rivers in its short 156-mile course to the Gulf of Mexico through Berwick Bay. The Atchafalaya began about 1,500 years ago at Old River, in a loop made where the Red River flows into the Mississippi. Eventually it wore a channel through a small distributary of the Red, reaching the sea between ridges formed by Bayous Teche and Lafourche. Its navigational qualities were limited by snags, sandbars, and log rafts. Clearing the stream of snags and bars allowed it to grow. The waters of the Atchafalaya did not remain in a single channel but spread in a 15-mile-wide basin that in some places resembled a lake or swamp rather than a river. There was no clearly defined channel but rather dozens of log-choked, more or less parallel channels. Between Butte la Rose and Flat Lake, the channel of the Atchafalaya is called Grand Lake, a body of water 40 miles long and 6 miles wide. Gradually the Atchafalaya took an increasing volume of water from the Mississippi as other distributaries became less important. Around 1950 the U.S. Army Corps of Engineers, realizing that the Atchafalaya would become the Mississippi if nature were allowed to take its course, began work on a spillway structure to limit the flow of water into the Atchafalaya.

Towns along the Atchafalaya River include Simmesport, Melville, Krotz Springs, and Morgan City near the coast. The Teche flows into the Atchafalaya just above Morgan City.

Since the early days of settlement, the Atchafalaya Swamp has been a major stumbling block to transportation between New Orleans markets and the Attakapas District, which is rich in fish, fur, lumber, moss, and wild game. An amazing geographic phenomenon, it was considered "impassable by man, except along the water communications." One of the largest natural areas of Louisiana, it was by far the largest true swamp in the state and one of the largest in the world. The natural levees of the Mississippi River and Bayou Lafourche form its eastern boundary. To the west the levees of Bayou Teche produce a natural barrier. The Gulf of Mexico is the southern boundary; the northern boundary is near Simmesport, a few miles west of the confluence of the Red, Mississippi, and Atchafalaya rivers. However, north of U.S. Highway 190 stretching westward from Baton Rouge to Lafayette, the swamp is considerably narrower than it is south of the highway.

The railroad tying Morgan City to New Orleans did not cross the part of the swamp east of the Atchafalaya until 1857. It did not reach Lafayette, the center of Attakapas, until 1878. Another line reached northward to Opelousas in 1882. After the 1927 Mississippi River flood, the Corps of Engineers built levees on either side of the Atchafalaya River, which have shrunk the width of the floodway to approximately 15 miles.[14]

Between the alluvial deltas of the streams in south Louisiana lay vast expanses of saltwater and freshwater marsh, teeming with aquatic animal and plant life. As one moves southward toward the Gulf, the deltas narrow, and the salt marsh becomes more expansive.[15] The first inhabitants of the bayou country, the Amerindians,

---

14. Richard Weinstein and Sherman Gagliano, "The Shifting Deltaic Coast of the Lafourche Country and Its Prehistoric Settlement," in Philip Uzee (ed.), *The Lafourche Country: The People and the Land* (Lafayette, La., 1985), 122–49; Malcolm Comeaux, *Atchafalaya Swamp Life: Settlement and Folk Occupations* (Baton Rouge, 1972), 1, 9, 19; Robert M. Crisler, "Bayou Teche," in Edwin Davis (ed.), *The Rivers and Bayous of Louisiana* (Baton Rouge, 1968), 106–108; Merl E. Reed, "Footnotes to the Coastwise Trade—Some Teche Planters and Their Atlantic Factors," *Louisiana History*, VIII (Spring, 1967), 191–93, 196; Donald J. Millet, "The Saga of Water Transportation into Southwest Louisiana to 1900," *Louisiana History*, XV (Fall, 1974), *passim;* Albert Cowdrey, *Land's End: A History of the New Orleans District, U.S. Corps of Engineers* (N.p., 1977), xiv, 50–51. The annual reports of the chief engineer, U.S. Corps of Engineers, and the annual reports of the engineer for the state of Louisiana are a gold mine of information about waterways from the 1830s to modern times.

15. Fred B. Kniffen, *Louisiana: Its Land and People* (Baton Rouge, 1968), 54–59; Philip Uzee, "Bayou Lafourche," in Davis (ed.), *Rivers and Bayous*, 121–28; Barnes Lathrop, "The Pugh Plantations, 1860–1865: A Study of Life in Lower Louisiana" (Ph.D. dissertation, University of Texas, 1946); Donald Davis, "Louisiana Canals and Their Influence on Wetland Development" (Ph.D. dissertation, Louisiana State University, 1973).

lived in this setting by fishing, hunting, and trapping. The first French settlers were greeted by members of the Bayougoula, Washa, and Chawasha tribes. In 1776 the Houma Indians, who gave the parish seat of Terrebonne its name, moved into the area after they were driven from their home on the Mississippi River.[16] Shortly before the American Revolution, Acadians who had been expelled from Nova Scotia by the British in 1755 joined new Spanish settlers in Louisiana. Under Spanish rule Louisiana prospered; settlers swarmed into the Bayou country and the Attakapas country.

Crucial to the growth and development of the many settlements in the bayou country was the transportation link to New Orleans. Without such a connection, settlers could not ship their produce to market or receive essential supplies of manufactured goods. New Orleans became one of the great ports of North America. Products from the entire Mississippi-Ohio-Missouri river systems easily reached the city. Exotic items from Europe, Asia, Africa, and Latin America were to be found in its thriving markets along the riverfront. By 1810 New Orleans housed most of the shops providing necessities for the city and surrounding plantations. Louisiana had seven tanneries, twelve shoemaking establishments, fourteen hat manufacturers, three saddle shops, two soap and candle makers, twenty-eight distilleries, thirty-three blacksmith shops, four gunsmiths, and three wagon makers.[17] Local products found in abundance complemented trade items from the heartland of North America. Shops sold sugar, fish, lumber, moss, furs, wild game, and garden crops. In some ways transporting the products from the surrounding bayou country to New Orleans markets was more difficult than importing trade items from abroad or from the upper Mississippi River.

Even though New Orleans grew in importance, it did not live up to early expectations of its becoming the leading port in the United States. After the panic of 1837, the city had trouble holding on to its position as a major grain-shipping region. Its geographic importance declined with the coming of railroads before the Civil War. Chicago

---

16. Burk and Associates, Inc., *Louisiana Coastal Resources Atlas: Terrebonne Parish* (New Orleans, n.d.), ii.

17. Allie Bayne W. Webb (ed.), *Mistress of Evergreen Plantation: Rachel O'Connor's Legacy of Letters, 1823–1845* (Albany, N.Y., 1983), xxi.

and other midwestern cities grew faster and developed more diversified economies. James De Bow, the leading exponent of southern economic expansion and an advocate of secession, had urged the South to look to the West, rather than to the North, for future trade. He favored government subsidies for railroads to the Pacific coast. Because of south Louisiana's marshy terrain, however, railroad construction was either impossible or prohibitively costly. As late as 1914 the U.S. secretary of war, in a report to Congress, explained the need for canals in south Louisiana. "The land is of such character and so cut by bayous and lakes," he wrote, "that railroad construction is impossible, and no other method of communication than by water is practicable."[18] For that reason canal building, which was cheaper in Louisiana than in upland regions, was economically feasible. When effective east-west canal links across south Louisiana were developed, the region grew and prospered. During the entire period, New Orleans usually ranked second in the nation as a port; today it is again a major grain port.

North-south transportation along the bayous, which generally ran in that direction as they coursed toward the Gulf of Mexico, was never a major problem before the advent of the steamboat. Early settlers readily took to using pirogues, flatboats, and various watercraft as a way of life. The real transportation barrier was east-west linkups to settlements separated by salt or freshwater marsh. To get from one community to another on a nearby bayou just a few miles across the marsh, a settler sometimes had to travel a great distance. He could descend one stream to the Gulf and then ascend an adjacent stream. Or he could ascend the stream on which his settlement lay until he reached a main branch upstream. Quite naturally, early settlers were interested in improving ways of getting their produce to market in New Orleans. When possible, settlers cut pirogue trails or ditches, which the French called *trainasses*, through the marsh. When the light organic soil and aquatic vegetation were removed, the ditches

18. Davis, "Louisiana Canals," iv–vii, 6, 9; John G. Clark, *New Orleans, 1718–1812: An Economic History* (Baton Rouge, 1970), 52–53; Lawrence H. Larsen, "New Orleans and River Trade: Reinterpreting the Role of the Business Community," *Wisconsin Magazine of History*, LXI (Winter, 1977–78), 113–24; U.S. secretary of war quoted in box 43, Robert Ruffin Barrow, Jr., Papers, Division of Archives, Nicholls State University Library, hereinafter cited as RRBP.

filled with water, becoming narrow, shallow canals. In time these grew into canals that were used for drainage, transportation, logging, trapping, and petroleum production in the twentieth century.

Since travel from one remote bayou to another was neither easy nor quick, it was rather limited in the days of subsistence farming before the transportation revolution. At the same time, there was less emphasis on cash crops than in the days of large cotton and sugar plantations. Consequently, there was not much east-west travel. Even the shipments of cash crops was a special occasion rather than a daily or weekly event.

Claude Joseph Villars Dubreuil, an early colonial entrepreneur, built a canal on the west bank of the Mississippi River and used it to great economic advantage. He began work on his canal connecting the river to a branch of Bayou Barataria around 1736. By 1740 he had completed the link to the Bayou Fatma branch of Bayou Barataria. This gave him access to the rich resources of Barataria Bay, famous for its seafood, cypress and other timber resources, and clamshells that the Indians gathered and piled into middens. Dubreuil became a major supplier of building materials for New Orleans. He shipped huge quantities of cypress lumber and clamshells, which were used as a building material, through his canal. Eventually Antoine Foucher became the owner of Dubreuil's canal. Still later François Gardère bought the land and operated the canal that became known as the Gardère Canal.

In time Jean Laffite, the pirate, and his associates inhabited the lower region of Barataria Bay; undoubtedly they used Dubreuil's canal to reach New Orleans with their trade goods. Laffite and his Baratarians needed these early canals in their smuggling operations before they redeemed themselves and became heroes in the Battle of New Orleans in 1815. Through various routes they reached the outskirts of New Orleans to carry on their illicit trade without having to ascend the more carefully guarded Mississippi River.

Dubreuil's son Claude Jr. also became interested in canal building. A short distance upriver he dug a canal that eventually became the Barataria and Lafourche Canal. The plantation on which Claude Jr. started work, possibly as early as 1759, went by a number of names. First it was called Petit Desert; later it was called Little Wilderness;

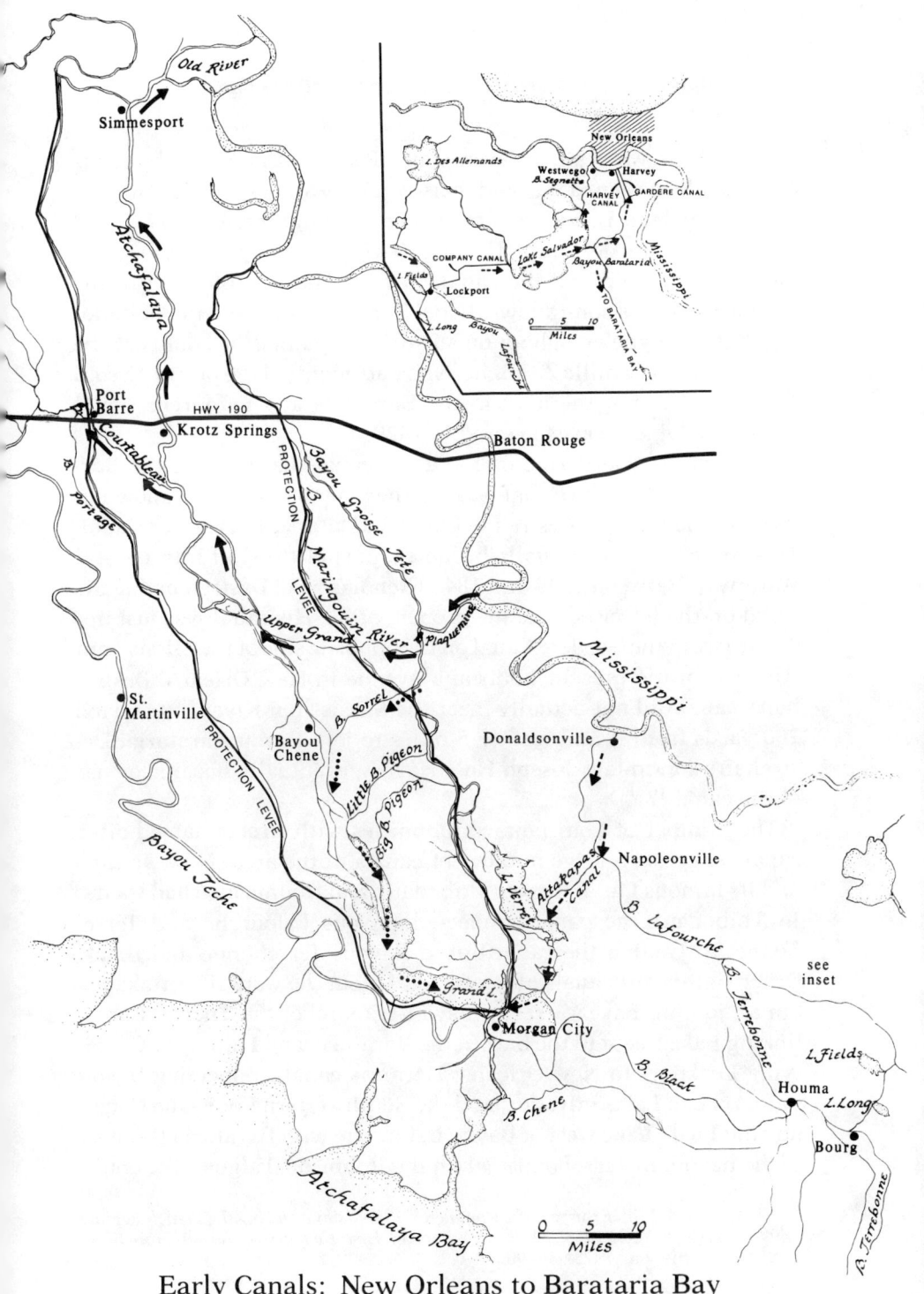

Early Canals: New Orleans to Barataria Bay and the Attakapas District

eventually it was called Seven Oaks. Possibly Claude Jr. built his canal while he owned the land (between 1759 and 1772) or during the time when Jean Louis Trudeau owned the land (between 1775 and 1785). In time Alexandre Harang, a prosperous planter, became owner of the land and the canal. In 1794 Harang sold part of the plantation to his son-in-law, Michel Zeringue, with the understanding that Zeringue's neighbor on an adjacent plantation could use the canal. In 1830 Camille Zeringue, who had acquired the property, sold the canal but not the land to the Barataria and Lafourche Canal Company, which was chartered in 1829.

Between the Gardère Canal and the canal that became the Barataria and Lafourche Canal was another important canal, known in the early days as the Destrehan Canal and later as the Harvey Canal. This route would eventually become a part of the Gulf Intracoastal Waterway. Between 1839 and 1845 Nicholas Noël Destrehan dug his canal on the lower edge of his property line. His canal was just upstream from the Gardère Canal on the opposite side of the Mississippi River from the present Louisiana Avenue in New Orleans. Destrehan's canal did not actually meet the Mississippi River but started 200 yards from it and ran for 5 miles to join Bayou Barataria. Destrehan's son-in-law, Joseph Hale Harvey, eventually became owner of the canal.[19]

The number of Louisiana communities with streets named after canals suggests a large number of canals in the area. New Orleans had its famous Canal Street; Thibodaux and Houma also had theirs. In Thibodaux the canal connected Bayous Lafourche and Terrebonne. In Houma the canal linked Bayous Terrebonne and Black. Other significant canals along Bayou Lafourche were the Attakapas Canal, joining Lake Verret to Bayou Lafourche; the Theriot Canal, linking Lake Boeuf to the bayou; the Barataria and Lafourche Canal, tying Lockport to New Orleans; Harang's canal, connecting Bayou Lafourche to Lake Salvador; and the Southwestern Louisiana Canal, uniting Little Lake west of Bayou Lafourche with Barataria Bay east of the bayou. In Terrebonne Parish the Robinson, Falgout, St. Louis,

19. Nancy M. Miller Surrey, *The Commerce of Louisiana During the French Regime, 1699–1763* (New York, 1916), 34; Betsy Swanson, *Historic Jefferson Parish: From Shore to Shore* (Gretna, La., 1975), 86–90.

and Boudreaux canals served similar transportation needs by connecting important lakes and bayous.[20]

Because of the unique transportation problems of the region, public bodies often associated internal improvements with canal building. During Louisiana's territorial period before statehood, the legislature appropriated monies for canal construction. In 1805 the territorial legislature chartered the New Orleans Navigation Company to build two canals, one westward between New Orleans and the Attakapas and the post at Opelousas, and another on the east bank between the city and Lake Pontchartrain. Because of the close ties between company officials and the city administration, the route to the Attakapas was abandoned in favor of the shorter link from the city via Bayou St. John to the lake. The territorial legislature complained about neglect of the Attakapas route, but the city of New Orleans and the Bank of Louisiana were major stockholders in the navigation company and ruled its destiny.[21]

Thus the Attakapas District remained isolated, as it had been during the colonial period. Since colonial times the Atchafalaya Basin had formed a great natural barrier to transportation between New Orleans and the productive Attakapas District. In time early settlers discovered three natural waterways that crossed the swamp and reached the Attakapas country, but none was totally satisfactory. The three most commonly used waterways were the Bayou Plaquemine route, the Attakapas Canal–Lake Verret route, and the Mississippi River–Old River–Atchafalaya River route.

One popular early route followed Bayou Plaquemine, which branched off from the Mississippi River 30 miles upstream from Donaldsonville and gave its name to the little community that sprang up at the confluence of the two streams. One could travel west on Bayou Plaquemine, enter the upper Grand River, and eventually reach the Atchafalaya River. Bayou Courtableau connected the Atchafalaya River to Bayou Teche, the most important waterway running through the heartland of the Attakapas region. Major Amos

20. Jane DeGrummond, *The Baratarians and the Battle of New Orleans* (Baton Rouge, 1961), *passim;* Davis, "Louisiana Canals," 47–50.
21. Clark, *New Orleans*, 287, 291; Carter Goodrich, *Government Promotion of American Canals and Railroads, 1800–1890* (New York, 1960), 36.

Stoddard, who did a survey of the region in 1812, claimed that ships of 60 or 80 tons could ascend both the Atchafalaya and the Teche for some distance. "But the most convenient navigation to New Orleans," he observed, "is by means of the lower parts of the Chafalia, Plaquemines, LaFourche, and the Mississippi."

Bayou Plaquemine, however, had a number of problems. For that reason Bayou Jacob, a small stream that ran parallel to Bayou Plaquemine, was the first route used. Bayou Plaquemine was usable only four months of the year, when the Mississippi was at flood stage, and then it was a raging stream that could be dangerous to travelers. Its surging waters could overturn boats and drown the victims. The rest of the year it was too shallow to use. In 1770 Bayou Plaquemine was deepened. From then until modern times, it has been an important water link in the area.

In 1765, the year before the Spanish took formal possession of Louisiana and ten years after the expulsion of the Acadians from Nova Scotia by the British, 193 Acadians arrived in New Orleans and received permission to make their way to the Attakapas country. Louis Andry, an experienced engineer, escorted them across the Atchafalaya Swamp via the Bayou Plaquemine route.

Another early traveler using this route was Francisco Bouligny, the founder of New Iberia. He followed Bayou Plaquemine to the Teche country from New Orleans during the Spanish colonial era. Bouligny and other settlers from Málaga in Spain left New Orleans in January 1779 and made their way upriver to Plaquemine. By February 7 they had progressed only 4 leagues west of the settlement, probably dragging their vessels across shallow sections of the bayou. Four days later they reached Bayou Teche, where they established a small settlement. The French had established a settlement nearby, at St. Martinville, called the Attakapas post. Still further north was the Opelousas post, the center of the Opelousas country.

The Bayou Plaquemine route had not improved much by the early days of the territorial period. When Thomas Clark Nicholls, the father of future Louisiana governor Francis T. Nicholls, relocated his family from New Orleans to the Attakapas country, he used the old route in 1805. After ascending the Mississippi River to the town of Plaquemine, Thomas Nicholls was surprised to learn that an

Irishman named Blake charged $75 to guide travelers across the Atchafalaya Swamp. Nicholls considered the figure exorbitant, but since he did not know the way, he agreed reluctantly. Travel by boat was uncomfortable and slow, and the Acadians who worked for Blake consumed provisions needed by the Nicholls family. They also stayed up late at night, drinking and making noise. Finally the travelers reached Butte la Rose and high ground, where they boarded clumsy oxcarts that transported them over bad roads the rest of the way to the Atchafalaya River.

A second important route to the Attakapas District was through the Attakapas Canal near Napoleonville; this canal connected Bayou Lafourche to Lake Verret. Originally the Attakapas Canal may have been a natural outlet for the Lafourche during flood stage. Settlers later dug it out in an attempt to make it a canal usable the year round. From Lake Verret, a traveler could wind his way through a number of waterways and reach the Atchafalaya and the Teche. Not surprisingly, the Attakapas Canal had some of the same shortcomings as Bayou Plaquemine. Low water during most of the year made it unreliable as a means of transportation.

Journalist Daniel Dennett used this route for a trip from Franklin to New Orleans in August 1850, amid loud complaints about the heat and the slow progress. A Frenchman and a black man rowed the skiff, and Dennett described himself as "packed away in the stern of the boat, under an umbrella, with a wet handkerchief tied around my head." When the skiff reached Lake Verret, Dennett took a horse-drawn cart for the next bumpy 28 miles to Donaldsonville. When he arrived, the steamboat for New Orleans had just departed. "Whoever thinks my account of the trip exaggerated," he told readers of the Franklin (La.) *Planters' Banner,* "would do well to try this route some time." Advertisements in the same newspaper frequently announced the replacement of a large steamboat by one with a shallow draft during the low-water season. Because of these handicaps, travelers either avoided the Atchafalaya Swamp altogether by taking the Gulf of Mexico route and entering the lower Atchafalaya-Teche system, or they crossed the swamp in a steamboat and entered the Teche at either the upper or lower end of the swamp.

The third major route from New Orleans to the Teche country, the

Mississippi River–Old River–Atchafalaya River route, was not altogether satisfactory, either. Its length, about 175 miles, was almost twice that of the two routes directly across the swamp. In 1876 Dennett noted that a round trip by steamer from St. Martinville to New Orleans via the Atchafalaya, the mouth of the Red River, and the Mississippi River took nine days.

The Atchafalaya was circuitous and often clogged with logs. Like Bayou Plaquemine, the stream had a strong current during flood stage but was too shallow the rest of the time to permit adequate water transportation. A major problem in recent years has been the tendency of the Atchafalaya to draw an increasing volume of water from the lower Mississippi River. If left to its own designs, the Atchafalaya would become the main channel of the Mississippi River and leave Baton Rouge and New Orleans practically landlocked. Without intervention by the Corps of Engineers today, nature would repeat a pattern of change that began about five thousand years ago. The increased flow of water through the Atchafalaya Swamp brings huge amounts of sandy silt, which is gradually raising the level of the swamp and endangering its existence as a modern geographic wonder.[22]

In 1819 the U.S. government authorized James Leander Cathcart, the Irish-born naval consultant, to conduct a survey of the timber resources of southern Louisiana and southern Alabama. Determined to correct weaknesses exposed by the War of 1812, the navy sought hardwood timbers necessary to build the new American navy. Cathcart used two of the known routes across the Atchafalaya Swamp. His comments about the trip revealed the severity of the

---

22. Comeaux, *Atchafalaya Swamp Life*, 1, 9–11; Crisler, "Bayou Teche," in Davis (ed.), *Rivers and Bayous*, 105–108; Millet, "Saga of Water Transportation," 333–45; Carl A. Brasseaux, *The Founding of New Acadia: The Beginnings of Acadian Life in Louisiana, 1765–1803* (Baton Rouge, 1987), 74–75; Gilbert C. Din, "Lieutenant Colonel Francisco Bouligny and the Malagueno Settlement at New Iberia, 1779," *Louisiana History*, XVII (Spring, 1976), 187–202; Evans J. Casso, *Francis T. Nicholls: A Biographical Tribute* (Thibodaux, La., 1987), 29–31; Amos Stoddard, *Sketches Historical and Descriptive, of Louisiana* (Philadelphia, 1812), 180–81; Daniel Dennett, *Louisiana as It Is* (New Orleans, 1876), 9; Franklin (La.) *Planters' Banner*, August 8, 1850, and *passim*, in "Steamboat Transportation History" box, Morgan City Archives, Morgan City (La.) Public Library.

east-west transportation problem in the bayou country and explained the impetus for constructing the Barataria and Lafourche Canal. In order to conduct his survey, Cathcart had to cross the Atchafalaya Swamp.

To reach Franklin on Bayou Teche, Cathcart and his party sailed from New Orleans upriver to Donaldsonville, where Bayou Lafourche branched from the Mississippi. He sailed down the Lafourche until he reached Napoleonville, where the "Old Canal," the Attakapas Canal, connected Bayou Lafourche to Lake Verret. Once on Lake Verret, Cathcart planned to wind his way through several small lakes and bayous to the Atchafalaya River. From the Atchafalaya near Brashear City, he could reach the mouth of Bayou Teche. However, upon entering Bayou Lafourche on January 2, 1819, he discovered that low water made passage through the Old Canal route impossible.

Thwarted by low water on the Lafourche and the Attakapas Canal, which was a problem for steamboats on the waterway for about six months of the year, Cathcart decided to try the Bayou Plaquemine route. He ascended the Mississippi River to the settlement of Plaquemine, situated 30 miles upstream, halfway between Baton Rouge and Donaldsonville. Undoubtedly encountering the same problems that Bouligny had faced in 1779, Cathcart had to carry his boats 6 miles from Plaquemine until he reached a navigable point on Bayou Plaquemine. From this point he sailed westward and reached the bayous and lakes in the vicinity of Brashear City that are a part of the lower Atchafalaya and the mouth of the Teche.

Besides conducting a survey of the timber resources suited for naval construction in the area, Cathcart kept a detailed journal of the geographic and nautical features of the country. On the Atchafalaya he visited Dr. Walter Brashear's plantation, which became the site of Brashear City, the forerunner of the present Morgan City. The Teche country, with its rich sugar resources, had gigantic problems in getting produce to New Orleans. Some planters shipped their sugar on schooners directly to the Atlantic coast. Others sent flatboats by both of the routes Cathcart had taken, the Attakapas Canal or the Bayou Plaquemine route to the Mississippi River. Teche planters could have sent their cargoes down the Atchafalaya to the Gulf of Mexico to New Orleans, but such a trip would have been impossible in a flatboat.[23]

Timothy Flint, a preacher and editor as well as an astute observer of early nineteenth-century frontier life, also noted east-west transportation problems in his travels through south Louisiana. A careful recorder of significant geographic features, he readily noted and understood the need for a canal linking the Mississippi to the Attakapas country. He pointed out why the Plaquemine and Lafourche routes were not always usable: "The mouths of these Bayous are liable to be choked with timber, and the navigation is generally attended with some difficulty, and is moreover circuitous." He noted further that there were "many communications by water between New Orleans and the lower parts of Louisiana, accessible by the smaller boats." People explored them "for the sake of finding new and shorter routes to their destination."[24]

Indeed, the search for shorter, cheaper routes to market had been going on for many years, and it would continue for many more. Finding them would attract the interest of the antebellum planters of Louisiana. The success of the Erie Canal fired their imaginations and led to the formation of canal companies to solve the east-west transportation problems that had always plagued Louisiana's bayou country.

Early in the nineteenth century the Louisiana legislature passed laws granting monopolies to two steamboat companies doing business in the Attakapas District. In 1821 the legislature chartered the Attakapas Steamboat Company, which operated from the mouth of the Teche to St. Martinville. In 1826 the Opelousas Steamboat Company received a charter granting it exclusive commercial transportation rights along Bayou Plaquemine and through Grand River, the Atchafalaya, and Bayou Courtableau near Washington. By the time of the Civil War, these companies no longer existed, but twenty-nine steamboats were engaged in the New Orleans and Atchafalaya trade; thirty were kept busy with the Bayou Barataria trade. After the war

23. Walter Pritchard *et al.* (eds.), "Southern Louisiana and Southern Alabama in 1819: The Journal of James Leander Cathcart," *Louisiana Historical Quarterly*, XXVIII (July, 1945), 754*n*, 813*n*.
24. "Timothy Flint's Louisiana," in Glenn Conrad (ed.), *Readings in Louisiana History* (New Orleans, 1978), 115.

they gradually reduced the prewar cost of transporting a bale of cotton to New Orleans from $3.75 to only $1.25. Making regular runs along the route were the steamers *Anna E, Irene, Selma, Jennie Howell,* and *Ruth.*[25]

The financial success of the Erie Canal, which opened in 1825, undoubtedly influenced many investors during the early years of the transportation revolution. Yet as Robert Wiebe noted, that canal did not cause leaders in other states to concede the West to New York.[26] An amazing engineering and economic project, the Erie Canal fired the imaginations of millions of Americans grappling with the problem of shipping agricultural produce to market. It forced consideration of significant political factors regarding government subsidies of internal improvement projects, for many builders realized that individual companies, and even state legislatures, could not afford to build canals without federal aid.

In the late 1790s Gouverneur Morris and DeWitt Clinton, both of New York, envisioned a canal linking the Hudson River to the Great Lakes at Lake Erie. They hoped to circumvent the old Appalachian Mountain barrier to transportation between the West and the East coasts by digging a canal where the Mohawk River cut through the rock on its way to the Hudson. Generally, shipping from the Midwest to the East Coast over the Appalachian Mountains was more expensive than shipping down the Mississippi to New Orleans and then transshipping to the Atlantic coast.

The state of New York chartered two companies to initiate work on the canal. Soon both companies needed financial assistance, which they hoped would come from the federal government. In 1806 there was much talk in Washington about a national road; in 1808 Treasury Secretary Albert Gallatin's plan called for the expenditure of $20 million for canal and road construction. New York hoped to capitalize on the scheme, as did Ohio and Pennsylvania, but monies from

---

25. Millet, "Saga of Water Transportation," 339–43; *Biographical and Historical Memoirs,* II, 47.
26. John C. L. Andreason, "Internal Improvements in Louisiana, 1824–1837," *Louisiana Historical Quarterly,* XXX (January, 1947), 11, 28–31, 40, 50; Merl E. Reed, *New Orleans and the Railroads* (Baton Rouge, 1966), 5; Robert Wiebe, *The Opening of American Society from the Adoption of the Constitution to the Eve of Disunion* (New York, 1984), 140, 288.

Washington never came easily. In 1817 President James Madison vetoed a bill that would have provided $1.5 million in federal aid to the Erie Canal project. New York decided to continue the work without federal aid. By 1819 a section of the canal between Rome and Utica opened; in 1825 the canal reached Buffalo and Lake Erie. By 1829 foreign investors had acquired approximately a half-interest in the canal.

The Erie Canal was a great financial success. It carried a tremendous volume of trade in special barges, or canalboats. In New York harbor twenty or thirty canalboats were tied together and hauled by steamboat upriver to Albany to begin their trip westward on the canal. In a short time the cost of shipping a ton of wheat from Buffalo to New York City dropped from $100 to $10. In the late stages of the transportation revolution, however, even the mighty Erie Canal could not escape the changes technology brought. By 1869 the New York Central and the Erie railroads carried more freight than did the canal. In 1882 the Erie Canal became a free canal; by 1898 it had fallen into disuse. In 1903 portions of the old canal route became a barge canal.[27]

Louisiana entrepreneurs undoubtedly became excited about the success of the Erie Canal. They likewise realized that the marsh country of south Louisiana was quite flat and had no rock formations or difficult structures to cut through if a canal were dug. Perhaps, too, they realized early in the railroad era that railroad construction across terrain that was largely marsh would not be practical. Somehow they may have overlooked the fact that canals in remote south Louisiana would not link as large an area or reach as broad a population base as that served by the Erie Canal. In time Louisiana investors in canal projects learned that there were unique local disadvantages to building canals in south Louisiana. Because of the danger of flooding during the high-water season, Louisiana canals needed locks where they intersected major waterways. Constructing such gates on watery foundations taxed the engineering and fiscal capacity of in-

27. Ralph Andrist, "The Erie Canal Passed This Way," *American Heritage*, XIX (October, 1968), 22–31, 77–80; Jonathan Hughes, *American Economic History* (Dallas, 1983), 175–78, 180.

vestors. Even when completed according to specifications, these expensive locks could not always stand up to the flow of the Mississippi River during flood stage. Swirling currents undermined foundations and created crevasses that allowed water to inundate large areas. Additional canal expenses included acquiring rights-of-way; building and maintaining bridges over canals; paying bridgetenders and toll collectors; redredging canals periodically; and after 1884, clearing the canals of water hyacinths.[28]

It is not surprising that enterprising planters sought new routes for transporting cotton and sugar to New Orleans markets during the boom years of the 1820s and 1830s. Obviously there was a need to find a route that was superior to the three currently in use. The Attakapas Canal–Lake Verret and the Bayou Plaquemine routes both cut across the swamp and were short. Both routes, however, were circuitous and not usable except during high water. Neither could accommodate large river steamers. The Old River route was long and slow, which added to costs, and it was not totally reliable.

Some of the great colonial planters of Louisiana devoted their skills and resources to finding a better transportation system across sugar country. That they would eventually succeed in canal-building ventures during the heyday of the railroad is as much a tribute to their economic and political acumen as it is due to the unique geography of south Louisiana. The region's nearly aquatic surface, called "trembling prairies" by early French settlers, blocked railroad expansion to remote agricultural markets and permitted antiquated toll canals to operate into the second decade of the twentieth century. The construction of canals is intimately related to the social, political, and economic life of the region. It is also largely a story of the hardheaded determination of one planter, Robert Ruffin Barrow—and later his son Robert Jr.—to build and operate a canal, despite even the ravages of the Civil War. The two generations of Barrows, more than anyone else, were responsible for Louisiana's one-hundred-year canal history. Until the first quarter of the twentieth

---

28. See RRBP and BFP, which document the economic activities of the Barataria and Lafourche Canal Company from 1829 until it became a part of the Gulf Intracoastal Waterway in 1925.

century, the Barataria and Lafourche Canal carried a portion of the goods transported by the inland water route crossing Louisiana. This canal influenced the Corps of Engineers when it constructed the Gulf Intracostal Waterway, following generally the old Barataria and Lafourche Canal route.

2

The Barataria and Lafourche Canal

Robert R. Barrow was not directly involved in the formation of the Barataria and Lafourche Canal Company (B & L), but he was soon to play a key role in its destiny. In 1829, just one year after Barrow arrived in Terrebonne, Dr. Walter Brashear, of the Teche country, and Judge Charles Derbigny, of New Orleans, formed the Barataria and Lafourche Canal Company to link the Attakapas country to the Mississippi River near New Orleans.

Walter Brashear was born in Kentucky in 1776. He studied medicine in Philadelphia and became a surgeon in his native state. In 1803 he married Margaret Barr, who was to bear him eight children before her death in 1835. In 1809 the Brashears came to Belle Isle in the lower Atchafalaya Delta. In time Brashear bought Tiger Island plantation, which became the town of Brashear, the forerunner of the present Morgan City. Brashear represented the Attakapas District in the Louisiana legislature, serving in the House from 1835 until 1846 and in the Senate from 1846 until 1850. He was a Whig and a prominent member of the committee to select the site for a new state capitol in 1847.[1]

Charles Derbigny, the other cofounder of the canal company, was the son of Governor Pierre Derbigny. In 1819 Governor Jacques Vil-

1. MS-45, folder 1, Brashear Collection, Morgan City Archives, Morgan City (La.) Public Library.

leré appointed the young Derbigny justice of the peace for Orleans Parish. In 1832 Governor Alexandre B. Roman appointed him a director of the Barataria and Lafourche Canal Company. Like Brashear, Derbigny served in the Louisiana legislature; he was president of the Senate in the mid-1830s. In the 1850s Derbigny ran unsuccessfully for governor on the Know-Nothing ticket.[2]

Derbigny and Brashear undoubtedly were aware of the failure of the controversial New Orleans Navigation Company to reach the Attakapas country. They likewise noted the importance of government subsidies to transportation. In 1811 the territorial legislature for Orleans appropriated $500 to improve the road along the Attakapas Canal connecting Bayou Lafourche and Lake Verret. Later the state legislature formed a committee on internal improvements; in 1826 the state hired an engineer. In the 1830s the state subscribed funds for a number of canal and railroad projects under the jurisdiction of the Louisiana Board of Public Works, which oversaw railroad and canal construction. When the United States distributed surplus funds to the states in 1837, the Louisiana legislature formed a committee to decide how monies should be dispersed.

Derbigny and Brashear envisioned a bold new route to the Teche— a southern route that would be even shorter than the old Attakapas Canal–Lake Verret or Bayou Plaquemine routes, and considerably shorter than the Mississippi River–Old River–Atchafalaya River route that began above Baton Rouge. The two men did not plan an entirely new canal; they would instead provide crucial linkups to already functioning canals and natural waterways. If they could connect several important rivers and bayous, their plan might work. If any link in the chain failed, however, their entire concept seemed doomed to fail.[3]

Founders of the canal obviously were aware of the rapid growth of the plantation system in the early days of the transportation revolution. In 1803, at the time of the Louisiana Purchase, 50,000 people inhabited the territory. In 1810 about 75,000 people lived in the pres-

---

2. MS 13, folders 7, 11, Historic New Orleans Collection, 533 Royal St., New Orleans.
3. Thomas R. Landry, "The Political Career of Robert Charles Wickliffe, Governor of Louisiana, 1856–1850," *Louisiana Historical Quarterly*, XXV (July, 1942), 681.

ent Louisiana; many more poured in when they learned of pending statehood. By 1820 the population had more than doubled from the 1803 figure, to about 200,000, and the growth trend continued. In 1830 the population was 215,000; in 1840 it was 250,000; and in 1860 it reached 700,000. St. Mary Parish, Brashear's home region and traditionally the largest sugar-producing area in the state, had a population in 1830 of 6,442, two-thirds of whom were slaves; in 1840 the number reached 8,950; and in 1850 it reached 13,697. Terrebonne grew in similar fashion, from 2,121 to 4,410 to 7,724 during the same period of time, as did Lafourche and Assumption parishes on Bayou Lafourche. The river parishes of St. John, St. Charles, and St. James grew at a slightly slower rate. These rural sugar parishes had few urban centers. Even in 1880 their major settlements were small: Napoleonville had a population of 497, Lafayette had 815, Thibodaux had 1,515, Houma had 1,084, and New Iberia had 2,709. Other sugar settlements on the Teche were small: Franklin had 1,702 people, Centerville had 254, Patterson had 500, and Morgan City had 2,015. These hamlets remained small because they were not trading centers for the planters, who normally conducted business directly through factors in New Orleans.[4]

Bayou Black, the little stream that ran westward from Houma toward the lower Atchafalaya, was a significant part of the water network plans of Derbigny and Brashear, for it reached Berwick Bay through Bayou Boeuf and ran to Houma less than a mile from Bayou Terrebonne. Connecting the Black to the Terrebonne at Houma with a short canal and clearing the Black for navigation were essential. In Houma a canal less than a mile long would link the Black to the Terrebonne. Brashear, who lived on a plantation on the lower Atchafalaya, undoubtedly had pored over maps while studying ways to make the Black the avenue to Houma.

Another big barrier was getting from Bayou Terrebonne to Bayou Lafourche. Here several old canals had enjoyed limited success. Near Bourg the old Belanger canal extended toward Lake Long, which was only 3 miles from Lake Field. William Field, who owned land near the small freshwater lake bearing his name, had experimented with a

4. Population figures come from U.S. Bureau of the Census, most notably annual compendiums and abstracts.

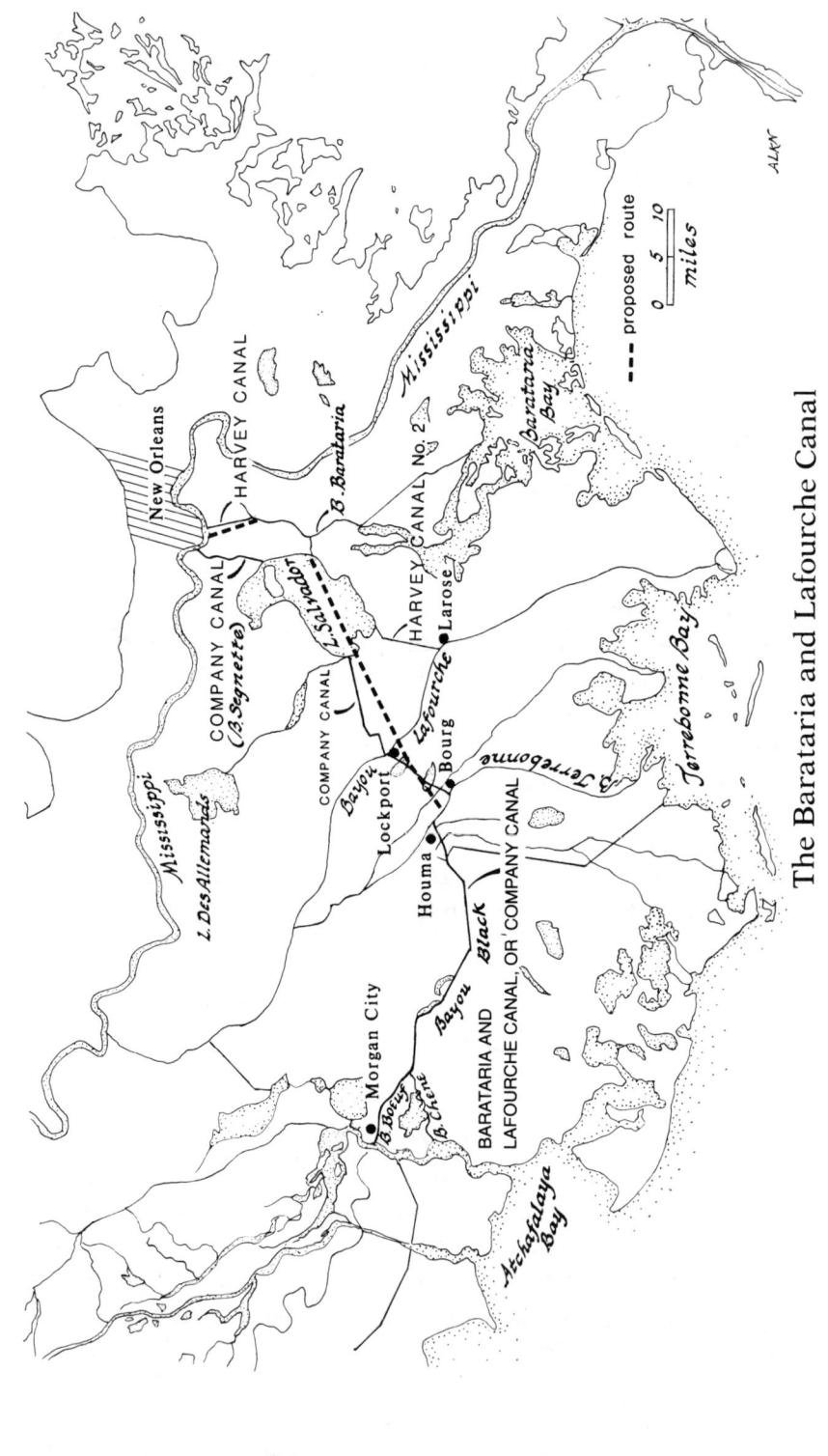

The Barataria and Lafourche Canal

canal between Bayou Lafourche and the lake, hoping to use the current flowing between the two bodies to drive a waterwheel and gristmill.

A third significant area was between Bayou Lafourche and Lake Salvador, which had ancient links to New Orleans and Barataria Bay. Dubreuil's canal, from the Mississippi to Lake Salvador, opened in 1740. As early as 1817, maps indicated the presence of some type of canal from Bayou Lafourche eastward toward the Mississippi River.[5]

Obviously both Brashear and Derbigny had political influence, and they would need legislative support for their plan to work. They realized that natural waterways would have to be deepened and widened in certain areas. They foresaw the need for constructing locks where their canal intersected major waterways. On paper, at least, their concept seemed logical and economically feasible. As envisioned, the Barataria and Lafourche route would complete the long-sought link from New Orleans to the Attakapas country. The investors planned to traverse the Atchafalaya Swamp by digging canals to connect natural waterways running south of it.

Derbigny and Brashear combined resources with a number of subscribers and applied for and received a charter in 1829 from the state of Louisiana. According to Robert Barrow, investors in the Barataria and Lafourche Canal Company were for the most part farmers interested in improving ways of getting produce to market. His description was accurate only if one included in the term *farmers* both subsistence farmers and great planters. Most of the directors were landowners of importance.

Act 38 of 1829, passed by the Louisiana legislature and signed by Governor Pierre Derbigny, provided sizable benefits to the private canal company owned in part by the governor's son. Other original B & L stockholders included L. LaBranche, Camille Zeringue, Noël B. LeBreton, F. Fazend, and Walter Brashear. The B & L was chartered "for the purpose of digging a canal from the Mississippi to Bayou Lafourche." A subsidiary was to build from the Lafourche

---

5. Stanley Faye, "Privateers of Guadeloupe and Their Establishment in Barataria," *Louisiana Historical Quarterly*, XXIII (April, 1940), 438; Donald Davis, "Louisiana Canals and Their Influence on Wetland Development" (Ph.D. dissertation, Louisiana State University, 1973), 51–58.

westward. The B & L's capital stock was $150,000, divided into 1,500 shares of $100 each. The governor was to appoint five commissioners to sell B & L stock. When 600 shares had been sold, the commissioners could advertise in local newspapers and call for an election of five directors of the B & L. Voting strength was based on shares owned: One to five shares entitled a stockholder to one vote, but no person could have over ten votes in all. The stock was negotiable. The board of directors served without compensation, but it elected the president, Charles Derbigny, who received compensation. The company could issue dividends semiannually if it showed a profit; it had to submit an annual report to the legislature. The B & L was authorized to charge tolls of $1.00 on vessels weighing a half-ton or more and $0.50 on those weighing less than a half-ton. The company was to grant a discount of 30 percent to steamboats "on account of their machinery."

The B & L, whose legal life was to be fifty years, was authorized to purchase lands for rights-of-way. And finally, the act provided for a state subsidy. The treasurer subscribed to 100 shares of B & L stock in the name of the state of Louisiana. In other words, Louisiana invested $10,000 in the B & L. The governor could appoint two B & L directors with Senate approval, presumably to look after the state's interests.

The law provided that the B & L construct locks on the Mississippi River according to specifications, beginning where Westwego is today, on "Mr. Dugue's plantation." In keeping with the law, the company was to construct another lock at Lockport: "At the point at which said Canal will communicate with the Lafourche there shall be established well secured locks or sluices."

In 1829 the state legislature also created the Lafourche and Terrebonne Navigation Company, a subsidiary of the B & L that was to build a canal from Bayou Lafourche westward toward Attakapas if the B & L failed to build a canal all the way to Berwick Bay. The Lafourche and Terrebonne Navigation Company stock was capitalized at $100,000, or 1,000 shares at $100 each. Before long the subsidiary company complained of neglect by the parent company. Taylor Beattie, of Thibodaux, became president of the subsidiary.[6]

6. Certified copies of legislation affecting the Company Canal can be found in box 1,

The route chosen by the Barataria and Lafourche Canal Company was more carefully determined than a cursory look at maps would indicate. Established with an eye toward economy, the route followed natural waterways whenever possible. These would be linked by short canals across marshland. The planter-investors hoped to keep construction costs down. Yet the Company Canal, as the B & L was often called, logically had to follow a route that was as near a straight line as possible between New Orleans and the towns along the course to the Attakapas District.

The Company Canal was to begin where Westwego is today, on the Mississippi River opposite New Orleans. There the company would dig a canal to Bayou Segnette, which flowed into Lake Salvador. From this lake the B & L would cut a canal to Bayou Lafourche near the settlement of Lockport. On the west bank of Bayou Lafourche the canal was to continue through Lake Field to Lake Long and thence to Bayou Terrebonne near Bourg, along the old Belanger canal route. Then the route would proceed up Bayou Terrebonne to Houma, where a short canal through town would reach Bayou Black, which veered sharply westward toward Morgan City. In the Morgan City area, Bayou Black branched into Bayous Boeuf and Chêne, which flowed into the Atchafalaya.[7]

Even before the B & L had made much progress constructing the canal, an accommodating state legislature granted other benefits. Act 22 of 1831 authorized B & L board members to open or close stock subscription when expedient. It also authorized the B & L to charge tolls on the Attakapas Canal, the old route near Napoleonville on Bayou Lafourche that Francisco Bouligny and James Cathcart had used. Act 3 of 1833 extended the company's life to sixty-eight years, granted a tax-exempt status for twenty-five years, gave the company the exclusive right to dig canals for twenty years, and provided the company a monopoly on toll ferries it maintained on the canal at the intersection with the Mississippi River and with Bayou Lafourche. For these benefits the state received authorization to take over direc-

---

Robert Ruffin Barrow, Jr., Papers, Division of Archives, Nicholls State University Library, hereinafter cited as RRBP.
7. "Circular of the Barrataria [sic] and Lafourche Canal Company No. 2," April 12, 1866 (Box "1833–1912," RRBP).

tion of the canal thirty years hence, ostensibly when it would be a money-making venture, simply by paying off the stockholders.[8]

Acquiring rights-of-way across private property for construction of the canal posed no great barrier in the early 1800s, when settlements were sparse and the marsh country was not known for its rich mineral resources. Some rights-of-way, especially those across remote stretches of marshland, were carelessly acquired. Possibly the B & L did not even bother to acquire title in some instances. Even though many settlers gave land along the canal to improve transportation, there were a number of questionable titles along the route, some discovered only when Robert Barrow's descendants tried to sell the canal to the U.S. government in the 1920s.

A number of significant donations got the B & L started on its ambitious project. In 1833 Charles Derbigny and Noël B. LeBreton donated to the Company Canal a strip of land 300 feet wide along the Vacherie ridge east of Bayou Lafourche for construction of a canal, providing that no slaves or intoxicating liquors would ever be sold on the canal. William Witherspoon and his wife gave a narrow tract in Houma, "wishing to encourage the Barataria and Lafourche Canal Company and the Lafourche and Terrebonne Navigation Company" in their efforts to link Bayous Terrebonne and Black. The Witherspoons stipulated, however, that the company "give forever to the public a highway on each side of said canal." Other donors were less fussy or specific. Laurent Pichauff, who gave a 1-arpent tract near Bourg on Bayou Terrebonne, specified only that the donated land go "to such direction as will suit best the company to dig the canal intended to connect the Lafourche to the Terrebonne." Thomas Shields, agent for the B & L in Houma, accepted the Pichauff donation in 1838. In 1840 Richard Ellis, who was also a company agent, bought a small tract in Houma, located between Bayous Terrebonne and Black, for the company from Heloise Verret for $525. Many of the early transactions did not specifically locate the land donated to the B & L. Some were written in French, and the records are not always well preserved.

8. Box 1, RRBP.

Businessmen in remote sections of the bayou country eagerly encouraged the B & L in hopes of becoming part of a major transportation network that would increase the value of hard-to-reach virgin lands. On Bayou Lafourche, William Field played a significant role in the growth and development of the Company Canal. A native of Rhode Island, Field owned huge tracts of land on both sides of Bayou Lafourche in the area of the present Lockport, near the early settlement of Longueville. At one time he owned Rienzi plantation near Thibodaux. Using his own barges, Field shipped sugar from the lower Terrebonne through early canals to Lake Long and Lake Field, located to the rear of his property. On January 14, 1833, he donated to B & L president Charles Derbigny a tract of land fronting 5 arpents on both sides of Bayou Lafourche at Longueville. The land Field donated to the B & L was contiguous to an old canal he had constructed to connect Bayou Lafourche and Lake Field. He intended the donated land to be used as a townsite if the B & L completed the canal from Bayou Lafourche to Bayou Terrebonne. In 1835 Allen D'Hèmecourt surveyed the area, calling his work the map of Longueville, after the nearby settlement. In 1837 Derbigny sold lots on the site for the B & L. After locks were constructed on the east bank of the bayou, the settlement became known as Lockport. Undoubtedly it was named after the more famous town on the Erie Canal in New York.[9] A number of streets in the town—Lafourche, Barataria, and Canal—indicate close ties to the B & L.

Poor roads and the uncertainty of water transportation had piqued the interest of Louisianians in canal and railroad construction. Then, during the 1830s, an incredible expansion in money and banking in the state resulted from the British easing credit for rail and canal ventures. In New Orleans alone twelve new banks or improvement companies with banking privileges were chartered. Soon Louisiana ranked second only to Pennsylvania in the amount of money invested in banks. Unfortunately, investors did not use these resources to solve

---

9. Lafourche Parish Donation Book, Thibodaux, La., "B," fol. 13; Terrebonne Parish Conveyance Book, Houma, La. (hereinafter cited as TCB), "G," fol. 382, 444; TCB "H," fol. 86, 273; boxes "1833–1912," "1925," RRBP; Lockport (La.) *Eagle*, December 21, 1901 (Box "1901," RRBP).

nagging transportation problems. Some improvement companies speculated in land instead of building railroads or canals; panics in 1837 and 1839 precipitated a rash of bank failures.

This led the state legislature to draft sound banking laws and to subsidize internal improvement companies. Railroad companies received more attention than canal companies, but the B & L came in for its share of aid. In 1833 the legislature created the board of public works, which owned over 150 slaves and its own steamboats with which to improve navigation on waterways. Governor Alexandre Mouton once publicly criticized the board for its failure to act. Sometimes the board bought stock in private improvement companies if matching funds from citizens were forthcoming. In the 1830s the Gas Light and Banking Company of New Orleans and the board each bought 500 shares of B & L stock. This practice of government aid to private companies was not unique; other states had similar policies.[10]

Without a doubt, the Company Canal benefited from political influence the planters and canal investors wielded. As already noted, Charles Derbigny, the B & L's first president, was the son of the governor who signed the bill creating the canal corporation. One of the original B & L investors in 1829, Derbigny was president of the Louisiana Senate in 1835, when Act 58 was passed and signed by Governor Edward Douglass White, who was also a planter. This piece of internal-improvement legislation boosted the B & L both directly and indirectly. Section 1 of Act 58 authorized the state treasurer to purchase 500 shares of company stock, which in essence was a $50,000 subsidy. Other sections of the law called for appropriation of $100,000 for the board of internal improvement for the purchase of slaves to improve navigation on streams. The act authorized the B & L to use one-third of the slaves owned by the board to complete the Company Canal, at a rate of compensation of $150 per year per slave. Specifically, the board's slaves were to open the canal from Lake Field to Bayou Lafourche at Lockport. Section 10 authorized the union of the B & L and its subsidiary, the Lafourche and Terrebonne Navigation Company. Section 10 was particularly distasteful

10. Merl E. Reed, "Boom or Bust—Louisiana's Economy During the 1830's," *Louisiana History*, IV (Winter, 1963), 38–39, 48–51.

to investors from Terrebonne Parish, who felt that the B & L neglected the western portion of the canal in favor of the part east of Bayou Lafourche. In time the controversy would lead to legislative and legal warfare between the factions.

The nepotism from which the B & L benefited would be illegal today or in violation of the codes of ethics of most states. However, wealthy planters who dominated Louisiana politics from the antebellum period to the turn of the century maintained a cavalier attitude toward public spending. They assumed in their paternalistic way that their actions would eventually serve the general welfare. Certainly Robert Barrow profited from state aid to canal projects. As a Whig he endorsed a program of state and national aid to road- and canal-building efforts. In that sense he was less hypocritical than those who advocated states' rights on sensitive issues like slavery but sought pork barrel legislation to support pet projects.

Louisiana was probably no different from other states. Nepotism and genteel advantage had always been the norm in Louisiana's French and Spanish past; noblesse oblige had not disappeared but been relegated to its normal secondary position. Louisiana may have developed an impersonal attitude toward its privileged classes, but when it came to building public transportation, it was similar to every other state. Carter Goodrich's study of government aid to railroads and canals indicates that extensive state, federal, and local aid went to transportation systems throughout much of the United States. In that sense Louisiana was like the rest of the country. However, even with the support of a munificent state legislature, investors in the Company Canal faced serious obstacles to the completion of their canal network.

Reports of the state engineers and later of the U.S. Corps of Engineers indicated substantial difficulties in keeping open to navigation the natural waterways so vital to the B & L. Streams that were accessible the year around to pirogues and flatboats could not necessarily accommodate the larger, deeper-draft steamboats that appeared in large numbers starting around 1830. The Company Canal would be of limited use if it did not link New Orleans to the Attakapas country or if north-south transportation on the streams it traversed was not a routine matter. On paper the concept of the Company Canal linking navigable streams with relatively short canals across marshland or prairie was feasible and inexpensive. The practical realities, B & L investors soon learned, were a bit more complicated. Particularly troublesome were navigation problems on Bayous Lafourche, Terrebonne, Black, Teche, and Plaquemine. The rivers, too—the Mississippi and the Atchafalaya—posed unique problems. All of these difficulties surfaced even before the B & L tackled the problem of building locks where the Company Canal intersected navigable streams.

In the mid-1830s the state engineer's office came to realize that navigational problems were perennial; clearing streams was a seasonal task, not a one-time proposition. Benjamin Buisson, assistant engineer for the board of public works, elaborated on the problem. To begin with, he said, the state needed a dredging machine for use on Bayou Lafourche. This bayou ran through a rich agricultural region that was densely populated, but it essentially had been neglected. At both its upper and lower ends there were serious encumbrances to navigation. Old schooners that had sunk at the mouth of the bayou had remained for years; sand and trees had collected and become a barrier to navigation except during high-water season. The Attakapas Canal linking the bayou to Lake Verret, which Buisson thought offered the best route between the Teche and the Mississippi, needed to be widened and straightened. Bayou Black, a crucial link in the Company Canal from Terrebonne to Berwick Bay, needed much dredging and clearing before it would be usable.

The state appropriated $86,328 for corrective action in 1834 and sent its engineers, boats, and slaves to several trouble spots. Although some progress was made clearing Bayou Plaquemine, things went badly on the Atchafalaya, where seven slaves and an assistant engineer named Welsh fell victim to cholera and died. Severe summer storms toppled trees, which fell into and blocked Bayou Boeuf, a key link between Berwick Bay and Bayou Black. Friction within the ranks of the B & L did not help either. Feuds between the parent company and its subsidiary, the Lafourche and Terrebonne Navigation Company, prevented a united front before the state legislature.

Both Buisson and E. Rousseau, the secretary of the board of public works, expressed doubts about the economic feasibility of completing the Company Canal at state expense. Fortunately for B & L investors, the reports of these two men did not always influence policy decisions. Clearing Bayou Lafourche, Buisson said, "will exceed the present means of the state, and will not be justified by the advantages that may result." He noted that the B & L was open to small craft from the Mississippi to about 7 miles from the Lafourche. A few cuts through the marsh would take the canal all the way to Bayou Terrebonne, but between Houma and Morgan City, Buisson saw serious problems. From where the Company Canal reached Bayou Terrebonne, near Bourg, to the town of Houma, extensive work would be required "to double its present width the whole distance." The shortcut from Bayou Terrebonne to Bayou Black would not be difficult, Buisson thought, but much work on the Black was needed to reach navigable water leading to Berwick Bay.

Rousseau acknowledged that completing the work would be of benefit to the citizens of Terrebonne, but he ended on an ominous note: "But whether the advantages to be derived from extending it to Berwick's Bay will be commensurate with the expenditure and time required is doubtful." The only hope for the future came from Buisson, who suggested that since federal lands along the route were enhanced because of state expenditure, the United States should cede some lands to the state of Louisiana.[11] Here lies only a hint of what was in time to become extensive federal aid to the development of waterways throughout the country.

Work on the Company Canal began in earnest during the 1830s. Steamboats from the Attakapas District could ascend Bayou Black to the rear of Houma, which faced Bayou Terrebonne less than a mile away. Slaves owned by the Lafourche and Terrebonne Navigation Company began excavation work in 1840 on the canal between Bayous Black and Terrebonne.[12] *De Bow's Review* referred to the

11. Carter Goodrich, *Government Promotion of American Canals and Railroads, 1800–1890* (New York, 1960), *passim;* Louisiana Board of Public Works, Annual Reports, 1834, 1835, Louisiana State Engineer, Annual Report, 1842, all in Louisiana Room, Troy H. Middleton Library, Louisiana State University.
12. Box 1, RRBP; Chief Engineer, U.S. Corps of Engineers, Annual Report, 1881 (Box 43, RRBP).

Attakapas and Barataria Canal as a part of the not-yet-completed Bayou Black route.[13] The B & L looked to the board of public works for help in clearing Bayou Black below Houma, where silting was a serious problem. Buisson requested dredging machines like the steam dredge owned by the Company Canal. The B & L dredge worked well, Buisson stated, digging canals across prairies, but it cost between $4,000 and $4,500. In 1842 State Engineer George Dunbar reported that Captain J. B. Harris, aboard the steamer *Experiment*, had used eighteen slaves to clear 4 miles of Bayou Black below Houma. Harris had another mile to clear before reaching the Company Canal cut linking Bayous Black and Terrebonne.

Dunbar had a decentralized view of financing navigational programs. He did not favor asking the federal government for financial aid; he recommended turning over to the parishes the responsibility for maintaining navigation on streams cleared at state expense. He criticized the system of placing temporary structures on Bayou Plaquemine, as these were usually washed away by high water on the Mississippi. Dunbar recommended that rather than waste state funds each year, Bayou Plaquemine be closed with a dam, since it was usable for transportation only four months of the entire year. Planters could use the longer route via the Atchafalaya to reach the Attakapas District. Like Buisson, Dunbar stumbled upon an issue that would ignite controversy well into the twentieth century, even after the U.S. Corps of Engineers assumed responsibility for levee construction and flood protection. Dunbar also understood the economic situation, realizing that because of navigational problems, planters "have been subjected to enormous charges in getting out their crops."

During the 1830s the B & L constructed locks at Lockport, where the Company Canal crossed Bayou Lafourche. These first locks were built of cypress timbers rather than masonry. At midcentury the state of Louisiana helped build the more substantial locks of brick and metal.

Even during the colonial period, governmental subsidies drew public officials into controversies that would carry over into the

13. Randolph A. Bazet, "Houma—An Historical Sketch," in *Centennial Celebration, Houma, Louisiana, May 10–13, 1934* (Morgan City, La., 1934), 31; H. B. Price, *De Bow's Review*, VIII (January–June 1850), 146–50.

twentieth century and directly affect the Barrows and the Company Canal. The most notable disputes involved tolls and public accessibility to natural waterways. By 1822 Louisiana officials had second thoughts about a charter granted to the New Orleans Navigation Company, which managed a canal running from the inner city via Bayou St. John to Lake Pontchartrain. Attorneys for the state argued that the company charged excessive tolls "to enrich about thirty individuals." They stressed the theme of the exploited farmers: "All the profits of their labour, which ought to feed and clothe their children are swallowed up by the company." However, the legislature failed to revoke the charter of the navigation company.

Attorneys for the state, however, found other reasons for revoking the charter. Citing federal laws regarding navigable streams, they contended that Bayou St. John was a natural waterway that should remain in public use, free of tolls or impediments of any kind. They cited evidence to prove that sizable vessels had been using the bayou long before the navigation company was chartered.

Attorneys for the New Orleans Navigation Company effectively countered charges levied by the state. They refuted the notion that the charter was illegal by pointing out that the federal government on several occasions had granted land adjacent to the canal to the company, both during the territorial period and during the early days of statehood after 1812. Denying that the company made excessive profits at the expense of the general public, company attorneys pointed out that tolls were used to maintain and improve navigation on the canal.

Company attorneys were particularly effective on the navigability issue. Bayou St. John was a "miserable channel," they claimed; it became "a great public highway" because "we have made it so." They presented overwhelming evidence to show that the bayou was often impassable for long periods of time, trapping vessels unlucky enough to be in the basin during extended periods of low water. State Supreme Court Justice François Xavier Martin agreed with company attorneys and ruled in favor of the defendants. He saw no valid reason for revoking the charter of the navigation company.

Martin's opinion conflicted with evolving federal interpretation of the right of the government to regulate interstate commerce, but for many years his position influenced Louisiana courts. Inevitably, grants from governmental bodies increased public involvement in transportation and sparked constitutional debate that changed little over the years. In time litigation over waterways helped delineate the bounds of the commerce clause of the U.S. Constitution.

Taylor Beattie, who was president of the Lafourche and Terrebonne Navigation Company, complained frequently that B & L directors had been neglecting canal operations west of Bayou Lafourche in Terrebonne Parish. Beattie and his associates were most interested in completing the short canal in Thibodaux connecting Bayous Lafourche and Terrebonne and in the canal in Houma connecting Bayous Black and Terrebonne. When the B & L failed to act on these projects, Beattie attempted to complete the canals in Houma and Thibodaux without its concurrence.

However, the B & L had considerable political clout and frustrated Beattie's efforts. In 1843 the Louisiana legislature passed Act 172, which permitted the B & L to collect tolls on upper Bayou Terrebonne between Houma and Thibodaux and on the short canal in Thibodaux. The act spelled out toll rates the company could charge on a navigable stream. Another section of the law provided that the B & L would receive double the normal tolls if it were required to sue in a court of law in order to obtain payment.

The Terrebonne Parish delegation to the state legislature finally secured legislation in 1846 that separated the Lafourche and Terrebonne Navigation Company from the B & L. Section 4 of Act 78, which Governor Isaac Johnson signed on May 25, 1846, created two separate entities, each autonomous in its own area. The law called for the B & L to compensate the Lafourche and Terrebonne Company for completing the canal in Houma with its own slave labor. But that did not end the matter. The Louisiana Supreme Court declared Act 78 null and void in the case of *Boykin & Lang* v. *W. A. Shaffer* (1858). The court, following a precedent set by Justice François Xavier Martin in *State of Louisiana* v. *New Orleans Navigation Company* (1822), overturned a Terrebonne Parish court that had ruled in favor of C. J. Merrick, a planter who sued William Shaffer for blocking navigation on Bayou Black with two locks constructed under an arrangement with the B & L. The court neither ordered Shaffer to remove his locks, which obviously improved navigation, nor authorized him to charge tolls to lock boats through his gates.

The B & L felt that Act 172 of 1843 was sensible; the upper Terrebonne was a navigable stream only because the B & L dredged it periodically. Even though this view was contrary to precedents established in federal courts since *Gibbons* v. *Ogden* (1824), Louisiana courts upheld this view in several significant decisions.[14]

Fortunately for the B & L, the *Boykin* case had not reached the U.S. Supreme Court, for since *Gibbons* v. *Ogden*, the Court consistently held that Congress could regulate all phases of interstate commerce and could not be limited by state powers. Chief Justice John Marshall did not apply the rule to canals and steamboats, but he removed state restrictions on interior commerce. Later, in the Roger Taney court, Justice Joseph Story's opinions extended national control over inland waterways, using admiralty jurisdiction rather than the commerce clause.[15]

In 1848 the legislature passed still another bill subsidizing construction of the Company Canal. Ten thousand dollars from the Internal Improvement Fund was to reactivate work on the canal. The state engineer was to contract with the B & L to complete the work according to specifications, but the value of any work completed by the state was to constitute a lien against the company until the debt was fully paid. To finance this latest subsidy, the attorney general was authorized to execute a bond bearing interest at 6 percent due in 1860.

Governor Joseph Walker continued the salutary trend in 1850, when he signed two bills to aid the Barataria and Lafourche Canal Company. Act 320 made it easier for the company to collect tolls. It authorized justices of the peace to seize and offer for sale any vessels or cargo whose owners refused to pay tolls due the company. Act 236 simply appropriated an additional $20,000 to complete the canal.[16]

In 1850 the Barataria and Lafourche Canal Company signed a lu-

---

14. *Boykin & Lang* v. *W. A. Shaffer* (1858), 13 La Ann 129; *State of Louisiana* v. *New Orleans Navigation Company* (1822), XI, François Xavier Martin, pp. 38–40, 52, 56, 70, 76–77, 95–96, 116, 148, 177–78; Louisiana Board of Public Works, Annual Reports, 1834, 1835; Louisiana State Engineer, Annual Report, 1842.
15. Robert Wiebe, *The Opening of American Society from the Adoption of the Constitution to the Eve of Disunion* (New York, 1984), 228, 242–43.
16. Box 1, RRBP.

crative contract with the state of Louisiana. Absalom D. Wooldridge, a controversial state engineer, represented the state in negotiations with the B & L. George May, the president of the B & L, signed for the company. Wooldridge, who was an ordained minister rather than a trained engineer, failed to live up to expectations as state engineer. Not surprisingly, citizens complained most during flood season, when swollen streams overflowed their banks and caused property damage. As big sections of New Orleans lay under water because of breaks in the levee early in the summer of 1849, people complained bitterly. "A sermon cannot control the Mississippi," one irate citizen noted during the flood that covered much of the city through most of May.[17]

The Wooldridge contract fulfilled provisions of the December 20, 1848, act of the legislature that set aside funds to construct the canal and a March 20, 1850, act that provided funds to complete the canal. The contract between the state and the B & L spelled out details of work on the canal. For the sum of $55,000, Wooldridge agreed to construct two locks on the Mississippi River, two locks on the east side of Bayou Lafourche, one lock on the west side of Bayou Lafourche, one lock between Bayous Blue and Terrebonne, and a wooden culvert under the canal linking Bayous Terrebonne and Black; he also agreed to "complete all dredging and excavating necessary to place the canal in good navigable order." In order to assure payment of the $55,000, the company, with the approval of Attorney General Isaac Johnson, mortgaged the entire canal, all the real estate and property of the company, and sixteen slaves, who were listed by name and age. The company agreed to pay 6 percent interest on the money, due semiannually in January and July up to 1860 or until the debt was paid. May further pledged not to bind, sell, alienate, or encumber any company assets. The state recorded mortgages against the B & L in Lafourche, Terrebonne, and Jefferson parishes.

The contract also specified the priority of the work to be performed, all of which was to be completed in three years from January 1851. First priority was placing a wooden culvert 75 feet long by 10

17. Harry Kmen, "New Orleans' Forty Days in '49," *Louisiana Historical Quarterly*, XL (January, 1957), 40n.

feet wide by 4 feet high under the canal in Houma connecting Bayous Black and Terrebonne; this would allow Bayou LaCarpe, a small stream running between the two larger bayous, to drain surface water from the town of Houma in a continuous flow under Company Canal levees that cut across its channel. Second and third priorities were the locks on the east and west sides of Bayou Lafourche. Fourth was completing the locks on the Mississippi; fifth called for building the locks between Bayous Blue and Terrebonne. And finally, Wooldridge promised to start the dredging as soon as he could obtain the necessary equipment.

Construction blueprints contained detailed descriptions and specifications for the project. The larger masonry locks on the Mississippi River were to be 25 feet wide, with gates 130 feet apart. The water depth over the gate sills was to be at least 6 feet at low water. The quoins, or corners, were to be of cast iron and the gate sills of cypress. Hydraulic cement was to be used. In determining the height of the locks, engineers were careful to specify at least 2 feet above the high-water mark of 1849. The locks at Lockport were to be identical to the river locks, with a guarantee of at least 2 feet above the high-water level of Lake Field "in order at all times to afford lockage from said Lake into Bayou Lafourche where the depth of water over the gate sill shall be six feet at low water." Smaller locks were to be constructed of cypress.[18]

Constructing masonry locks on Louisiana's marshy surface was more difficult and time-consuming than engineers expected. Wooldridge, who died of consumption at the age of forty-six, spent considerable time working on the Company Canal in 1850 but could report little progress on the locks. Two years later his successor, George Morse, reported that he had nearly completed one gate of the lock at Lockport and that "we are at present making the excavation for the foundation of the masonry for the second gate." He hoped to finish the foundation by mid-February and the brickwork by March so that the lock could be used by spring. Morse had spent $13,861 so far and had $5,736 on hand to finish the job. He had spent quite a bit of

18. Contract between the B & L and the state of Louisiana, July 1, 1850, in box "1833–1912," RRBP.

money, but much of it, he reported, was for building materials. He had all the necessary wrought and cast iron, wood, and other materials to complete the structure.

Morse explained why progress was slow in Lockport even though ninety-six of the state's slaves worked on the locks in 1852. "It became necessary to place them in consequence of the uncertainty of white laborers, and the absolute necessity of finishing the first walls and gates next to the Bayou Lafourche before the rise of Water," he wrote. He indicated that work had progressed to a point where there was little danger of flooding. In an effort to speed up construction, Morse had also hired white men, who did not perform satisfactorily. He complained that they were often on the sick list, and when they worked, they "could not or would not perform much more than half the work of a negro force of the same number." White laborers received $1 per day and board, which came to approximately $41 per month, Morse calculated. Morse requested four hundred additional slave laborers. In 1853, the year the Lockport locks were completed, eight slaves died on the job: Four died from cholera, two drowned, and two died of chronic diseases.

Despite construction problems over which he had little control, Morse still believed that canals provided cheap, reliable transportation. Mud slides were a major problem for Morse, forcing his crews to redig excavations time after time in order to set adequate foundations. To justify his appeal for additional funds, he pointed out that the state of New York had expended additional funds to enlarge the Erie Canal.

Less than a year after the contract between the state and the B & L went into effect, *De Bow's Review,* the leading financial journal in the South, could find little good to say about the Company Canal. The authoritative word on trade and commerce in the area criticized B & L management and construction practices. After making field observations, writer G. W. Pierce noted, "Thousands of dollars have been recklessly squandered on work which still remains incomplete, and is fast going to ruin and delapidation [sic] for want of funds to complete it." He acknowledged that a good deal of freight was shipped from Terrebonne and Lafourche, but the rates—$3.75 for shipping a hogshead of sugar to New Orleans—were excessive. He blamed the high costs on inefficiency; the Lafourche and Terrebonne Navigation Company paid $5,000.00 for a boat to run between Houma and Thibodaux. In 1853 Robert Barrow paid $3.80 per hogshead of freight from Terrebonne to New Orleans, plus an additional charge of $21.00 for weighing. In 1856 he paid $22.50 to ship one hundred sacks of corn and a few other items from New Orleans to his plantation. Furthermore, Pierce continued, the promised locks had not been built, and the waters of the Lafourche were silting up the upper part of Bayou Terrebonne. He concluded with a poignant observation: The New Orleans, Opelousas, and Great Western Railway, which followed the same general route as the B & L, had caused people to forget about completing the B & L.[19]

Persistent navigational problems, combined with waste and mismanagement of state monies, caused a public demand for change. A new state constitution written in 1845 prohibited the state from subsidizing private business. In time, merchants, who disliked the tight banking regulations and the ban on state aid to corporations, combined forces with big planters and railroads and got a new constitution. The Louisiana Constitution of 1852 permitted state subsidies to railroads and canal companies. The B & L wasted little time in capitalizing on the change. In 1852 it asked for and received still another grant. Act 236 appropriated $12,000 that the state engineer could draw from in order to complete the canal.

State courts, too, seemed to look favorably on the B & L, which became involved in litigation from time to time. In 1840 the high court ruled that the B & L was not responsible for the actions of Joseph Meyer, a toll collector who locked up and beat a free black man who, Meyer contended, refused to pay tolls for his oyster boat at the B & L locks at Westwego. The court likewise ruled in 1851 that the company was not responsible for damage done when its dredge destroyed a boat in a squall.[20]

19. New Orleans *Times-Picayune*, August 30, 1856; G. W. Pierce, "Historical and Statistical Collection of Louisiana—Terrebonne," *De Bow's Review*, XI (July, 1851–January, 1852), 610; Shipping receipts in box 3, folder 4, Robert R. Barrow Family Papers, Manuscripts Section, Howard-Tilton Memorial Library, Tulane University.
20. Bennett Wall (ed.), *Louisiana: A History* (Arlington Heights, Ill., 1984), 117–19; Box 1, RRBP; *Ware f.m.c. v. Barataria and Lafourche Canal Company* (1840), 15 La 169; *Edgell, Mulford & Co. v. Barataria and Lafourche Canal Company* (1851), 6 La Ann 425.

In 1853 Governor Paul Hébert approved a bill that marked the end of the periodic grants to the Company Canal. He signed Act 331, which appropriated $23,000 to complete the B & L, provided the state and the B & L settled contract disputes. The act authorized the governor to appoint three commissioners "with full powers to alter, modify, and render conformable" the old contract. On June 2, 1853, the state of Louisiana and the B & L amicably terminated the July 1, 1850, contract. By mutual agreement, the state was to do no more work on the project; the B & L was to complete the canal with no further state aid. Because the B & L had completed a portion of the specified work, the state paid the company $23,000 "for the completion of the Barataria and Lafourche Canal." The state was giving the B & L, in cash, approximately half of what the company owed the state in hopes that the company could complete the project without further costs to the state. George May released the state from its contractual obligations and acknowledged the B & L's $55,000 indebtedness to the state, due in semiannual installments until 1860 or until the debt was paid in full.

May also reiterated the work yet to be completed by his company. The B & L would complete the locks on the east side of Bayou Lafourche, where the plans called for two locks with three gates. He also promised to finish the locks on the Mississippi and to complete the dredging of the entire length of the canal.[21]

What had gone wrong? Why had the B & L failed to complete the virtually sea-level canal across marshy terrain that required only five sets of locks, especially in view of generous state subsidies, whereas the Erie Canal had overcome more difficult obstacles to become a financial success? Undoubtedly, the B & L suffered from managerial weaknesses, as *De Bow's Review* had pointed out in 1852. Not only did B & L managers squander company money; they also were ignorant of construction problems associated with building heavy masonry locks on Louisiana's marshy terrain. Even the relatively simple task of dredging a canal across marshland posed problems. Early dredging equipment was slow, expensive, and subject to frequent breakdowns. Canals often became silted up or clogged with sunken logs or

21. Release by the B & L and the state of Louisiana from the terms of the July 1, 1850, contract, June 2, 1853, in box "1833–1912," RRBP.

other obstructions. Construction often had to stop during the time of high water. In the heat of summer, workers suffered from cholera, yellow fever, and other maladies.

The inability of state bodies to maintain open transportation on the natural streams was a significant aspect of the B & L problem. As originally conceived, the Company Canal was to link natural bodies of water by a series of short canals; when these natural waterways became unnavigable, the B & L suffered accordingly. Navigational problems that concerned state engineers during the antebellum period followed a monotonous pattern and resembled those faced one hundred years later. Antebellum engineers grappled with concepts of flood control, spillways, locks, and dams on various streams long before the Civil War. Early engineers realized that the Atchafalaya River was destined to grow and would eventually capture the main channel of the Mississippi River if man did not interfere with the natural course of events.

The navigational problems of Bayou Lafourche are a good case in point. In 1854 George Morse reported to the state legislature the findings of his assistant, A. S. Phelps, who conducted an extensive study of the Lafourche. Morse noted the serious silting in the central portion of the bayou, attributing the problem, in part, to General Andrew Jackson, who had blocked the Lafourche 10 miles below Lockport in 1814 to prevent the British from using it as an invasion route before the Battle of New Orleans. Morse was concerned because during flood stage, water levels of the Lafourche rose higher each year. The level at the obstruction near Lockport was 6 inches higher than it had ever been, Morse complained in 1853, yet the level at Donaldsonville was 10 or 12 feet lower than high water in 1849. For the first time, engineers considered closing the bayou at its source. Another idea was to build a new mouth at Donaldsonville. Still another plan called for diverting the waters of the Lafourche about 6 miles above Lockport into Bayou des Allemands, a parallel stream about 10 miles east of the Lafourche. Morse even considered lowering the level of the Mississippi River by diverting the waters of the Red River through a canal into the Sabine River.

After battling extremes of high and low water on the state's natural streams, in 1853 Morse posed a rhetorical question suggested by a predecessor: "As to the matter whether the United States Government ought to perform the work or not, I have nothing to say." Somehow, however, one gets the impression that Morse and his predecessors had reached the inevitable conclusion about controlling the state's many waterways: The job was too big and too expensive for anyone except the federal government to undertake.

In the late 1850s State Engineer Louis Hébert wrote perceptive reports on drainage, navigation, and flood control in Louisiana. He noted serious problems at the confluence of the Red, Mississippi, and Atchafalaya rivers and predicted that the latter would grow in size and increase its volume of water carried to the sea. He opposed the idea of shutting off Bayous Lafourche and Plaquemine, mainly because doing so would place greater strain on the levees of the lower Mississippi and increase the possibility of floods. Instead, Hébert favored an active dredging program. He noted in 1857 that boats owned by the state were in bad shape and desperately in need of repair. Snag boats were important, he stated, but dredge boats were essential: "We *must* have them; we cannot do without them."

Whether the B & L's problems stemmed from the whims of nature or from managerial weaknesses, the company had not achieved its goal. It had not completed the Company Canal by 1858, thirty years after being chartered, despite generous aid from the state. Since 1829 the state had spent approximately $125,000 in direct subsidies to the B & L and indirectly probably even more. It granted the B & L tax-exempt status in 1833 for a portion of its existence. It granted a monopoly, not only in building canals but also in operating toll ferries near the canals. The state permitted the B & L to charge tolls on navigable streams improved by the Company Canal. It performed extensive work on the canal itself using state-owned slaves. Indirectly the state helped the B & L by removing sandbars, log rafts, and other obstacles to navigation. The state permitted the B & L to fall behind in payments on its mortgage. State engineers conducted surveys and performed work on company locks. The state encouraged individuals to donate land for rights-of-way for the canal. Company Canal officials could hardly blame the state of Louisiana for the failure of the Barataria and Lafourche Canal. They had received handsome subsidies, yet they had failed to live up to their overall promise to improve transportation for the good of all Louisiana citizens.

By the late 1850s Louisiana public figures appeared eager to end a thirty-year policy of sending good money after bad. Act 215, passed by the state legislature and signed by Governor Robert Wickliffe on March 19, 1857, ended the state's commitment to the B & L. The canal had not been completed, and the company still owed money to the state. In 1858 the legislature provided even more specific steps. Governor Robert Wickliffe signed Act 205, which marked the ignominious end of state aid to the B & L. It authorized the governor to transfer the state's stock and debt to a new canal company, providing the new company paid in full the $21,500 that the B & L owed to the state. Even though the asking price seemed small in view of past grants from the state, no longer would the state be called upon to shoulder the financial burden of completing the ill-fated Company Canal. If a private company wanted to complete the project, it would have to proceed without state subsidies.

In June 1858 the state's snag boat, the *Atchafalaya*, loaded the irons and other hardware that had been purchased for the Company Canal locks and transported them to St. Martinville, where they would be used for locks on the Teche, a project for which the legislature had appropriated $11,250.[22] The state, in effect, abandoned the Company Canal; the stage was set for the enterprising investor Robert Ruffin Barrow to make an appearance.

22. Absalom D. Wooldridge, "Attakapas Navigation," report to Louisiana legislature, in Legislative Documents, 1851, Louisiana Room, Troy H. Middleton Library, Louisiana State University; Louisiana State Engineer, Annual Reports, 1853, 1858.

3

The B and L No. 2 Through the Civil War and Reconstruction

Robert Ruffin Barrow became sole owner of the Company Canal in 1859, the year after the state of Louisiana withdrew from the expensive project. Whether Barrow had ties to the canal prior to 1858 is not indicated by extant company records, but he certainly would have been interested in it. A wealthy planter and landowner in Terrebonne and Lafourche, which lie in the center of the sugar country, he naturally would have wanted a fast, cheap way of getting sugar to markets in New Orleans. At any rate, Barrow took an active role starting in 1859, when at his behest, members of the Louisiana legislature from Terrebonne introduced a bill ceding the stock and debt of the B & L to a new company being formed in Houma. Colonel J. B. Robinson of the House and state senator F. S. Goode introduced a bill to sell state interest in the B & L to Barrow's new canal company. On their return to Houma, they convened a public meeting at the courthouse to choose a legislative committee that would actually oversee the official transfer from the old company to the new one.

Robert Barrow provided the capital for the Barataria and Lafourche Canal Company No. 2, the new company chartered to purchase the assets of the original B & L, which had grown too costly for the state to subsidize. He chaired the committee that effected the transfer of B & L assets and liabilities to the B & L No. 2. The new company, for all practical purposes, was Barrow's property. He directed its operations until his son, Robert Ruffin Barrow, Jr., succeeded him. No family had greater influence on canal activities in Louisiana than the Barrows. To make sure he acquired all of the old B & L property, Robert Barrow sought legislative relief in 1860 to revoke the charter of the Lafourche and Terrebonne Navigation Company. Because of charter violations, Barrow wanted its charter set aside and forfeited. Yet in March 1860 he wrote to officials of the navigation company in a tone suggesting that he favored collective effort by directors of both companies. I hope that "with the assistance of the Directors of Both Companies we can buy a dredging Boat & negroes so as to make good & suitable navigation and effect our purpose in compliance with the Charter."[1]

Barrow understood the appeal of the agrarian myth, always pretending that the original directors of the B & L were farmers. In an attempt to rekindle interest in the canal after the Civil War, he wrote about the early history of the B & L in a promotional pamphlet. Soon these farmers, unaccustomed to the world of high finance, were $400,000 in debt and turned to the state legislature for help, he liked to say. The locks on the east bank of Bayou Lafourche cost $60,000, he claimed. On the west bank "the Company did not stop to put in locks, but dug the Canal in a continuous line to Lakes Field and Long, thence to the Bayou Terrebonne."[2]

Barrow went to great lengths to disguise the true extent of his control over the B & L No. 2. He knew that making the state-subsidized canal a privately owned toll canal would not be easy to justify, especially if its owner were known to be one of the richest men in the state. However, grants to improve transportation for public welfare seemed reasonable and consistent with the philosophy of the Louisiana legislature. Even though Barrow was sole owner of the B & L No. 2, his direct links to the company were not widely known. He was

---

1. Box 1, Robert Ruffin Barrow, Jr., Papers, Division of Archives, Nicholls State University Library, hereinafter cited as RRBP; Barrow to canal directors, March 27, 1860, in box 13, folder 10, Robert R. Barrow Family Papers, Howard-Tilton Memorial Library, Tulane University, hereinafter cited as BFP.
2. *Circular of the Barrataria [sic] and Lafourche Canal Company No. 2* (New Orleans, 1866) (Box "1833–1912," RRBP); *William Minor v. Samuel Hornsby and E. Knowlton*, Injunction No. 2196, 5th Judicial District Court, Terrebonne Parish, February 20, 1860.

the driving force and the only real stockholder of the new corporation organized in Houma. He ran the company from behind the scenes through its president, Ephrain Knowlton, a Barrow agent who served in several capacities. Barrow owned 10 of the 20 shares of stock in the company; his business partner John Pittman owned 1 share, as did Benjamin F. Smith, Samuel Hornsby, James Hornsby, George Davis, Valerien Sulakowski, Joshua Bond, Howard Bond, Knowlton, and Ruffin C. Barrow (Robert Barrow's nephew). Like a modern agribusiness corporation determined to hide from public scrutiny the extent of its government subsidies, Barrow, too, used the Jeffersonian myth, the mystique of the small farmer, to secure subsidies for his canal project.

Only technically were Pittman and other Barrow associates stockholders. Houma notary Alfred Delaporte drew up the bill of incorporation on March 7, 1859, making Barrow's partners nominal stockholders. In exchange for 1 share of B & L No. 2 stock, each signed a promissory note to Barrow for $1,053, which was one-twentieth of the $21,060 B & L debt Barrow had paid the state. Thus Barrow arrived at the par value of 1 share of stock through simple mathematics. Each stockholder could cancel his note by simply returning his share of stock to Barrow. In an endorsement on the back of one share, Barrow specified that when he received the stock certificate, he would cancel the note due. The contract went on to say that "it is further understood that Barrow is the sole owner of the Canal & by Notarial Act Retains half the interest in the Stock Company." Among themselves, the stockholders referred to Barrow as the "real owner of the B & L."

The value of Barrow's anonymity surfaced in 1860, when William Minor filed for an injunction in the Fifth Judicial District Court of Terrebonne to prevent Samuel Hornsby and Ephrain Knowlton, both of whom ostensibly were B & L No. 2 stockholders, from collecting tolls on Bayou Black or from blocking the bayou. Hornsby and Knowlton acknowledged that they were officers of the company but claimed that they had no control over the Company Canal, since it was leased to Robert Barrow. Minor might have pursued the matter further had he realized that Barrow was the owner. Barrow, in effect, was leasing his canal to himself.

Barrow and his associates hoped to capitalize on the March 18, 1858, act of the legislature that authorized "the transfer of the stock and mortgaged debts held by the State in the Barataria and Lafourche Canal Company." On paper at least, Barrow invested $10,530, and each of the others $1,053, in order to acquire the B & L's stock and mortgaged debt and to improve navigation in the area. Serving on the board of directors were Robert Barrow, Samuel Hornsby, and Ruffin C. Barrow. The B & L No. 2 authorized Robert Barrow to procure from the government of Louisiana "a transfer of the stock and mortgage interest of the state in and to the Barataria and Lafourche Canal Company." Apparently Barrow succeeded in his mission to the governor's office, for on March 14, 1859, he recorded the transfer of stock from Governor Robert Wickliffe to the B & L No. 2.[3]

The old planter had made quite a good investment—that is, if he could complete the canal and make it profitable. For only $21,060 he had acquired all of the Company Canal and its rights-of-way from Westwego to Berwick Bay, along with its locks, equipment, bridges, toll ferries, boats, dredges, and slaves. For just a fraction of the total investment by individuals and by the state, he had bought the entire B & L. But just what had he bought?

Was Robert Barrow convinced that he could make a profit on the B & L, or was this another speculative venture? Did he think he could succeed during the heyday of railroads, or was he being eccentric just because he wanted to own a canal? He was stubborn, but he did not have a reputation for throwing money away. Undoubtedly Barrow realized that because of south Louisiana's marshy terrain, railroads would be expensive and could never reach the remote agricultural outposts that canals alone could reach. He seemed to have an instinctive feeling that an east-west canal system would provide a viable transportation route.

Robert Fogel, who tested the hypothesis of the indispensability of railroads to the expansion of the Midwest, offers an interesting hypothesis against which the Louisiana situation can be compared.

3. Act of Incorporation, B & L No. 2, March 7, 1859 (Box "1833–1912," RRBP); Terrebonne Parish Conveyance Book, Houma, La. (hereinafter cited as TCB), "U," fol. 352; box 3, folder 8, BFP; *Minor v. Samuel Hornsby and E. Knowlton*, February 20, 1860.

Fogel considered how well substitutes for rail transportation would have worked in the absence of rail service. His pioneering counterfactual findings challenged the prevailing wisdom and showed that the importance of the railroad has been exaggerated. Railroads were significant, but the prairies would have developed without them. In much of the Midwest the population had shifted before the railroads were built.

Water transportation, Fogel concluded, would have been a viable substitute for rail service. After all, canals had provided the original big cost reduction in shipping by wagon, greater even than any subsequent reductions brought on by railroads. Since many market cities were on navigable rivers, water travel would have been practical in interregional transportation. Fogel created a model establishing a region of feasible commercial agriculture, which included areas whose distances from markets to water shipping points were reasonable. He even proposed thirty-seven canals in the Midwest that could have tied in markets and enlarged the area of feasible commercial agriculture.

To be certain, Fogel was not blind to obvious advantages enjoyed by railroads. Even though water travel was often cheaper per tonmile, there were other factors to consider: speed, terminal fees, loss, transshipment costs, capital costs, and seasonal closing of waterways. Both Robert Barrow, who benefited from handsome state subsidies to the B & L, and Robert Barrow, Jr., who benefited from work done by the U.S. Corps of Engineers, enjoyed hidden reductions in capital outlay.[4]

On the eve of the Civil War, Robert Barrow was deeply involved in efforts to complete the Company Canal. His plantations, meanwhile, made him one of the richest men in the South. Like other planters, he realized the need for tariff protection for the sugar industry. He became a Whig, as did other sugar planters, for that reason. Furthermore, Barrow favored the policy of the Whig party in funding internal improvements: roads, canals, and river and harbor legislation. As a canal owner, he stood to benefit from such expenditures. In 1852 he made a speech at Bayou Sara in favor of Whig presidential candidate

4. Robert Fogel, *Railroads and American Economic Growth: Essays in Economic History* (Baltimore, 1964), 8–13, 23–24, 41, 46, 51, 81, 92–106, 110.

Winfield Scott and local candidates. However, Franklin Pierce won the presidency, and Paul O. Hébert, a Democrat, became governor.

Barrow had distinct views on secession, which he expressed in his usual strident fashion. He was a southern nationalist, but he opposed immediate secession. In 1861 he wrote a twenty-page pamphlet, *A Miscellaneous Essay on the Political Parties of the Country, the Rise of Abolitionism and the Impolitics of Secession*, stating his opposition to secession. For political and economic reasons he favored a wait-and-see attitude. Although his pamphlet was vituperative and laced with invective, he obviously did not yearn for a fight. The physical appearance of the booklet indicated that he may have had help in its preparation, but many of the observations sounded typically Barrowesque. He may have borrowed liberally from newspapers and other sources that publicized the emotional confrontation. He hated abolitionists and called John Brown a murderer; he defended slavery and would have spat in New York senator William Seward's face had the opportunity presented itself. Nonetheless, Barrow urged caution. "I am for the union," he wrote on December 15, 1860, in a widely publicized letter that appeared in the New Orleans *True Delta* and other newspapers. He criticized that paper and the New Orleans *Daily Picayune* for labeling him a renegade because he was not for immediate secession.

Perhaps economic considerations were the most important factors influencing Barrow's stand on the eve of the Civil War. "Free trade with nations has ever been a favorite principle with the cotton States," he wrote, "and if the contemplated Southern Confederacy approves of it, the sugar planters will be ruined, as they cannot compete with the West Indies." Obviously Barrow feared that cotton interests would control the political destiny of the Confederacy to the detriment of sugar growers.

Race, too, figured prominently in Barrow's thinking. He externalized his feelings and blamed abolitionists for slavery's problems. "Abolitionists are not citizens of the United States," Barrow reasoned, "because they are traitors to its laws." In Barrow's mind, there was little doubt concerning the viability of the peculiar institution. "That nature has placed the stamp of inferiority upon the black race, is admitted by all," he wrote, "that they are incapable to govern and otherwise act for themselves." Liberia was living proof of that observation, Barrow felt. He went on to defend slavery. "Having an interest in upwards of 700 slaves, and being a slaveholder my whole life," he stated, "I will give my treatment of slaves as a sample of how they are treated in the South." He bragged, "I feed, clothe and lodge them better than are thousands of poor families of the North."

Even though Barrow was convinced that fire-eaters in the South were excessively eager for a "melee," the feisty old planter would not admit that he was walking away from a fight. "Successful revolution is not treason," he said, in a passage demonstrating his southern nationalism. Advocating an economic boycott by the South and the Midwest of the North, he concluded: "Thus we can operate upon the tender point of the Yankee character, and make them curse the day they first meddled with our rights. 'The South must submit to abolition rule or secede,' is the prevailing opinion among the friends of Southern rights; but it never has been mine, because I think both those calamities can be averted," he wrote. Barrow concluded on a positive note. "Let us first exhaust all the power of the Constitution in attempting to bring our enemies to terms," he wrote, "and if it fails, let us test the merits of the sword."[5]

Characteristically, Barrow expressed his views and became emotionally involved in the election of candidates and delegates to conventions. Friends congratulated him for a victory over the Thibodaux clique in a judgeship race. Barrow bet sizable sums on the outcome of political races. He lost $5,000 betting that Constitutional Union candidate John Bell, who was his choice for president in the 1860 presidential election, would carry certain states in the South. Horace Hunley, his brother-in-law, advised him to exercise caution with his investments and with his political wagers. On vacation in Washington, D.C., in 1860, Barrow's wife quoted his political opponents as saying that "Mr. Barrow has gone crazy on politics and that I'd better hurry home to take care of him." Volumnia said she answered her antagonists "in an ironical and intensely scornful tone."

Even though Volumnia defended her husband against his critics,

5. *A Miscellaneous Essay on the Political Parties of the Country, the Rise of Abolitionism and the Impolicy of Secession* (N.p., 1861), in the Louisiana Collection, Manuscripts Section, Howard-Tilton Memorial Library, Tulane University.

she and her spouse had widely divergent views about secession and the Confederate States of America. As late as March 5, 1861, Barrow was saying in a rambling letter printed in the Houma *Ceres,* "the secession apple is not yet ripe." Then, after secession was a reality and Jefferson Davis became president of the Confederacy, Barrow criticized him. This upset Volumnia, who felt that the leader of the new nation should be given a chance to prove himself. "My instinct tells me," she wrote, "that the descriers of our President are doing wrong." She worried, too, that her brother, Horace, had joined Barrow in criticizing the Confederacy. "Don't give up the ship," she urged.[6]

Too old at sixty-two to fight, Barrow nonetheless supported the Confederacy in other ways. He contributed money to finance the construction of the *Pioneer,* the ill-fated submarine subsidized by Captain Horace L. Hunley, his brother-in-law. Hunley became associated with the sub in 1862, contributing to its completion, which was thwarted by the arrival of Commodore David Farragut and his Yankee forces in April. Hunley and the builders then transferred operations from Lake Pontchartrain to Mobile, where another sub, the *H. L. Hunley,* was built and named after its principal investor. After several disastrous trial runs that drowned a number of crews, Hunley transferred the craft to Charleston Harbor, where more failures occurred. General P. G. T. Beauregard permitted Hunley himself to take the sub down for a test, which was successful. But on October 15, 1863, the sub went down and failed to surface, killing Hunley and his crew. When the sub was finally lifted, Hunley was found with his head in the hatchway; one hand was clutching a candle, and the other was trying to open the hatch. He died of asphyxiation, and his sub was nicknamed the "peripatetic coffin."[7]

Even before U.S. military forces gained control of the Lafourche District, where most of Barrow's land was located, his canal holdings

6. Volumnia Barrow to My Dear Husband, September 10, 1860, Charles Williams to Robert Barrow, March 2, 1860, Horace L. Hunley to Robert Barrow, November 12, 16, 1860, all in box 4, folder 1, BFP; Volumnia Barrow to Robert Barrow, March 13, 1862, in box 19, folder 4, BFP; Houma (La.) *Ceres,* March 5, 1861, letter in box 26, folder 4, BFP; William Barrow Floyd, *The Barrow Family of Old Louisiana* (Lexington, Ky., 1963), 25–26; William H. Adams, *The Whig Party of Louisiana* (Lafayette, La., 1973), 236.

7. Lydel Sims, "The Submarine That Wouldn't Come Up," *American Heritage,* IX (April, 1958), 48–49, 51, 108, 111.

were jeopardized. The eastern terminus of the canal was opposite New Orleans, where the company had locks on the Mississippi River. When New Orleans fell in 1862, Barrow's canal, for all practical purposes, was under enemy control.

Barrow may have conspired with a staunch supporter of the Confederacy as Commodore Farragut's fleet approached the city in April 1862. He made a puzzling purchase at a sheriff's sale in the Fifth Judicial District Court of Orleans Parish. The sale was obviously arranged in haste by Deputy Sheriff J. G. Dreux as Yankee forces advanced on the city. It transferred all old B & L property to the owners of the B & L No. 2. Dreux offered for sale in Carrollton at 11 A.M. on April 6, 1862, all the possessions of the old B & L, including "the canal in full extent," various equipment described in detail, and slaves owned by the company. The B & L No. 2 bid $25,000 for the canal and property; the slaves were sold separately, "cash on the spot." Was Barrow using a sheriff's sale to erase a mortgage on the canal? Was he capitalizing on wartime confusion with economic hocus-pocus? Had he not obtained clear title to the canal in 1859? Detailed information that would answer these questions is lacking. When the Barrow heirs tried to sell the canal in the 1920s, attorneys could not determine what had transpired. Even after conducting a title search, they found a number of unanswered questions regarding the sale. Perhaps no sale took place. Barrow's son, in an equally mysterious manner, finally acquired title long after his father was dead.

Perhaps haste and obfuscation were intended; Commodore Farragut's fleet was approaching New Orleans, and General Mansfield Lovell's forces had fled the unfortified city. Dreux, who was a captain in the Confederate cavalry, may have perpetrated a questionable act to deprive Yankee forces of a valuable asset. In December 1860 Dreux had organized the Jefferson Mounted Guards, a seventy-man unit that sometimes accompanied General Beauregard's Confederate Army of Tennessee. The unit surrendered to the U.S. forces at Meridian, Mississippi, in 1865.[8]

The Barataria and Lafourche Canal Company No. 2 was not Bar-

8. Copy of sheriff's sale of the B & L to the B & L No. 2, April 6, 1862, 5th Judicial District Court, Orleans Parish, in box "1833–1912," RRBP; Betsy Swanson, *Historic Jefferson Parish: From Shore to Shore* (Gretna, La., 1975), 93.

row's major economic setback. The Civil War brought a complete disruption of sugar production in Louisiana and financial ruin to many planters. To be certain, Barrow was a big planter who used slave labor extensively. At war's end his fields lay idle, and his slaves were gone. His canal had not been destroyed, but disuse had caused silting and problems for locks and bridges. A major problem at the end of the war was a shortage of steamboats to care for the commercial needs of the state. Many railroads, too, had been destroyed, but the New Orleans, Opelousas, and Great Western, which ran from the Mississippi River to Morgan City in competition with the B & L No. 2 route, had been run by Federal forces during the war and was in good shape in 1865. Yankee forces held fortified positions along the Company Canal opposite New Orleans during the war, not to guard the canal but to protect the nearby railroad.[9]

The Civil War undoubtedly wrought havoc on the financial empires of the heavily mortgaged planters. By late 1863 Federal forces occupied most of the sugar country. In an effort to protect his property, Barrow sent some of his slaves to Texas under the care of John Pittman. The blockade denied planters markets for their produce and essential equipment and supplies; mules and farm animals became as scarce as credit with which to meet financial obligations. At the end of the war, planters did not even have sufficient seed cane to insure recovery. When slavery ended, their labor supply vanished. At least 139,000 slaves in the sugar country alone became freedmen, whose labor was still available—for daily wages. Experts believe that in 1860 sugar planters had $199 million invested in land, mills, and slaves. More than half of that amount, the $105 million that had been invested in slaves, was totally lost. Lands and mills became run-down, but they retained at least a portion of their value. Because of the nature of sugarcane and cotton production, large plantations were not broken up into small farms; they changed hands often, but they remained large estates.[10]

9. Floyd, *The Barrow Family*, 26; Joe G. Taylor, *Louisiana Reconstructed, 1863–1877* (Baton Rouge, 1974), 318.
10. Charles P. Roland, "Difficulties of Civil War Sugar Planting in Louisiana," *Louisiana Historical Quarterly*, XXXVIII (October, 1955), 40–42; William E. Highsmith, "Louisiana Landholding During War and Reconstruction," *Louisiana Historical Quarterly*, XXXVIII (January, 1955), 42n; J. Carlyle Sitterson, "The Transition from

At war's end Barrow was strapped for funds. In 1865 he borrowed $1,187 from Samuel Locke and signed notes for $553 and $634. Locke died that same year, and his widow sued Barrow in the Fifteenth Judicial District Court of Terrebonne to collect. However, when she failed to appear in court, Barrow's attorneys claimed that her request had prescribed. Barrow lost and then appealed to the state supreme court, which also ruled against him. He had to repay the loan at 8 percent interest since 1865 and also pay court costs.

Undaunted by the financial setback, Barrow fought back, hoping to revitalize the B & L No. 2. In 1866 he wrote a promotional pamphlet titled *Circular of the Barrataria [sic] and Lafourche Canal Company No. 2*, which contained a brief history of the old canal and optimistic predictions of future earnings. Claiming the canal was worth $1 million, Barrow discussed the transportation of oysters, timber, and produce of all kinds. Dated April 12, 1866, the pamphlet was signed "R. R. Barrow of Terrebonne, No. 2 South Street, New Orleans." At a stockholders' meeting in Houma on March 4, 1867, Barrow was chosen a director, along with John Pittman and Joseph S. Goode. Only 14 of the 20 shares of stock were represented at the meeting held at B & L No. 2 headquarters in the law office of F. S. Goode.[11]

By this time Barrow, now sixty-nine, was only a shadow of his former self. Financial setbacks and marital problems troubled him in his final years. Before he died of cholera in 1875, he fought heated legal battles against stockholders and creditors and had emotional personal clashes with his wife and children. All the while, he continued efforts to complete the canal or sell it to those who would. It remained for his son, Robert Jr., to complete that phase of the Company Canal.

Even though Robert R. Barrow lived until 1875, little has been written about his career after the Civil War. Perhaps the general

---

Slave to Free Economy on the William J. Minor Plantation," *Agricultural History*, XVII (October, 1943), 216; Walter Pritchard, "Effects of the Civil War on the Louisiana Sugar Industry," *Journal of Southern History*, VI (August, 1939), 322; Roger Shugg, "Survival of the Plantation System in Louisiana," *Journal of Southern History*, III (August, 1937), passim; Swanson, *Historic Jefferson Parish*, 95.

11. *E. Locke, Tutrix, v. Robert R. Barrow* (1873), 25 La Ann 118; Minutes of B & L No. 2 board meeting, March 4, 1867, *Circular of the Barrataria [sic] and Lafourche Canal Company No. 2*, both in box "1833–1912," RRBP.

impression that all planters were ruined by the Civil War was so widely accepted that no one bothered to learn how Barrow spent his declining years. Unlike the McCollams, his Terrebonne Parish neighbors who successfully made the transition as a planter family from slavery days to freedom, Barrow suffered considerable loss of property. His lands were subject to confiscation by the U.S. government. Thomas Conway, assistant commissioner of the Bureau of Freedmen and Abandoned Lands, published a list in 1865 of those properties subject to confiscation. Two of Barrow's plantations owned jointly with others were listed as abandoned and confiscable by the Treasury Department. Eventually Barrow was reduced to taking in boarders in his New Orleans home after the war. He and his wife were legally separated in 1866, just two years before her death. His children filed suit against him to claim property left to them by their mother. Charging that their father did not educate them or adequately care for their needs, they furthermore accused him of squandering their inheritance.

The familial bliss evident in the letters exchanged between Robert and Volumnia when the children were babies disappeared in the years after the Civil War. Something shattered the exuberance, but extant records are silent. Public records indicate that Robert Barrow and his wife were legally separated on June 28, 1866, but there is no hint of the source of marital friction. Volumnia retained custody of Roberta, who was sixteen, and Robert, who was twelve. Just a few months later, in August 1866, Volumnia sued her husband for furniture, jewelry, and other belongings at the family home at No. 5 (the address was sometimes listed as No. 2) South Street that she claimed had been personal gifts to her from her father and were therefore not community property. She also sought to reclaim the part of her furniture that Robert had sold to his nephew John Pittman of Lafourche. Pittman acknowledged that the furniture in question was Volumnia's property. In September the court ordered Robert to surrender to his wife Myrtle Grove, Roberta Grove, and Residence plantations in Terrebonne Parish.

Perhaps the Barrows' legal separation was, in part at least, an attempt to ward off Robert Barrow's creditors, who would have had no legal claim to Volumnia's personal property. Her petition asserted that her brother, Horace L. Hunley, had left her $25,000 in cash and furniture in care of her husband. In response to interrogatories, Barrow acknowledged that Hunley indeed had left the money for Volumnia in his care. Barrow's nephew Ruffin C. Barrow, who also testified, confirmed the $25,000 story.

Volumnia's petition, filed in the Fifth Judicial District Court of Orleans Parish, sought to sever the community property bonds established by marriage. She asserted that "her husband met with serious and heavy losses during the late war and that his affairs are embarrassed." The petition went on to say that "she desires to administer and preserve for her self her present property and the property that she may hereafter acquire." The court ruled in favor of Volumnia.[12]

Volumnia died on November 7, 1868, before receiving a divorce from Robert. Like so many aspects of their personal lives after the Civil War, there is little information about the circumstances of her death. She was only forty-three years old. Whether she suffered from a chronic disease that eventually became fatal or whether she died suddenly is not indicated by extant records. At any rate, her holographic, or handwritten, will, signed on May 27, 1868, appointed her estranged husband executor of her estate and guardian of their children. However, in 1873 Barrow was declared destitute and replaced as executor by John Pittman, who also became the tutor of the minor children.

After Volumnia's death, it was even harder for Robert Barrow to maintain his faltering financial empire. Throughout his life he had speculated wildly and created a pyramid of investments based on installment buying and imaginative accounting. He disguised from public view his ownership of the Barataria and Lafourche Canal No. 2, creating instead the impression that the canal was built by farmers to improve ways of getting their crops to market. The Company Canal had received state subsidies that undoubtedly would not have gone to a single proprietor of the canal project. After the war Barrow expended most of his energies fending off creditors with ever

12. New Orleans *Daily Picayune*, August 19, 1865; TCB "W," fol. 22, 29; Lafourche Parish Conveyance Book, Thibodaux, La. (hereinafter cited as LCB), 11, fol. 547; *Volumnia W. Barrow v. Robert R. Barrow*, 5th Judicial District Court, Orleans Parish, June 28, 1866, in box 13, folder 11, BFP.

more ingenious schemes. As they pressed for payments, Barrow took extraordinary steps to stymie their efforts. A favorite trick was to sell property—on paper, at least—to friends and relatives, who signed private documents renouncing their actual ownership of the property in question. Often he resorted to this stratagem with his nephews Ruffin C. Barrow and John Pittman. One Barrow accomplice explained how the procedure worked. C. R. Conner, who ostensibly had purchased property from Barrow in 1865, wrote, "I hereby declare that I did not pay to said Barrow the price stipulated nor any consideration whatsoever, but consented to its being sold to me merely to serve the said Barrow, he being fearful of its seizure for debt."[13]

Pittman, who was a business partner as well as Barrow's nephew, had to resort periodically to legal actions against Barrow to prevent creditors from seizing property Barrow had mortgaged to him. These actions, Pittman reassured Barrow, were not grasping or vindictive; they were designed to protect Barrow's interests. In 1865 Pittman bought land from the Shaffer family in Terrebonne for Barrow at a sheriff's auction; he promised that in the event of Barrow's death, the property would go to Roberta and Robert Jr. After filing judgments against Barrow for $36,000 in 1866, Pittman went to great pains to explain that this was to protect the property from seizure by other creditors. "I hope and flatter myself you have confidence in me as a friend," he wrote. At the bottom of the letter, Barrow wrote to Pittman in a small, squiggly hand, "I accept the above   R R Barrow." In 1868 Pittman transferred his B & L No. 2 stock to Barrow without complaint or compensation.[14]

That same year, Pittman codified his honorable intentions to Barrow by inscribing them in his will. Except for a bit of property in North Carolina that he was leaving to his brother and a small tract in Lafourche that was to go to his black mistress, Ludy Jones, Pittman left his Terrebonne property to Volumnia, or to her children in the event of her death. He reassured Barrow, again in 1868: "You seem to be uneasy about your debts mortgages judgments—I hold against you. You need not be uneasy." To another, he explained, "The judg-

13. C. R. Conner to Robert Barrow, May 25, 1865, in box 4, folder 3, BFP.
14. John Pittman to Robert Barrow, April 10, 1865, in box 4, folder 3, BFP; Pittman to Barrow, March, 1866, in box 4, folder 4, BFP.

ment obtained against Mr. Barrow is a just debt but I am desirous of giving it to his two children and I now hold it in trust for them in case of my death."[15]

Pittman proved to be far more honorable than Barrow ever had been. He lived up to his promises to Barrow even when the old man's egregious hostility must have been difficult to tolerate. Pittman wrote into his will provisions for Ludy Jones to receive a small plot of land on Oak Grove plantation, a house, a team of mules, and a horse and gig.[16]

In 1867 Robert, Volumnia, and nephew Ruffin C. Barrow transacted a number of complicated land sales in Terrebonne Parish. In June, Volumnia purchased a plantation in Terrebonne on Bayou Chacahoula from Ruffin C. for $17,000. Robert was legally responsible for the mortgage she signed; Volumnia justified her action by citing her husband's violation of his marriage contract by disposing of her personal wedding gifts.[17] Here perhaps lie unexplained hints of marital friction—or perhaps financial distress—that led to their separation.

Robert had other complicated dealings with Ruffin C., who lived in New Orleans. As early as 1862, New Orleans merchants were sending Robert C.'s bills to Barrow for payment. In 1868 Ruffin C. informed Uncle Robert that he had bought the steam vessel *Paynswick* and six barges "from W. H. Hannon and used your funds." Ruffin C.'s disclaimer, showing that Barrow was the "bona fide owner," left little doubt about the true nature of the sale: "I have no interest in the canal or its property except to secure my commission for transactions." On May 7 Barrow sold all the stock in the Barataria and Lafourche Canal Company No. 2 that he had acquired from the partners to Ruffin C. for $20,000. The next month Robert sold a tremendous amount of property to Ruffin C. for $197,000, of which only $8,000 was in cash. Ruffin C. signed promissory notes of varying amounts for each of the thirteen tracts of land he had bought: Point

15. Will of John Pittman, February 26, 1868, in box 4, folder 6, BFP; John Pittman to Robert Barrow, March 20, 1868, Pittman to [?], December 5, 1868, both in box 4, folder 6, BFP.
16. See box 14, folder 8, BFP, for a brief note on Ludy Jones.
17. TCB "W," fol. 388.

Farm, Caillou Grove, and various other parcels described in detail. Each tract was mortgaged.[18]

Suddenly, on October 11, 1869, the $197,000 sale was canceled, along with the $20,000 deal for the B & L No. 2. When Ruffin C. returned the B & L No. 2 stock, he retained 1 share for himself. A summary sheet, undoubtedly prepared by Barrow's attorneys and forwarded to Ruffin C. in 1869, explained only the mathematical aspects of their dealing. Ruffin C. held Barrow's promissory notes worth $191,166; Barrow held Ruffin C.'s notes totaling $179,432. In order to square accounts, Barrow gave Ruffin C. negotiable paper worth $12,000 even. Then the two Barrows canceled all mortgages they had made to cover their notes.[19]

Exactly what transpired during this period will probably always be something of a mystery. One can only speculate that the two sold property that was mortgaged to keep other creditors from seizing it. They transferred titles and canceled mortgages whenever it was convenient. Quite possibly, this switching of property was tied to legal disputes over community property owned by Robert and Volumnia (Volumnia had died on November 7, 1868). At any rate, the confusion over complicated property titles lasted for six more years, until Robert died. And even then, the struggle went on in the courts over the disposition of the Barrow estate.

During this time Robert was also selling property to John Pittman. In May 1868 he sold a half-interest in Oak Grove plantation in Lafourche, another tract near Donaldsonville, and some of his other property in Ascension Parish to Pittman for $30,000, of which only $7,000 was in cash.[20] These transactions, too, may have been mere legal ploys conceived by Barrow to thwart his creditors.

As agriculture languished during Reconstruction, Barrow hoped to regain his fortune by reactivating the Company Canal. He searched about for investors who could help raise funds to put the canal back into operating condition. One investor who saw potential in the canal

18. TCB "Y," fol. 294, 304; TCB "X," fol. 63, 142; Ruffin C. Barrow to Robert Barrow, June 8, 11, 1868, both in box 4, folder 6, BFP.
19. Summary sheet, n.d., in box 4, folder 7, BFP.
20. LCB 11, fol. 547.

was John Fazend of New Orleans and his articulate agent, Henry C. Stephens. Stephens approached Barrow about buying the B & L No. 2 or forming a partnership. He dangled two offers before Barrow in 1865. The first was a partnership. For a half-interest in the B & L No. 2, Fazend would raise $15,000 to clear the canal for navigation from the Mississippi River to Bayou Lafourche "as soon & as fast as permission of military authorities can be obtained so as to allow boats to pass to & fro and conditions of the canal will allow." As partners, Fazend and his associates would pay half, and Barrow was to pay half of that portion in excess of $15,000 for opening the canal to Lockport. Stephens's second offer was to buy the canal for $25,000, payable in six installments. These proposals, Stephens explained, were "to know if you will offer sufficient inducement to make it worth my while to investigate the subject further and try to convince my associates." Undoubtedly Fazend and Stephens had friends in high places in Louisiana's carpetbagger Reconstruction government. Even though Stephens and Barrow never consummated a partnership, Fazend purchased 1 share of B & L No. 2 stock from Barrow for $1,500 in 1867. Fazend authorized Pittman to vote his stock proxy in 1870.[21]

Barrow and his fellow stockholders rejected Fazend's offers and borrowed money to get the canal back into operating order. In 1869 they raised $55,000 by signing eleven $5,000 notes negotiated through the Union Bank of New Orleans at 8 percent interest. The notes were due on January 1, 1871, 1872, and 1873. Regardless of the financial status of the company, the partners agreed not to seek a return on their investments before January 1, 1874.

A financial report prepared in 1870 detailing the costs of upgrading the B & L No. 2 indicates that investors may have taken on more than they could handle; $55,000 would only begin the necessary repairs. A rather sophisticated company report showed $82,500 to be a more realistic estimate of company needs. The company would have to spend over $10,000 just on the locks and facilities on the Mississippi River at Westwego. An additional gate for the locks there would cost $2,000; furthermore, dredging and other matters needed attention.

21. Henry C. Stephens to Robert Barrow, March 10, 1865, in box 4, folder 3, BFP; John Fazend to John Pittman, March 3, 1870, in box 4, folder 8, BFP.

On the east bank of Bayou Lafourche the company would have to spend over $6,000 for locks, as well as $1,500 for a bridge at Lockport. On the west bank of Bayou Lafourche, where no locks had been built originally, the estimate was $36,000, mostly for constructing the badly needed gates. To prevent the waters of the Mississippi from flooding large areas of the west bank of the Lafourche during high-water season, the company had placed temporary earthen dams in its canal. The makeshift dams could be removed, but not without extra dredging work and expense for the company. In Houma the company needed $17,900 for a dredge boat and wooden locks. It would have to spend an additional $12,300 to construct wooden locks and to dredge Bayou Black from Houma westward toward Morgan City.[22]

Reports from the U.S. Corps of Engineers and from engineers working for the state of Louisiana confirm the belief that completing the B & L No. 2 would impose a heavy indirect burden on taxpayers to clear many rivers and bayous of barriers, both natural and man-made. During the war years, snag boats had not operated, and even the Mississippi River needed considerable attention. At about this time engineers began referring to Bayou Terrebonne as little better than a drainage ditch rather than a commercial waterway.

Sometimes political action changed water transportation drastically and affected the B & L No. 2 directly. Taking matters into its own hands, the police jury of Iberville Parish dammed Bayou Plaquemine at the Mississippi River in 1867 or 1868 to save itself the expense of constantly rebuilding control structures that the Mississippi washed away. This action forced steamers bound for the Attakapas District to use the Old River–Atchafalaya route, which was considerably longer and not entirely free from encumbrances. Talk of building locks on the Mississippi at Plaquemine was just in the formative stage. Bayou Lafourche, too, continued to have navigation problems, which some people thought could be solved only by damming it at its source on the Mississippi at Donaldsonville. Early estimates for constructing locks at the site of a dam ran to $115,950.

One unnamed Louisiana engineer listed four reasons why people

22. Box "1833–1912," RRBP.

were justified in looking toward Washington for resolution of the problem. First, U.S. aid would create jobs for freedmen who needed work. Another humanitarian reason was the need to aid impoverished people unable to help themselves because of the ravages of the Civil War. Another point was economic: The state, in improving transportation across south Louisiana, was actually improving the value of federal lands contiguous to the cleared streams. The fourth point was both economic and patriotic: Louisiana had suffered heavy financial losses during the Civil War, and the U.S. government should compensate the state.[23]

The unflappable Barrow was tenacious; he refused to give up on the Company Canal. In 1870 he borrowed $60,000 from Taylor Beattie, the Thibodaux lawyer and planter who had been president of the Lafourche and Terrebonne Navigation Company. Barrow gave him as collateral a first mortgage on the Barataria and Lafourche Canal Company No. 2. Barrow undoubtedly had faith in the Company Canal's future; he did not hesitate to borrow money to make his dream a reality.

Ephrain Knowlton, who had served as titular president of the B & L No. 2 since 1859, discouraged Barrow from investing more money in the canal venture. Prophetically he warned Barrow against taking out second mortgages on property that was already mortgaged. In an emotional appeal written on February 15, 1870, he advised Barrow to sell all his company stock: "This course will make you and your children rich and happy. Then you can live here or at the North, as you like." The cautious Knowlton ended with an ominous warning: "The canal will make you miserable and unhappy." Barrow rejected Knowlton's advice, suspecting instead ulterior motives on the part of his employee, who had spent six years at Residence as overseer. Barrow remembered that in 1868 Knowlton's wife had warned him that her husband was not to be trusted.

Knowlton was born in Saratoga, New York, in 1812 and came to Louisiana in 1836. In addition to performing numerous chores, he

23. Chief Engineer, U.S. Corps of Engineers, Annual Report, hereinafter cited as AR; 1891, Pt. 3, pp. 1818–19; AR, 1875, Pt. 1, p. 888; Albert Cowdrey, *Land's End: A History of the New Orleans District, U.S. Corps of Engineers* (N.p., 1977), 16–17; Robert W. Harrison, *Swamp Land Reclamation in Louisiana, 1849–1879* (Washington, D.C., 1951), 66.

wrote fiction about kings who were unable to manage their kingdoms because they had grown old and senile. Barrow considered the tales veiled criticism of B & L No. 2 management, "so that he [Knowlton] might lead me blind and trust my entire business into his hands." Barrow blamed the alienation from Knowlton partly because "the war & niggers shooting at him separated us."

After the war, Knowlton sought out Barrow in New Orleans and reestablished their economic ties. He rented Barrow's house and ran it as a boardinghouse; meanwhile he attempted to find a buyer for the B & L No. 2. According to Barrow, Knowlton failed in both efforts. Later Barrow accused Knowlton of acquiring canal stock by "disgraceful and degrading fraud." Nonetheless, Barrow came to realize how prophetic Knowlton's advice about selling the canal had been. His own children, who became B & L No. 2 stockholders when their mother died, clamored for their share of her estate. Despite the economic setbacks caused by the Civil War, Barrow and his children still owned extensive holdings. In 1871 property taxes in Terrebonne Parish alone came to $5,455, for Caillou Grove, Residence, Myrtle Grove, Point Farm, lots near Tigerville on Bayou Black, and various other tracts.[24]

After mortgaging the Barataria and Lafourche Canal Company No. 2 to Taylor Beattie, Barrow and Knowlton fell prey to a number of nefarious schemes promulgated by carpetbaggers and speculators whose capital and influence in the Louisiana legislature Barrow needed. The cast of characters involved in these Reconstruction-era canal ventures is long and mysterious. No doubt many of those involved merely sought quick fortunes; they needed the Company Canal to foster their schemes. Despite their promotional wizardry and ties to carpetbagger politicians, Barrow held on to his faltering canal, even in his dying days.[25]

In his attempt to make the B & L No. 2 a profitable venture, Barrow leased the Company Canal to the Louisiana Canal and Land Improve-

24. New Orleans *Daily Picayune*, July 19, 1863; Ephrain Knowlton to Robert Barrow, February 15, 1870, in box 5, folder 1, RRBP; Barrow to [?] regarding Knowlton, n.d. [1868], in box 26, folder 8, BFP; TCB "Z," fol. 429.
25. Box 3, folder 2, RRBP contains many letters explaining the complicated legal and financial maneuvering between the B & L No. 2 and the Louisiana Canal and Land Improvement Company in 1870 and 1871.

ment Company in 1871 for 10 percent of the canal receipts. In return, the improvement company pledged to put the canal in "proper working order." Barrow wrote to his daughter, Roberta, about these matters periodically in business letters devoid of personal references. One letter to her mentioned that the Company Canal had been leased for thirty years starting in 1871, but it did not provide details. In another letter Barrow mentioned a stockholders' meeting and the need to pay off a $1,000 judgment against the company "or they will close it!"[26]

Why would the Louisiana Canal and Land Improvement Company be interested in leasing a canal that had fallen into disuse and was experiencing financial difficulty? A brief glimpse into the operation of the Louisiana Levee Company, another company chartered during Reconstruction, reveals how profitable a privately owned public service company chartered by the state of Louisiana could be if it received contracts from the state. Created during the Radical Reconstruction era in Louisiana, the levee company had capital with which to influence legislators. Charles Howard and John Morris of the Louisiana lottery were major stockholders in the levee company, which received most of a 4-mill tax on all property in the state to build levees along major waterways. As it turned out, the levee company did not actually construct the levees; it sublet contracts to those who did the work, at a rate of approximately half of what the levee company received. The levee company paid subcontractors 25 to 35 cents per cubic yard for material placed on a levee site. The state paid the levee company 50 cents per cubic yard.

For a time the company did adequate levee construction and earned a profit, but soon there were complaints of crevasses left unfilled. A. F. Wrotnowski, the chief engineer for the state, openly and bluntly criticized the levee company in 1876 for failing to maintain levees and to close the Bonnet Carré crevasse. "The remedy lies in repealing the charter or breaking the contract between the State and the Levee Company and selling public levees at auction to the lowest responsible bidder," he wrote. With home rule in 1877 came change. That year Act 139 of the Louisiana legislature abolished the charter

26. Terrebonne Parish Probate Record No. 579, 1869, Houma, La.; Robert Barrow to William J. Slatter, n.d., in box "1833–1912," RRBP.

of the Louisiana Levee Company.[27] Meanwhile, the U.S. Corps of Engineers was assuming a greater role in clearing natural streams of navigational hazards. Not until the great flood of 1927 would the Corps become responsible for levee construction as well.

A key figure in the complicated plan to lease Barrow's Company Canal to the recently chartered Louisiana Canal and Land Improvement Company was Benjamin F. Smith. This New Orleans doctor had grandiose ideas and get-rich-quick schemes that, to succeed, required large investments and political support from the carpetbagger government running Louisiana. An imaginative thinker, Smith calculated that for an investment of about $150,000 the canal company could earn as much as $50,000 per year.

Another mysterious character in the drama was A. F. Chamberlain, a London promoter who claimed to be an agent for European banks and to have capital in excess of $200 million. According to Chamberlain, his banker friends were eager to invest in the United States. Chamberlain and Smith met in New York and became friends. In time they developed an ambitious Louisiana canal scheme. Smith explained to Chamberlain that Colonel Horace M. Bearce could secure a canal charter from the Louisiana legislature with bribes and a promise of $1 million in company stock. Bearce, a native of Boston, came to New Orleans with Benjamin Butler, the Yankee general who governed the captured city, in 1862; he remained after the war to make his fortune. The new canal company, Smith continued, could lease the Company Canal for a small fee. Then, presumably, the transportation company could negotiate lucrative contracts with the state, as the Louisiana Levee Company had done.

Horace Bearce engineered the chartering of the Louisiana Canal and Land Improvement Company. For a paltry fee of $500, he pushed the charter through the Louisiana legislature, which listed the canal company's worth as $5 million. One of Bearce's associates was G. L. Laughland, a shadowy figure who later turned against his partner.

Smith and Bearce promised Knowlton $25,000 worth of stock in

27. Louisiana State Engineer, Annual Report, 1876, Louisiana Room, Troy H. Middleton Library, Louisiana State University; Harrison, *Swamp Land Reclamation*, 80–90. Taylor, *Louisiana Reconstructed*, 193–96, documents the corruption of Reconstruction-era businessmen.

the new company and $5,000 per year to manage the canal company, if he could convince Barrow to lease the Company Canal for 10 percent of the net proceeds of the new canal company. Knowlton eventually talked Barrow into leasing the canal, which he thought would bring a return of $50,000 per year to Barrow and a nice position for himself. Knowlton was convinced that Barrow's unpopularity stood in the way of any chance for the B & L No. 2 to succeed without outside influence. "Mr. Barrow was very unpopular & no one would have anything to do with the canal as long as it was in his hands," Knowlton wrote. "In the hands of any one else it would be valuable."

Barrow had serious reservations about the leasing arrangement Knowlton proposed. For one thing, he felt the B & L No. 2 was worth more than 10 percent of the net proceeds of the new company. Instead, he demanded $125,000 in cash and $4,500 worth of stock in the new company before signing a lease. Furthermore, Barrow did not like the way the new company was organized. Its salary structure, he concluded, was so high it would "swamp the concern." Getting a new canal charter through the Louisiana legislature would be costly and take a long time, Barrow figured, but he was not privy to information available to Smith, Bearce, and Chamberlain.

Eventually Barrow succumbed to Knowlton's logic. Promises of big capital improvements and nice profits won him over. For 10 percent of net proceeds he agreed to a thirty-year lease. The new canal company promised to begin work by March 1871, "to bring out next years' crop." Knowlton convinced Barrow that even if investors failed to come forward with money for improvements, "we are no worse off."

Barrow agreed. "This is good news," he wrote on March 16, 1871. He forwarded Knowlton $100 and promised to get Laughland to pay him $200 per month. He got his son-in-law, William J. Slatter, who had married Roberta just a short time prior to this incident, to draw up the thirty-year lease arrangement with the Louisiana Canal and Land Improvement Company. On April 5, 1871, Barrow, Knowlton, Smith, and Laughland signed the lease.

The arrangement soured quickly for Barrow and Knowlton. The promised money did not arrive—at least not in amounts promised by

Smith and Laughland. Only Laughland was putting up money for canal improvements, Knowlton told Barrow, and not a large sum at that. Soon the new company was broke and unable to borrow money, since Taylor Beattie held a first mortgage on its assets. It was merely a corporation chartered by the legislature—a dummy corporation, Smith admitted.

For $500 Bearce gained controlling interest in the defunct company and tried to hold Barrow to his lease. The new company refused to pay Knowlton's salary, so although he had previously urged Barrow to accept the lease terms, he suddenly warned Barrow not to ratify the lease: "You must not confirm the lease & sign that paper Col. Slatter has drawn up." Chamberlain and Smith "have been fooling & deceiving me and yourself & I am satisfied there will be no money coming," he told Barrow. Knowlton criticized Laughland for refusing to pay his salary. Without funds, Knowlton admitted having "to take canal money to pay my rent & live upon."

All the while, Knowlton pledged his loyalty to Barrow: "I am still President & intend remaining, & you shall not be injured or swindled out of the Canal & I have the power & will use it & protect your interest," he wrote. After asking Barrow for the third time not to sign the lease, he ended, "I can do more than this."

Barrow denied closing any deal with the Louisiana Canal and Land Improvement Company, but Slatter said that Barrow had signed the lease he had drawn up. "It was a very one-sided document, & was surprised that Mr. Barrow should have been a party to a trade so manifestly to his injury, or the injury of his Company," Slatter wrote in 1871. Barrow, too, soon saw the light. In a letter to Chamberlain, he claimed that misrepresentation and failure to send promised funds for repairs had nullified the deal. "The President & Directors of the Barataria & Lafourche Canal Co. No. 2 have made up their minds to view the project as a swindle & break the lease," Barrow wrote.

Barrow warned investors of the improvement company's failure to comply with the terms of the contract: "Hence, the lease is cancelled, and persons are warned not to release, or purchase the lease, or trade for bonds based upon a mortgage, or pledge of the Barataria & Lafourche Canal Co. No. 2 & signed by E. A. Knowlton as President & B. G. Smith as Secretary."

Suddenly Knowlton changed his mind again about leasing the B & L No. 2 to the new company. Instead he suggested a new leasing arrangement, provided Barrow would clear up the $60,000 Taylor Beattie mortgage that prevented Smith and his associates from borrowing against company assets. If Barrow cleared up the Beattie mortgage, Knowlton said, the improvement company was ready to enter into a thirty-year lease for 25 percent rather than 10 percent of the net proceeds of the new company.

In March 1871 Barrow criticized Knowlton for conspiring with Laughland and Smith against him. He accused his former agent of changing sides after accepting additional shares of improvement company stock. The $25,000 in company stock Knowlton received was not worth 40 cents, Barrow asserted. Barrow said that Knowlton had worked with scoundrels to uphold an obviously fraudulent lease. "If I was ready to die, I would not die, until I had played my time on all of you," he wrote Knowlton on March 20, 1871. As it turned out, Barrow outlived Knowlton by two years.

However, Barrow was not without blame in the whole matter. He, too, may have committed a fraudulent act. Before leasing the Company Canal to the canal improvement company, he had affirmed that the B & L No. 2 was free and clear of encumbrances. He hardly could have overlooked the $60,000 mortgage Taylor Beattie held; nonetheless, he obtained a certificate from Terrebonne Parish saying that there were no liens against the Company Canal. Then he signed the lease with the improvement company.

Rather than expose any wrongdoings, Knowlton and Laughland asked Barrow to settle the Beattie mortgage and renegotiate the lease. If Barrow refused to acquiesce to their terms, they would expose his deception. At that point Barrow fell out with Knowlton and refused to ratify any leases. When Bearce threatened criminal action against him, Barrow responded with typical invective: "Surely no court of equity in the world would decide that the Barataria & Lafourche Canal Co. No. 2 is bound by the double dealing of an agent [Knowlton]."

Knowlton and Laughland also thought Barrow's questionable dealings would make him liable to civil action. "This was gross fraud upon the part of Mr. Barrow," they claimed in April 1871, "& it could easily be proved & make him liable to suit for damages." Undaunted, Barrow dismissed the threats. "As for lawsuits, I have never lost one of importance," he wrote. "I conducted one for 15 years successfully & obtained payment for $83,000."[28]

Barrow's problems were not all financial. In his feuds with Knowlton over canal matters, he once digressed to discuss his children, whom he professed to love "perhaps more than any man on earth never having struck or chastised them since they were born." Barrow proudly bragged that ten-year-old Robert Jr. had his own pony and bank account.[29] But all was not well with the children, and soon family problems added to his financial worries.

Barrow's teenage children ran away from home early in 1871. Their sudden disappearance led to an estrangement that kept Roberta, seventeen, and Robert Jr., thirteen, from ever reconciling fully with their father, who was then seventy-three. Thinking that the children were with the family of Reverend W. A. Hall of Woodville, Mississippi, Barrow wrote to Hall, "I am seeking them and am aware that your wife bore a prominent part with those who have harbored my children. You must know that a father lives for his children. I have good reasons to believe my daughter is at your house. I fear my daughter intends to marry. He who marries her without my consent shall not live if I live." Barrow sent William J. Slatter to reassure the children that they could return home "free from any fear of repremand."

Reverend Hall displayed considerable restraint in assuring Barrow that he was mistaken. "Your daughter is not at my house and never has been," he wrote. "I have not seen her, for, I believe, twelve months and I have no knowledge whatever concerning her or your son." Realizing that he had wrongly accused Hall, Barrow came as close as he could to apologizing: "There is a mystery about this matter which you may see dispelled some day."[30] Then, with a touch of irony usually reserved for gothic romances, Roberta married Slatter, who found her and Robert Jr. at Bayou Sara. As indicated earlier, Slatter eventually met with Barrow's approval and even prepared legal doc-

28. Box 3, folder 2, RRBP, outlines the entire canal-leasing dispute.
29. Ephrain Knowlton to Robert Barrow, February 15, 1870, in box "1833–1912," RRBP; Robert Barrow to [?] regarding Knowlton, n.d. [1868], in box 26, folder 8, BFP.
30. Robert Barrow to W. A. Hall, February 10, 17, 1871, Hall to Barrow, February 15, 1871, all in box 4, folder 9, BFP.

uments in the leasing arrangement with the canal improvement company.

Barrow's death threat was soon overlooked, but neither Roberta nor Robert Jr. was ever on good terms with their father again. Robert Jr. undoubtedly decided to live at Residence Plantation in Terrebonne Parish, even though his father wanted the boy to live with him in New Orleans. Soon he and Roberta engaged their father in heated debate over the estate of their deceased mother. Many intriguing questions remain unanswered about the family problems. What caused the estrangement? Where did the children live after the death of their mother? What was the mental state of Barrow during his last few years? Did Roberta first meet Slatter when he came looking for her?

Volumnia's will ceded her property to Robert Jr. and Roberta, who lived in Tennessee. Barrow was guardian of the children and executor of his wife's estate. Unable to deal with her father to obtain her inheritance, Roberta sued to receive her portion of her mother's estate. Volumnia Barrow's estate, valued at $117,702, included property in New Orleans and Terrebonne and 5 shares of B & L No. 2 stock.

Roberta's suit had far-ranging implications for Robert Jr. as well, for it removed his father from the executorship of his mother's estate and gave the elder Barrow ten days to file an account of his administration of the estate. Like his sister, Robert Jr. also filed suit against his father in order to receive his inheritance. Only seventeen years old in 1875, he sought emancipation from his father and control over property inherited from his mother. Robert Jr.'s legal battle with his father became even more heated and emotional than his sister's. His petition to the parish court in Terrebonne cleared up some questions about the complicated family property settlement.

In June 1873 Barrow was declared destitute and removed by judicial decree as the executor of his wife's estate. John Pittman, who was Robert Jr.'s tutor, had not asked the court to appoint a new executor to replace him. Criticizing this arrangement two years later, Robert Jr. leveled stinging blows at his already troubled father: "The said R. R. Barrow is notoriously unkind to petitioner, refusing to support him or send him to school, or take care of him in any manner whatever." Young Barrow also accused his father of "causing waste of the property, and its depreciation in value, and is colluded with John B. Pittman to defraud petitioner of all his titles, goods, lands, chattels and interests." Pittman claimed that Robert Jr. could not substantiate these charges, but Robert Jr. was emancipated several months before his father died.

On March 10, 1875, the court appointed Peter Bergen curator ad hoc to carry out young Barrow's suits. J. Fisk, who represented the elder Barrow, responded to the charges against his client. A "kind & indulgent Father," Fisk stated, tried to shelter Robert Jr. from "evil disposed persons" who exposed him to "immoral influences." Fisk, who claimed Barrow acted in good faith, used conspiracy theories to explain what had gone wrong.[31]

During the course of these stormy disputes, Barrow realized that raising money by mortgaging family property was no longer a mere formality. Attorney F. S. Goode informed him that he could not mortgage his children's property. Roberta, who was married and living in Tennessee, controlled her own property, but Robert Jr. was single and a minor. His half-interest in his mother's estate could be mortgaged, but only after a family meeting in the presence of his tutor. Goode told Barrow that he had a long talk with the boy, who was then only thirteen. Headstrong and stubborn like his father, Robert Jr. agreed to meet his father in Terrebonne, but he would not go to New Orleans to visit him. He agreed to attend school if his father sent money to cover expenses.[32]

Inevitably, the flimsy B & L No. 2 financial structure collapsed; sheriffs' sales followed in short order. Taylor Beattie acquired some company property in 1873, when he foreclosed on his mortgage. Robert and Nelson Taylor purchased the locks at Lockport at a tax sale in 1874. Property owned by Robert Jr. and Roberta was not secure from seizure. Fortunately, John Pittman, true to his word to Barrow, looked after the children. To protect their interests, he bought Roberta Grove and Myrtle Grove plantations, which had been

31. Terrebonne Parish Probate Record No. 666, Houma, La., Succession of R. R. Barrow, May 16, 1876; Probate Record No. 701, *R. R. Barrow, Jr. v. R. R. Barrow, Emancipation,* March 9, 1875.
32. F. S. Goode to Robert Barrow, June 10, 1871, in box 4, folder 9, BFP.

seized in December 1874 for $4,277.54 in taxes due on the estate of the children's mother.[33]

The holdings of Robert Barrow had declined tremendously since 1860, when he was one of the wealthiest planters in the South. A tough, controversial realist, Barrow adjusted to a lower status and went on in his blunt way. He lost his home at No. 5 South Street, opposite Lafayette Square. Undaunted, he rented a large house at 219 Magazine Street in 1874 or 1875. Some destitute relatives lived with him, along with a number of boarders who performed legal and secretarial services. W. S. Denny, a boarder and Barrow's private secretary, testified in a succession hearing that Barrow spent at least ten months of the year in New Orleans. John Isley, Jr., an attorney, boarded with Barrow and performed legal services as well. J. E. Wallace was another Barrow boarder who testified at the old man's succession. Establishing Barrow's legal residence became an important issue, for his residence determined where suits against him would be heard. There was some evidence that Barrow voted in Terrebonne in 1872.

In 1874 Barrow vented his frustrations and disappointments in a long letter dictated to Pittman. He outlined his family, business, and health problems. In one section he seemed to criticize Pittman for trying to win over the children: "You imagine you know them as well or better than I do." Other passages suggested disappointment at not having closer ties to the children. He alluded to the hostility of the children, especially Robert Jr., who was, in Barrow's words, "the meanest of the meanest and lowest of the lowest no matter what garment he wears or what blood he springs from." But in another passage he spoke proudly of Robert Jr.'s inclination to follow in his footsteps. Barrow closed with an assertion of his "determination not to die until my house is in order."[34]

All the while, Barrow saw conspiracies everywhere and became suspicious of those around him. He trusted no one as he struggled to reacquire parts of his once immense estate. J. Fisk apprised Pittman of Barrow's many suits against those he thought had wronged him. "I

33. Boxes "1833–1912," "1925," RRBP; TCB "AA," fol. 508–518; TCB "BB," fol. 317.
34. Robert Barrow to John Pittman, February 18, 1874, in box 4, folder 12, BFP.

have tried to keep Mr. Barrow from bringing suits," Fisk told Pittman, "especially when there is a prospect of your having to become responsible for the costs." Despite Fisk's efforts, Barrow became embroiled in a number of cases.

Fisk appealed one suit, involving 3,300 acres on Bayou Grand Caillou valued at $150,000 and lost in a tax sale, to the Louisiana Supreme Court. On November 28, 1873, Jules Lapene, a native of Orleans Parish, bought the land on Bayou Grand Caillou known as Caillou Grove plantation for a mere $1,859.14 in back taxes. Fisk thought he had a chance of winning the case against Lapene on a technicality, but he was wrong. In Houma, Barrow's attorneys filed suit against J. P. Viguerie over some sugar dealings. Meanwhile, Barrow was trying to get Pittman to delay all hearings on judgments brought against him for debts. Once in a routine business query to W. S. Denny, Barrow asked casually about his son.[35]

On April 1, 1875, Barrow filed his holographic will in civil court in New Orleans. Even though Roberta and Robert Jr. had become estranged and had filed suits against him, he left his entire estate to them, "each one half of all my estate real and personal which I leave at my decease." For some reason, Barrow appointed three executors: John Pittman, John B. Robertson, and James W. Board. The three were appointed "with full seizen of all my estate without furnishing security." Board, who managed Oak Grove plantation and was also one of Barrow's creditors, communicated with the old man about Robert Jr.'s emancipation suit and about plantation matters. He informed Barrow that someone was interested in leasing Honduras plantation, one of Barrow's plantations near Houma, and he wanted to know what terms Barrow was asking.[36]

In the summer of 1875, Barrow became ill with cholera. "I was last Tuesday night taken with a very severe attack of cholera morbus," he stated in a letter dictated to Pittman. "It has completely prostrated me, I am unable to walk across the room, or get to the chamber without help, and I am getting worse," he wrote on July 1. Yet some of

35. *R. R. Barrow v. Jules Lapene* (1878), 30 La Ann 310; J. Fisk to John Pittman, June 12, 1875, F. S. Goode and John B. Winder to John Pittman, July 30, March 5, 1875, Robert Barrow to John Pittman, March 29, 1875, all in box 5, folder 1, BFP.

36. Copy of will of Robert R. Barrow, in box 5, folder 1, BFP; James W. Board to Robert Barrow, April 4, 1875, in box 5, folder 1, BFP.

his old spunk remained, and he talked of going to Houma with John Robertson the next week if his health improved. Before signing off, he added a dying barb: "I learned you was here the other day and did not call to see me it looks strange. I can dictate no further now. I do my best to live." The next day Robertson confirmed the fatal diagnosis: "I have been up all night with Mr Barrow he has *cholera* and will hardly recover. Come quick today if possible."[37]

Robert Barrow died on July 27, 1875. A simple, brief obituary notice in the New Orleans *Daily Picayune* invited friends to the funeral service at his Magazine Street residence at 4 P.M. on July 28. He was buried in the Girod Street Cemetery. Complicated legal questions for his heirs did not end with his death; they were just beginning.

An inventory of Barrow's possessions in the big two-and-a-half-story house at 219 Magazine Street hinted at the great wealth he once possessed. The room-by-room listing indicated there was much furniture in the house, but most of it was shabby or run-down. The furniture was mahogany, but many of the mirrors were broken. The inventory listed beds, bedding, armoires, pillows, mattresses, and the like.[38]

Accounting for the immovable portions of Barrow's estate was far more complicated, and soon the estate's executors were at odds. Robertson and Pittman tried to make decisions without Board's concurrence, but they pretended to work closely with him. On August 14, 1875, Robertson told Pittman he had authorized Board to remove the sawmill from Residence and use it on Myrtle Grove "on the best terms he can make." Two days later Robertson explained to Pittman his thinking regarding the sawmill: "I thought it necessary to quiet him and I believed [it] to be right also, and Ruffin [Robert Jr.] was exceedingly anxious about the matter." Robertson explained the economic reality to Pittman: "I thought he ought to start the sawmill so as to keep you from putting your hand into your pocket every day."

Robertson also thought Robert Jr. should make peace with Pitt-

37. Robert Barrow to John Pittman, July 1, 1875, John Robertson to John Pittman, July 2, 1875, both in box 5, folder 1, BFP.
38. Inventory of Barrow house by George Morris, July 29, 1875, in box 5, folder 1, BFP; New Orleans *Daily Picayune*, July 28, 1875.

man and settle the Barrow estate. And Robertson reminded Robert Jr. that Pittman had borne a terrible burden for years in dealing with Barrow. Robertson also told Pittman that Robert Jr. knew about "the trouble you had had for a life time" with Barrow.[39]

On August 18 Robertson felt all parties were ready to settle their differences. He told Pittman that Roberta's husband, William Slatter, and Robert Jr. were both ready to listen to his advice and that "Board is also willing to do what is right." Meanwhile, Board realized that Robertson and Pittman considered him an outsider. He asked why he had been excluded from family meetings and why Pittman had failed to pay legal fees as he had promised. Still hoping for peaceful negotiations at this point, Board wrote, "Be pleased to give me some idea of your proposed plans relative to the Barrow Estate in order to know how I may be guided."

By mid-September, Pittman had a proposition for Board: $1,500 per year to manage Oak Grove plantation, with the understanding that his salary would come from plantation earnings. His letter implied that Board would have to complete final arrangements for the job with Robert Jr. Board rejected the offer and sought legal advice before embarking on an independent course. He informed Pittman that he did not require any authorization to act, since Louisiana law had already given him, "as one of the Executors of the R R Barrow Estate, all the authority I need."[40]

In December 1875 Board obtained an injunction to prevent Pittman and Robertson from collecting rents from tenants on Oak Grove for 1872, 1873, and 1874. This apparently was his way of collecting monies owed him by the estate. Pittman, a veteran in dealing with the complicated Barrow estate, calmly sought the advice of one of several attorneys advising him. John Isley, Jr., explained Board's action to Pittman: "I think his object is to scare you into some kind of compromise—but of course you are too *wide awake* to enter into any arrangements whatsoever—his claims will require very strong proof to be sustained—and I do not think they are very dangerous."[41]

39. John Robertson to Pittman, August 14, 16, 18, 1875, all in box 5, folder 1, BFP.
40. John Board to John Pittman, September 3, 20, 1875, Pittman to Board, September 13, 1875, all in box 5, folder 2, BFP.
41. John Isley, Jr., to John Pittman, December 22, 1875, box 5, folder 2, BFP.

As Board continued his struggle to administer Robert Barrow's estate, Pittman and Robertson sought ways to prevent him from carrying out his duties. Pittman, who had recently opposed Robert Jr.'s charges against his father, now supported Robert Jr.'s petition to administer his late father's estate. Although Pittman and Robertson acknowledged Barrow's indebtedness to Board, they felt that Robert Jr. had a better claim to managing his father's property than Board did. On August 29, 1876, Judge Henry Sidney in Terrebonne appointed Robert Jr. executor of his father's estate. In June 1878, three years after Barrow's death, J. Fisk reminded Pittman that he and Robertson should get together and close the Barrow estate.[42]

The wealthy planter's influence lingered long after he was dead, partly because of the intricate web of finances he had woven. Undoubtedly, Robert Barrow would have taken pleasure in knowing how he had complicated matters. He would have enjoyed seeing his son evade creditors to build an empire of his own, all in the family tradition.

42. Terrebonne Parish Probate Record No. 666; J. Fisk to John Pittman, June 8, 1878, in box 5, folder 4, BFP.

Ruins of the Company Canal locks in Lockport, facing east, 1978.

Robert Barrow's home at Residence plantation on Bayou Terrebonne two miles below Houma.

Robert Barrow, Jr., and his wife, Jennie, with daughters Irene (left) and Zoe (right).

Robert Jr.'s home at 4938 St. Charles Avenue, New Orleans, about 1920.

Robert Jr.'s motor launch *Brer Rabbit*, about 1910.

The steamboat *Ohio* in the Company Canal.

Unloading sugarcane from a wooden barge on the Company Canal.

A steamer unloading produce in Houma on the Company Canal.

The steamer *Phyllis* entering Bayou Terrebonne in Houma from Bayou Black through the Company Canal, about 1913.

Cook County (Chicago) Real Estate Board excursion aboard the *Houma* in the Company Canal, 1913.

Small motor vessel entering the Company Canal at Lockport while en route to Terrebonne. In the background are the old locks built on Bayou Lafourche in 1853.

Repair work on the Company Canal locks at Westwego, probably in 1917.

The Company Canal locks in Westwego, 1918, after repair work.

PART II

Robert Ruffin Barrow, Jr., and the B and L No. 2, 1875 to 1925

4

Robert Barrow, Jr.: Carrying on the Family Tradition

Shortly after the death of Robert Barrow in 1875, Robert Barrow, Jr., began carrying on the family tradition as sugar planter and canal proprietor, even though he was only seventeen years old. Robert Jr.'s experiences as a youth were unusual; his irascible father certainly was not the typical southern gentleman. Like his father and his grandfather, Robert Jr. had limited formal education. At one time he agreed to attend school if his father paid his expenses, but there is no indication of the extent of his education. However, this lack of formal learning did not prevent him from writing extensively on a wide variety of subjects, in his own ungrammatical way. At times he demonstrated force and clarity in his prose; usually, though, he was repetitious and rambling.

Like his father, Robert Jr. was tough and persistent; nothing could deter him from a course of action, especially if someone suggested an approach different from his own. He was strident, abrasive, and quick to take legal action against those he thought had offended him; and he saw conspiracies everywhere. His experiences growing up during the Civil War, when his family was losing its fortune and was being torn apart by marital strife, must have toughened him to the realities of the outside world.

Mostly assuredly Robert Jr. was introduced at an early age to the hardship of life. Even though much of his youth is a mystery, it is possible to piece together a chronology of his life. He was only four years old when Yankee forces reached New Orleans and brought his father's agricultural and canal operations to a halt. When the war ended in 1865, he was seven; when his mother died in 1868, he was ten and had his own pony and his own bank account, his father once bragged. But in 1871 he and his sister, Roberta, ran away from their father. For several years Robert Jr. and Roberta waged legal battles against their father over the disposition of their mother's estate, which had been left entirely to them. In 1875 his father died; in 1876 Robert Jr. and Roberta came into their inheritance. In 1880 Robert Jr. married at the age of twenty-two.

Whether Robert Jr. observed any of his father's complicated financial dealings with John Pittman or with his cousin Ruffin C. Barrow is not known, but he undoubtedly learned how to function in the world of high finance. He understood loans, mortgages, and complicated transfers of mortgaged property. He also knew about lawsuits and legal recourse through the court system, for he was involved through the years in a plethora of litigation. In time Robert Jr. was to hone these business skills to an edge that would have pleased his father.

After Robert Jr. and Roberta received their inheritance, they bought back from Pittman plantations he had bought earlier at sheriff's sales to protect their interests. In 1876 they paid Pittman $22,000, little of which was in cash, for Residence, Myrtle Grove, Honduras, and other lots and pieces of property in Terrebonne Parish. A year later Robert Jr. and Roberta leased land in Terrebonne Parish to Charles Tennent, who was Robert Jr.'s agricultural partner and future father-in-law. Robert Jr., who had visions of revitalizing the Barataria and Lafourche Canal No. 2, also began to acquire other plantations once owned by his father. He capitalized on a feature of Louisiana law that allowed landowners to reacquire land lost in tax sales long after the new owners had taken possession of it. In 1879 he paid $25.42 for land on Bayou Blue that earlier had been sold for taxes.[1]

Considering their aggressive encounters with their father, it is not surprising that Robert Jr. and Roberta argued between themselves

1. Terrebonne Parish Conveyance Book, Houma, La. (hereinafter cited as TCB), "CC," fol. 101, 366; TCB "EE," fol. 7.

about property they owned jointly. The tone of Robert Jr.'s letters to his sister, who lived in Winchester, Tennessee, suggested that she may have suffered from a mental disorder. He hoped she could find peace and tranquility, but he complained in 1887, "You are the only sister I ever knew that a brother had to put on kid gloves to talk to." He worried about her children: "I certainly pity you and may god guide & care for your 3 little ones for your ungovernable temper will surely never let you see right." Finally, with a gesture of resignation, he wrote, "Well Berta good bye for I don't intend to fuss with you." When Robert Jr. finally settled some of his canal problems, he sold to Roberta a tract of land she wanted on Bayou Black. In 1882 they divided property owned jointly on Bayou Terrebonne; in 1888 they divided their property on Bayou Petit Caillou. Robert Jr. became the sole owner of Residence in 1902, when he bought Roberta's half-interest in the plantation at a sheriff's sale for $9,000.[2]

In the meantime Robert Jr. had not neglected his social life. In 1879, just three years after receiving his inheritance, he was twenty-one and courting Jennie L. Tennent of Terrebonne Parish, the daughter of his agricultural partner, Charles Tennent. In July, Jennie told her aunt Mary Gayoso that "Ruffin gave me a beautiful album for Christmas my name on the back" and that "Ruffie" called on her every evening. Jennie Tennent, who had received little formal education, was a talented seamstress who made all her own clothes. She admitted late in life that she hated chalk dust and that she had progressed only through the third reader. Nonetheless, Jennie's ancestry was impressive. Her mother was Félicité Gayoso, a descendant of the Spanish governor Don Manuel Gayoso de Lemos.

Robert Jr. and Jennie married at 8 P.M. on June 28, 1880, at Jennie's home. Even though Robert Jr. was a Protestant, he reluctantly agreed to be married by a Catholic priest. Jennie described the ceremony: "Mr. Barrow did not like it, but it was the full ceremony he being a Protestant & I a Catholic & I asked the priest not to lecture, he just married us and everything was signed & he left." Rain was falling

2. Robert R. Barrow, Jr., to Roberta Barrow Slatter, n.d. [1887], in box 5, folder 12, Robert R. Barrow Family Papers, Manuscripts Section, Howard-Tilton Memorial Library, Tulane University, hereinafter cited as BFP; TCB "GG," fol. 609; TCB "LL," fol. 162; TCB "MM," fol. 98; TCB "XX," fol. 26.

when the young couple departed for their new home at 10 P.M. The bride wore a light gray silk dress with matching hat and gloves. Their honeymoon trip was a steamboat voyage up the Mississippi River to Cairo, Illinois, where they boarded a train for Winchester to visit Roberta and her husband. Jennie and Robert Jr. were to have six children, two of whom died during infancy.

Apparently the Barrows enjoyed a number of years of marital happiness. Writing many years later, Jennie observed, "We lived for 15 months in sublime happiness." Robert's letters to Jennie indicate that he, too, was happy, even though he was frequently gone from home to attend to canal and plantation matters. But like his father, Robert Jr. became estranged from his wife and feuded with his children over property and inheritance. Occasionally Robert Jr. became upset over Jennie's spendthrift ways or her inability to deal with plantation problems.[3]

Perhaps the death of two children during infancy contributed to marital problems. Their first child, Volumnia Hunley Barrow, lived only eight months. When she died on May 17, 1882, Jennie and Robert Jr. were distraught. "I thought every thing was gone," Jennie wrote. A second daughter, Irene, was born on March 29, 1883. Robert Ruffin Barrow III, their only son, was born on May 13, 1885, but he died six months later of respiratory complications diagnosed as membranous croup, which the family originally had assumed was just a cold. A close family friend observed, "Poor Jennie and Ruffin are terribly overwhelmed by this unexpected blow."[4]

Before long there were other children—all girls. Zoe was born in 1886, Jennie in 1888, and Hallette in 1892. Irene never married; Jennie, Hallette, and Zoe all married doctors. Zoe's husband was Robert Topping of Newark, New Jersey, who died during the flu epidemic of 1918. Jennie's husband, Harris P. Dawson, established his practice in Montgomery, Alabama. From time to time Harris and his

---

3. See box 3, folder 5, BFP, for Charles Tennent's letters. Terrebonne Parish Marriage Book, Houma, La., 4, fol. 258, records the wedding of Charles Tennant and Félicité Gayoso. Jennie Tennent to Mary Gayoso, January 15, 1879, box 5, folder 5, BFP; Jennie Tennent, "My Life" (Typescript diary in box 27, folder 7, BFP). Terrebonne Parish Marriage Book 16, fol. 86, records the marriage of Robert Barrow, Jr., and Jennie Tennent.
4. Fannie Bisland to Lisa, November 6, 1885, box 5, folder 11, BFP.

father-in-law exchanged ideas regarding family property. Hallette married Christian Cole, who served as coroner of Orleans Parish for years.

Remote bits and pieces of information only hint at what life was like for Robert Jr. and Jennie. In 1895 their house burned to the ground, but no details even of where the fire occurred are available. In 1895 Jennie was a patient at Hôtel Dieu Hospital in New Orleans, but there is no indication of the nature of her malady.

Robert Jr.'s absences from home undoubtedly were a problem for the young family. Jennie hated for him to leave, but Robert Jr. felt he had to oversee personally the dredging of the Barataria and Lafourche Canal No. 2, which he hoped would be profitable. Often his letters indicated that he would be away longer than expected because of dredging problems. "I leave feeling much better knowing all is well at home," he wrote in 1890. "God bless my little family & keep them well." He signed his letter "Ruf."

Sometimes Robert Jr. could not say whether he would be home in a week or in a month. At times he was at the mercy of the elements. On March 16, 1891, he wrote describing the crevasse that developed on the plantation of the Ames brothers near Westwego: "The crevasse is still a running and growing larger that they have given up all hopes of stopping it." He was right; there was little chance of stopping the Ames crevasse. The water level in the Mississippi River came to within 1 foot of the top of the Company Canal locks at Westwego; the canal's water level was 12 feet lower. Spectators came on excursion boats to observe the water surging through the break in the levee. Eventually floodwaters covered a vast area, stretching westward to Bayou Lafourche. Fortunately, the Company Canal locks were not damaged.

Robert Jr. sent his wife newspaper clippings and wrote explanations of goings-on in New Orleans. After the assassination of David Hennessey (the Irish-American chief of police in New Orleans in 1890), which led to the lynching of eleven Italians a short time afterward, Robert Jr. wrote, "The excitement over the Dagos are dying out."[5]

5. Robert Barrow, Jr., to Jennie Barrow, September 27, 1890, March 19, 1891, September 28, 1892, March 26, 1896, all in box 6, folders 2–7, BFP; Robert Barrow, Jr., to

When he became angry, Robert Jr. wrote vicious letters to Jennie. Because she had not written to inform him of a broken mill at Myrtle Grove plantation, he vented his feelings in 1893 in typical Barrow style. "What is matter you cant write me. Are you so worthless that you cant write me or is it you are too independent to take the trouble to be of any assistance to me," he wrote. "A butterfly spendthrift wife is a curse to any man and the more fool he to indulge such a creature who seeks to be a burden & not a helpmate."[6] Jennie's oversight not only brought on the wrath of her short-tempered husband but also caused a delay in replacing the mill.

In contrast, Robert Jr.'s letters were usually filled with details, questions, and observations about family members and about canal and plantation matters. Robert Jr. disliked having to go to Yazoo City, Mississippi, in 1892 to buy a boat for his canal company: "I regret my absence from home but try to bear it. If possible I would not go." In 1896 he closed a letter to Jennie, "Love and lots of kisses to all of you from your devoted Ruf." Once he extended his stay in New Orleans an extra day because freezing weather made draining pipes and boilers on his boat necessary. Often news about his daughters, their pets and peccadilloes, filled the pages. Schooling, health, and vaccinations received due attention, as did descriptions of fires, like the one that destroyed part of downtown Houma in 1900.[7]

Meanwhile, Robert Jr. was reacquiring portions of the Barataria and Lafourche Canal Company No. 2 that had been lost during the years of his father's decline. "I felt there was a moral obligation on my part to accomplish as much of this waterway scheme as it was possible for me to do," he wrote. When Robert Jr. first took charge of canal operations, a good portion of the canal had been abandoned and had

---

Mary Gayoso, May 22, 1895, in box 6, folder 6, BFP; Scraps of a letter to Jennie Barrow, May 21, 1889, in box 5, folder 13, BFP. See Michael Kurtz, "Organized Crime in Louisiana History: Myth and Reality," *Louisiana History*, XXIV (Fall, 1983), 355–76, for an astute look into the 1890 lynching of Italians in New Orleans and the literature relating to the Mafia in New Orleans. Betsy Swanson, *Historic Jefferson Parish: From Shore to Shore* (Gretna, La., 1975), 92–93.

6. Robert Barrow, Jr., to Jennie Barrow, November 19, 1893, in box 6, folder 4, BFP.

7. Robert Barrow, Jr., to Jennie Barrow, September 28, 1892, in box 6, folder 4, BFP; Robert Barrow, Jr., to Jennie Barrow, March 26, 1896, in box 6, folder 7, BFP; Robert Barrow, Jr., to Jennie Barrow, January 28, 1895, in box 6, folder 6, BFP; Robert Barrow, Jr., to Jennie Barrow, November 9, 1900, in box 6, folder 2, BFP.

partly filled in. Only the section of the canal near the Mississippi River at Westwego was navigable, and then only by vessels of shallow draft. Sometimes Robert Jr. reminisced about the times in his youth when he transported sugar and molasses on the old canal route between Bayous Terrebonne and Lafourche. He believed that reopening the old route would improve drainage and encourage reclamation of marshland contiguous to the Company Canal. Later, when the Corps of Engineers became active in revitalizing waterways, he saw an opportunity to turn his romantic dream into reality.[8]

Robert Jr. faced a formidable task. Engineers' reports indicated that he would have to solve gigantic problems before opening the Company Canal to transportation, especially the section west of Bayou Lafourche. According to a Corps report prepared in 1881, Bayou Black west of Houma had long been neglected and was gradually filling in. The Black was no longer connected to Bayou Terrebonne near Schriever, the site of its former confluence with that stream, even though "the beds of the old bayous can still be traced." When the B & L was in its infancy in 1831, steamboats from the Teche country could ascend Bayou Black to the town of Houma, "where now not even a pirogue could go." Many logs clogged the bayou. "In early days, when the banks were first cleared, the trees, principally live-oaks, were chopped down and allowed to fall into the bayou, where they have lain ever since," the 1881 report continued.[9]

The old B & L had attempted a number of projects to improve navigation on Bayou Black above Houma. The most ambitious involved William A. Shaffer, whose plantation, Ardoyne, was located 4 miles upstream from Houma. Shaffer contracted with the B & L through its subsidiary, the Lafourche and Terrebonne Navigation Company, to build locks on the bayou. The locks raised the water level of Bayou Black and made it navigable; for seven years Shaffer collected tolls on the bayou.

Eventually users of the bayou balked at paying tolls to Shaffer for using a natural stream. They contended that Louisiana laws prohib-

8. Robert Barrow, Jr., to W. H. Price, April 3, 1924, in box "1924," Robert Ruffin Barrow, Jr., Papers, Division of Archives, Nicholls State University Library, hereinafter cited as RRBP.
9. Chief Engineer, U.S. Corps of Engineers, Annual Report, hereinafter cited as AR, 1881 (Box 43, RRBP).

ited the construction of locks on Bayou Black. Shaffer, in defending his actions, stated that steamboats could not use the upper Black before he built the locks. The *General Walker,* a vessel sent to clear the stream, had been unable to move upstream past Houma, whereas the *Archer* ascended the stream successfully after the locks were in use. Soon the point was moot; the upper bayou became no more than a ditch, usable only during the rainy season, and then only by flatboats.[10]

The report of the Corps of Engineers for 1881 estimated that dredging and cutting trees on upper Bayou Black would cost $47,520. H. S. Douglas, an engineer who conducted surveys for the Corps, reporting on conditions on Bayou Black, noted that the entire area was good sugarcane country but presented serious obstacles to transporting produce to market. Besides having to pay a toll to go from Bayou Black to Bayou Terrebonne, there was "another toll to pass from the Terrebonne into the Lafourche, and still another to go from the Lafourche into Barataria Bay." Undoubtedly this situation was painfully obvious to sugarcane farmers in the area.

In view of the obstacles to reopening the Company Canal, why had Robert Barrow, Jr., considered undertaking such an ambitious project in the 1880s? Like his father, he became interested in the B & L No. 2 when everyone else was ready to give up on it. Some of the factors that had influenced his father in 1859 still held true. Maintaining a canal was cheaper than building a new one. Rail service did not reach many sections of south Louisiana because of high construction costs across "trembling prairies." But most of all, Robert Jr. realized that the U.S. Corps of Engineers was now taking on the responsibility for maintaining many of the state's navigable streams. All he had to do was open his canal connecting these streams. He could do some of the work himself. He was already part owner of a canal that most people did not consider valuable. Perhaps he could reacquire the whole Company Canal for a small price and apply his Barrow instincts toward making it profitable.

Then, too, the area was growing again. The Civil War had upset the agricultural expansion that Louisiana had experienced during the

10. Defendant's brief, in *Boykin & Lang* v. *W. A. Shaffer* (1858), appeal from 5th Judicial District Court, Terrebonne Parish, n.d., in box 43, RRBP.

transportation revolution, but recovery was inevitable. Census figures indicate that several sugar parishes had declined in population from 1860 to 1870. This was the case for Assumption, St. Charles, St. Mary, and St. James. By 1880 all showed substantial gains. St. Mary, for instance, went from a population of 16,000 in 1860, to 13,000 in 1870, to 19,000 in 1880. St. James went from 11,000 to 10,000 to 14,000 during the same period. Terrebonne and Lafourche, which had remained stable from 1860 to 1870, both showed increases in 1880, when Lafourche had 19,000 people and Terrebonne had 17,000.

As part of its improvements of rivers and harbors, the U.S. Corps of Engineers cleared Bayous Terrebonne and Lafourche in 1881. The Corps spent $16,000 to clear lower Bayou Lafourche from the Gulf of Mexico to 8 miles below Lockport. There still remained considerable obstruction on the upper Lafourche extending several miles below Donaldsonville.

The Corps needed $15,000 more to complete the dredging of Bayou Terrebonne, where work had stopped 16 miles below Houma. There was a need for "turn arounds" (turning basins) in various places on the narrow stream. The Corps rejected a bid from D. S. Cage—the vice-president of the South Louisiana Canal and Navigation Company, a subsidiary of the Harvey Canal interests—to complete the dredging of Bayou Terrebonne. However, Major C. W. Howell of the Corps of Engineers agreed to rent the South Louisiana Canal and Navigation Company's dredge, *Sampson*, for $10 per day, starting December 23, 1880.

H. S. Douglas surveyed Barataria Bay for the Corps in April 1881 and returned to New Orleans via the Company Canal, which he found usable. "Sailing vessels like the Company Canal route," he noted, "as very little timber is to be found on the banks of the bayou leading to it, and wind being unobstructed they are enabled to sail almost to the canal." Douglas was also impressed with the brick locks connecting the Company Canal to the Mississippi River at Westwego, "the only structure of its kind in this section that has withstood the test of years without apparent injury."[11]

In Houma the old B & L No. 2 canal connecting Bayous Black and

11. AR, 1881 (Box 43, RRBP).

Terrebonne was grown over with willow trees and cut-grass, which in some places was 6 to 8 feet high. In 1884 the Corps of Engineers began work with funds that had been appropriated in 1881. Captain Thomas Turtle told Congressman Randall L. Gibson that dredging the short canal from Bayou Black to Bayou Terrebonne across Houma could be done cheaply. Turtle did not think that the government could expropriate the old route without an act of Congress, and he did not recommend trying to acquire the right-of-way to it. He said, "The route, in my view of it, is chiefly of local value."[12] In time, Robert Jr. attempted to reopen the half-mile canal across the city. His interest in the project seemed directly proportional to efforts by the U.S. government to reopen the abandoned waterway.

Even though the Corps of Engineers had not thought much of the canal across Houma, Robert Jr. must have been favorably influenced by recent efforts to clear bayous the Company Canal intersected. If the U.S. government could keep the natural waterways navigable, Robert Jr. could reopen the B & L No. 2 and capitalize on their accessibility. Here, perhaps, was the opportunity he needed. The state of Louisiana had subsidized the old B & L; the federal government, indirectly at least, could do the same for him.

Not surprisingly, Barrow's hold on the B & L No. 2 was not altogether secure. Like his father, who manipulated company stock as he desired, Robert Jr. resorted to questionable wheeling and dealing at the expense of stockholders. In the 1880s Robert Jr. took a number of steps to cut expenses and strengthen his grip on the canal. Even though he had purchased all the available B & L No. 2 stock, Robert Jr. realized that minor stockholders could cause problems for him. In 1884 he wrote his cousin John Pittman in a tone reminiscent of his late father. Anticipating a reorganization of the B & L No. 2, he informed Pittman that canal business should receive immediate attention. In regard to a B & L No. 2 board of directors meeting scheduled in Houma on April 5, 1884, Robert Jr. wrote, "You had better come over and bring what papers you have connecting with the canal co."

Robert Jr. claimed to own 8 shares of B & L No. 2 stock and asked

12. Thomas Turtle to Hon. Randall L. Gibson, November 18, 1884, in box 3, folder 2, RRBP.

Pittman to claim control over 3 shares. He also wanted Pittman to ask C. A. Voorhies about his 1 share of B & L No. 2 stock that he suspected was bogus. "I believe the share referred to is not owned by him but was one of those floating shares my Father always put in name of other people for convenience sake," he told Pittman. Noting that some litigation over the B & L No. 2 had not yet come up for trial, Robert Jr. told Pittman, "They will offer a compromise."

The Voorhies matter ended well for Robert Jr. In 1886 C. A. Voorhies transferred his share of B & L No. 2 stock to Albert Voorhies, who then sold it to Charles Carroll for $250. Carroll, who bought it in Robert Jr.'s behalf, considered the price a bargain. "I must congratulate you at getting control of this share at so small a price," Carroll wrote. "It would have been better to pay $400 or even $500 than to leave the stock in outside hands." Occasionally Robert Jr. found a bargain and bought a share cheaply from someone who did not realize its true value. His attorney Lucius Fane Suthon bought 1 share of B & L No. 2 stock from the estate of F. S. Goode for $50.

Soon Robert Jr. was reacquiring other portions of the Company Canal. In April 1887 his attorneys met with attorneys representing Robert and Nelson Taylor, who had bought the locks and other B & L No. 2 property near Lockport at a tax sale in 1874. The parties reached an agreement, and Robert Jr. got the locks back. Likewise, for $168.95, Robert Jr. reacquired "all that portion of the Barataria Canal Company situated in the Parish of Terrebonne running from Bayou Terrebonne to Lockport," which had been lost to A. J. Bascle and Marcelin Falgout in a tax sale in 1880. This same property had been bought by the B & L No. 2 in 1877 and later lost when the company failed to pay property tax on the land.

Robert Jr. sometimes resorted to a tactic of his late father: having a friend or relative acquire property in name only. In 1886 Robert Jr.'s brother-in-law, F. Gayoso Tennent, bought the previously mentioned tract of land from Bascle and Falgout "for the benefit of R R Barrow & although in my name it is his property he having paid the one hundred dollars cash." Tennent said he would turn the property over to Robert Jr. "at any time when called upon to transfer the title of said purchase to him."[13]

13. Robert Barrow, Jr., to John Pittman, March 28, December 21, 1884, both in box

Despite these fortuitous acquisitions, several technicalities kept Robert Jr. from gaining full control of the Company Canal in 1886. The Louisiana Canal and Land Improvement Company, the now defunct company that had leased the B & L No. 2 from Robert Barrow in 1871, refused to give up its claim to the canal until John A. Karstendiek and James L. Roxburgh, stockholders in the improvement company, worked out a compromise with Robert Jr. No details of the settlement survive, but Robert Jr. admitted to Roberta, whose interest in the B & L No. 2 he purchased in 1886 for $400, that he was in danger of losing the canal as a result of lawsuits. "I have compromised with parties who held the canal," he wrote, "and am now in possession of same." In 1888 Robert Jr. leased the Company Canal in Terrebonne Parish to the police jury for an annual fee of $1. He was not motivated by a sense of charity; the jury kept the canal in running order at no cost to him.

With the help of his brother-in-law and nifty bargaining, Robert Jr. settled accounts with B & L No. 2 stockholders in 1887. On June 11, F. Gayoso Tennent bought the B & L No. 2 stock for $21,000. That same day, Tennent sold the company to Robert Jr. for $25,000, of which only $5,000 was in cash; Tennent held a mortgage for the balance due.[14] Robert Barrow, Jr., now owned the Barataria and Lafourche Canal Company No. 2. The entire venture was his—providing he could meet his commitments and make the canal profitable. Like his father, he acquired the canal when no one else had faith in its future. Whether he could turn it into a successful enterprise remained to be seen.

Realizing that B & L No. 2 rights-of-way were suspect, Robert Jr. systematically recorded many questionable company property titles. Charles Barker, the clerk of court for Lafourche Parish, charged him $12 for recording some sales and for examining "leaf by leaf, of these old records."

By far the most suspicious B & L No. 2 acquisition was in Jefferson

---

5, folder 10, BFP; Charles Carroll to Robert Barrow, Jr., July 12, 1886, L. F. Suthon to Robert Barrow, Jr., January 10, 1886, F. Gayoso Tennent to To Whom It May Concern, February 22, 1886, all in box "1833–1912," RRBP, which lists the conveyance records that document the sales; TCB "JJ," fol. 742.

14. TCB "KK," fol. 399, 402; Box "1925," RRBP; Robert Barrow, Jr., to Roberta Barrow Slatter, March 19, 1886, in box 5, folder 12, BFP.

Parish. The confusion began with the sheriff's sale held in 1862 as Yankee forces approached the city of New Orleans. John Winder, a Houma attorney representing Robert Jr. in a title search, received a confusing explanation of the whole matter from former Jefferson Parish deputy sheriff J. G. Dreux in 1880. Dreux claimed to have sold the B & L No. 2 for $25,000 to the elder Barrow, who "failed to pay costs and charges and never called for his title." Consequently, Dreux's brother paid the fees and took possession of the property. Finding no evidence of these transfers in Jefferson Parish conveyance records, Winder came to doubt that the sale by Dreux had ever occurred. Possibly the elder Barrow resorted to shady practices to acquire title to the B & L No. 2. In 1890 Lucius Fane Suthon, also a Terrebonne Parish attorney, informed Robert Jr. that he found no legal documents indicating a sale by Dreux.

To strengthen his claim, Robert Jr. paid Sheriff William Langridge of Jefferson Parish $1,500 to record a long list of titles, including the one involved in Dreux's mysterious sheriff's sale. Robert Jr. then sued Langridge in 1894 to force him to deed the canal to him. His suit alleged that Dreux had failed to execute a deed to the canal on April 6, 1862, "owing to the disturbance existing at that time, although the sale was complete by the adjudication." The disturbance referred to was the Civil War; Commodore Farragut's fleet took New Orleans on April 12, 1862. On March 23, 1895, Judge E. Rost of the Twenty-first Judicial District Court of Jefferson Parish ruled in favor of Robert Jr. against Langridge, who was ordered to deed B & L No. 2 property to Barrow. Even this expensive bit of legal maneuvering, however, did not solve Robert Jr.'s problem or give him clear title to lands long claimed by the B & L No. 2.[15]

Meanwhile Robert Jr. continued to expand and improve the Company Canal. F. Gayoso Tennent, now an employee of the company, conducted dredging operations for the B & L No. 2 and conferred

---

15. G. W. Trahan to Robert Barrow, Jr., July 18, 1888, Charles Barker to Robert Barrow, Jr., December 20, 1889, William Langridge to L. F. Suthon, September 29, November 4, 1894, all in box "1833–1912," RRBP; Box "1925," *passim.*, RRBP; TCB "PP," fol. 443; J. G. Dreux to John Winder, May 22, 1880, in box 5, folder 6, BFP; L. F. Suthon to Robert Barrow, Jr., April 17, 1890, in box 6, folder 2, BFP; *R. R. Barrow* v. *William Langridge* (1895), Civil Suit No. 284, 21st Judicial District Court, Jefferson Parish.

often with Robert Jr., describing the types of buckets and scoops that worked best on the various marsh muds encountered along the route. Often Tennent complained that the banks of the canal were too soft to support the fill that was removed from its bottom, but he dredged an average of 125 feet per day. On October 17, 1892, Tennent fell off the *Joe Webre* near Grand Lake while on route to Grand Isle and drowned. Only thirty years old and a strong swimmer, he may have sustained head injuries when he fell.[16]

New settlements along the canal route helped the B & L No. 2 grow and prosper. Westwego, at the eastern end of the canal, opposite New Orleans, grew in population after a devastating tropical hurricane struck the coastal settlement of Grand Isle and Chênière Caminada in 1893. Survivors of the disaster moved inland out of fear of future storms. Fishermen and their families settled along the banks of the canal near Westwego; they had used the Company Canal to transport seafood to the French Market in New Orleans.

Robert Jr. noted with interest studies on improving water transportation, especially those that considered the Company Canal a part of a proposed inland waterway route from Florida to Texas. Robert Jr. always insisted that the B & L No. 2 was the shortest, most direct course between New Orleans and the Attakapas country, and when official reports did not state what he wanted planners and politicians to hear, he suspected that engineers had conspired against him.

Robert Jr. sometimes overreacted to threats that existed only in his mind, and occasionally these phantom threats turned into serendipitous blessings for the B & L No. 2. For example, in 1893 Robert Jr. feared that inquiries by P. H. Thompson, an assistant engineer for the state, might lead to lawsuits that would put him out of business. Instead of seeking information on which to base a suit, Thompson actually wanted to borrow Robert Jr.'s sketches and blueprints of locks and structures for a pamphlet on canals between New Orleans and Berwick Bay. When Robert Jr. understood Thompson's motives,

16. F. Gayoso Tennent to Mrs. Félicité Gayoso Tennent, January 22, 1892, F. Gayoso Tennent to Robert Barrow, Jr., September 22, 1892, both in box 6, folder 4, BFP; Telegrams and newspaper clippings, October, 1892, in box 6, folder 4, BFP.

he readily provided descriptive materials.¹⁷ Thompson's pamphlet praised the Company Canal, pointing out that distances along the canal were shorter than rail links across the state. Thompson even cited military advantages of an inland canal: "It would afford an interior line of water communication in time of war, available for small armed vessels." His observation was prophetic; during World War II parts of the Company Canal were used to transport oil in barges, safe from German submarine attacks in the Gulf of Mexico.

Thompson mentioned other factors dear to Robert Jr.'s heart. He favored constructing a dam on Bayou Lafourche at Donaldsonville at its confluence with the Mississippi. This would have eliminated sandbars that plagued navigation on the upper Lafourche. Furthermore, Thompson saw a need for the Company Canal, since Bayou Plaquemine, the ancient route to western Louisiana markets, had been closed. The Mississippi River–Old River–Atchafalaya River route was open, but Old River, too, silted up badly, especially when the Mississippi and Red rivers rose simultaneously. In all, Thompson's study indicated that the B & L No. 2 was the key to any future inland route across Louisiana.¹⁸

Meanwhile, Robert Jr. was buying small tracts here and there along the canal route. In 1890 he bought 688 acres of marshland along the Williamson Canal near Lockport from Jennie Williamson for $100. For another $100 he bought the right-of-way along his canal between Bayous Blue and Terrebonne from Willie Martin in 1899; he acquired a small tract in 1900 from Henderson Washington and another tract from Michel Foret on the left descending bank of Bayou Lafourche contiguous to the locks in Lockport.¹⁹

Even though money matters received much of Robert Jr.'s attention, he became a liberal spender as his wealth increased. When the Barrows first moved to New Orleans in 1890, Robert Jr. leased a house for his family at 578 Prytania Street, between Berlin Street and

17. P. H. Thompson to Robert Barrow, Jr., April 8, 1893, Robert Barrow, Jr., to Jennie Barrow, March 4, 1893, both in box 6, folder 5, BFP.
18. P. H. Thompson, "Old River: A Discussion of the Proper Location of a Permanent Water Way Between the Mississippi River and the Navigable Waters of Western Louisiana" (MS in box 43, RRBP).
19. Box "1925," RRBP.

Napoleon Avenue, for only $35 per month. In 1896 he bought a lot on Valmont Street from his mother-in-law for $100. Later Jennie inherited from her mother a house at 1410 Valmont Street, which the Barrows leased for $55 per month in 1896. Eventually the Barrows bought a home on St. Charles Avenue, the fashionable New Orleans residential area. Robert Jr. took his family on vacations to Europe and to the West Coast. Even Jennie's expensive tastes—for example, she spent $115 for a dress from an exclusive New Orleans shop in 1899—he learned to take in good humor. From Paris in 1906 he wrote Jennie's aunt, Mary Gayoso, "We are all well but when Jennie gets through buying I know I'll be sick."[20]

Robert Jr.'s financial status improved over the years. Incomplete but nonetheless revealing financial records indicate that the B & L No. 2 was a moderate financial success. The Company Canal had problems, but its receipts consistently exceeded expenditures, according to raw figures in company files. In 1889, for instance, the company took in $5,439 and spent only $1,362 in operating expenses. In 1890 the profits were slightly less. In 1891 the company took in $6,633 and spent $5,636.

B & L No. 2 ledgers for 1888 indicate active use of the eastern portion of the Company Canal between New Orleans and Lake Salvador. Regular customers included the steam tugs *Emma*, *Baltimore*, and *Joe Webre*. The *Joe Webre* paid $26.60 to transport 147 barrels of molasses and 33 hogsheads of sugar to New Orleans on January 7, 1888. The *Emma* was an even better customer, paying $468.75 in tolls in March and over $250 per month in January and February of 1889. Receipts were considerably higher early in the year, when sugar planters shipped their sugar and molasses to markets in New Orleans. Company ledgers indicated operating expenditures as well: The dredge boat and lock repair account for February 1888 showed an outflow of $1,278.00 in one place and an additional $1,646.55 in a separate entry. Another company entry showed that Frederick Frossard paid $50 for an exclusive fishing privilege in the Company Canal for one year.[21]

20. Bill from shop of Marie Schweilzer and F. Cazelle, 938 Canal St., New Orleans, in box 6, folder 2, BFP; Robert Barrow, Jr., to Mary Gayoso, July 31, 1906, in box 7, folder 8, BFP.
21. B & L Ledger Book, 1888 (RRBP).

Robert Jr.'s agricultural ventures also succeeded. A most propitious act on his part had been the formation of an agricultural partnership with Henry Clay Duplantis at Myrtle Grove in 1890. For half of the profit from the plantation, Duplantis served as manager. An honest, capable manager, Duplantis made Myrtle Grove a profitable venture for many years. Sugar bounties that Barrow and Duplantis collected in 1891, as a result of the recently passed McKinley Tariff, came to $753; in 1892 they received a bounty of $2,389 for their production of 119,464 pounds of sugar at Myrtle Grove at 2 cents' bounty per pound. Duplantis was reliable; Robert Jr. could attend to Company Canal matters and not concern himself with problems at Myrtle Grove. In addition to Myrtle Grove, the partners jointly owned ten sugar barges, two cane loaders on the plantation, seven cane hoists on the Company Canal, one hoist on Bayou Terrebonne, one cane scale on Bayou Petit Caillou, and one at Bayou Blue.

The Barrows took on the trappings of wealth. They joined prominent New Orleans social organizations: the Boston Club, the Crescent Club, and the Juanita Club. They maintained residences in New Orleans and in Terrebonne Parish, and they took extended vacations to Europe in 1900 and in 1906. In 1905 they took a trip to the West Coast. Often they were gone for the entire summer—from May to August on one occasion. Sometimes only Robert Jr. and Jennie went, and the children stayed with Jennie's family at Valmont Street, but when the girls were older, however, they joined their parents. After the sugarcane grinding season was completed, Robert Jr. sometimes hunted rabbits at Myrtle Grove. In 1900 Robert Jr. was forty-two and a successful businessman. His passport describes his physical appearance: 5 feet 7 inches tall, brownish gray eyes, oval face, dark hair and complexion, small round chin, ordinary nose, and medium mouth.[22]

Robert Jr.'s ability to relax and vacation did not mean that he had no serious problems to solve. Agricultural prosperity from the turn of the century until after World War I strengthened his financial status, but navigational problems in the Company Canal and in the natural

22. *Duplantis* v. *Barrow* (1928), 116 So 568; TCB "MM," fol. 98. Boxes 6, 7, 14, BFP, contain most of the financial information on the Barrows. Orleans Parish Conveyance Book, New Orleans, 161, fol. 609; Irene Barrow Notebook, 1898 (Box 51, RRBP).

waterways it intersected were perennial. Sometimes the actions of local political bodies or the work by the U.S. Corps of Engineers made life easier for him; sometimes, however, they complicated matters.

In many ways, Robert Jr.'s biggest problems depended on the whims of nature: high and low water in the Mississippi and its distributaries. All physical problems for the Company Canal began with the Mississippi River. By the turn of the century this meant Robert Jr. would have extensive dealings with the Corps of Engineers.

Physical conditions in the bayou country had changed little since the early days of the Barataria and Lafourche Canal Company. What had changed dramatically since the Civil War was the role of the federal government in maintaining and improving navigation along the nation's many waterways. The U.S. Corps of Engineers virtually replaced the state engineer, the board of public works, and several other state agencies that once took responsibility for improving public transportation in Louisiana. As Ella Lonn noted in her 1918 study of Radical Reconstruction in Louisiana, local politicians may have criticized carpetbagger regimes in the state, but they saw the value of having the Corps of Engineers shoulder the burden of clearing streams and improving navigation. As local politicians and businessmen complained about current navigational problems, they exaggerated how effective travel on the rivers and bayous had been before the war. As a result, studies by U.S. engineers often called for restoring waterways to nonexistent pre–Civil War conditions. Reports from both state and federal agencies indicated that streams intersected by the Company Canal had changed very little over the years. As early as 1875, U.S. engineers noted serious navigational problems on the B & L No. 2 and considered constructing a new canal from the Mississippi River to the Rio Grande in Texas. As they toyed with this plan in its developmental stage, engineers did not rule out the feasibility of completing the Company Canal as its founders had originally envisioned.[23]

Sometimes problems on natural waterways worked to Robert Jr.'s short-term advantage. Bayou Terrebonne was one of these problem areas. In 1882 the Corps of Engineers stopped its dredging operations

23. AR, 1875, Pt. 1, p. 879 (Corps of Engineers library, New Orleans); AR, 1893, Pt. 3, pp. 1845–47; Ella Lonn, *Reconstruction in Louisiana After 1868* (New York, 1918), 34n.

15 miles below Houma because engineers were afraid that a leased dredge would break down. If that happened, the Corps would have to repair it and return it in good working condition. In the meantime, sugar growers south of Houma had to use flatboats to transport their crop upstream to a navigable point that steamboats could reach. Bayou Terrebonne north of Houma was nearly dry and not navigable to Thibodaux, Lieutenant O. T. Crosby reported in 1887, and the volume of trade along the route did not justify redredging it. Growers in the Houma area shipped their sugar by rail on a spur line that ran from Houma to Terrebonne Station (Schriever) and eastward to New Orleans. The Corps reported that freight rates dropped 25 percent when Robert Jr. opened the Company Canal from Bayou Terrebonne to New Orleans.

Bayou Black also had serious navigational problems, but because of its strategic link between Houma and the Atchafalaya River–Bayou Teche region, it was being redredged with great difficulty and at considerable expense. At times the bed was so hard that engineers had to hire teamsters with mules to break the ground; in other places the bottom was soft and oozed back into recently dug channels. In 1885 Major W. H. Heuer of the Corps questioned the cost and feasibility of the whole job: "Is the Government justified in cutting a canal, for that is just what is being done in 'Improving Bayou Black,' the lowest estimates cost of which is $47,520, for the sake of saving the planter the difference between 6¼ miles of wagon and canal transportation."[24] Even though Heuer did not mention Robert Barrow, Jr., he certainly could have been referring to the owner of the B & L No. 2 as one who benefited greatly from reopening Bayou Black.

Bayou Plaquemine, the main early route across the Atchafalaya Swamp to the Attakapas District, had not been used since 1867 or 1868, when the Iberville Parish Police Jury dammed it. From time to time the Corps of Engineers had considered building locks where Bayou Plaquemine joined the Mississippi River. This task turned out to be more involved than the Corps anticipated. Plans for locks on the

---

24. AR, 1882, Pt. 2, pp. 1382 (Corps of Engineers library, New Orleans); AR, 1883, Pt. 2, p. 1125; AR, 1884, Pt. 2, pp. 1279–80; AR, 1885, Pt. 2, pp. 1401–1402; AR, 1887, Pt. 2, pp. 1396–98.

Mississippi were complete in 1885, and by 1892 a portion of the money for the work had been appropriated. By 1894 the not-yet-completed project seemed feasible, for Teche planters had reduced shipping charges by transporting sugar through the recently dredged Bayou Plaquemine to the Texas and Pacific Railroad at Indian Village, just a few miles west of the proposed Plaquemine locks. Once the Plaquemine locks were completed, steamboats from Louisiana's largest sugar-growing parishes would have direct access to the Mississippi River and markets in New Orleans.

Work on the Plaquemine locks began in 1893, but soon a myriad of problems arose. A storm in 1896 washed excavated material back into a pit; then the levees on the Mississippi shifted. High water in 1897 demonstrated a need to redesign the locks. Then inspectors noted various cracks and leaks in the structure. Walls settled, and engineers designed new approach levees near the river. Shortly after construction resumed in earnest in 1905, a yellow fever epidemic halted work from August 7 until December 5. Finally, on July 1, 1909, the Corps opened the locks at Plaquemine to a considerable volume of traffic in logs, oil, and sugar. The route to Morgan City, via the locks, was 64 miles. Robert Barrow, Jr., must have noted the volume of traffic: Goods valued at $4.56 million were shipped through the locks that first year.[25]

Bayou Lafourche, which had been the subject of studies both before the Civil War and after Reconstruction, had the most complicated problems of all the streams in the area. In 1873 the Corps of Engineers conducted a comprehensive survey of the Lafourche, noting that it was usable the year around by flatboats and luggers but only during high water by the big river steamers. The *Henry Tete* and the *Lizzie Hopkins*, with capacities of 1,000 and 700 hogsheads, respectively, were the only steamers plying the upper bayou as far south as Thibodaux on a regular basis. Serious silting was occurring between Raceland and Cut Off. Farmers and fishermen living along the stream used both the Company Canal and the Harvey Canal to

---

25. AR, 1891, Pt. 1, p. 225 (Corps of Engineers library, New Orleans); AR, 1894, Pt. 3, p. 1370; AR, 1895, Pt. 1, pp. 250–53, Pt. 3, p. 1758; AR, 1896, Pt. 3, p. 1498; AR, 1897, Pt. 1, p. 282, Pt. 2, p. 1760; AR, 1900, Pt. 3, p. 2252; AR, 1901, Pt. 3, p. 1890; AR, 1903, Pt. 1, p. 333; AR, 1906, Pt. 1, p. 1305; AR, 1910, Pt. 1, p. 737; AR, 1916, Pt. 1, p. 873.

ship oysters, oranges, potatoes, wild ducks, chickens, eggs, sugar, and rice to markets in New Orleans.

Local political bodies had considered damming the Lafourche at Donaldsonville, but there was no unanimity of opinion about the long-range effects of a dam. Residents of the lower Lafourche generally favored closing the bayou as a way to end silting in the central section. Upper Lafourche farmers favored keeping the bayou open and periodically dredging obstructions that developed. One proposal even called for constructing two dams, one at Donaldsonville and one at Thibodaux. The U.S. Corps of Engineers did not agree with the majority of state engineers, who recommended closing the Lafourche. The Corps feared that closing it would put additional strain on the levees of the Mississippi and increase the danger of flooding. Locks would have satisfied both views but would have added tremendously to the cost. In the meantime the Corps dredged and removed snags regularly with funds provided by rivers and harbors legislation.

In time engineers considered extensive dredging on the upper Lafourche wasteful and unnecessary. They realized that the Company Canal and the Harvey Canal made it unnecessary to keep the Lafourche open from end to end. In view of the volume of trade on the competitive toll canals, the 1880 Corps report concluded, "It would be money thrown away to attempt to dredge it out."

In 1886 Lieutenant O. T. Crosby and Major W. H. Heuer conducted a sophisticated study of Bayou Lafourche that considered, in addition to sound engineering principles, economic impact and political realities. Damming Bayou Lafourche was feasible and economically sound, they felt. The value of commerce was approximately $3 million per year; locks would cost $450,000 to build and about $8,000 per year to maintain. Locks without periodic dredging would be of little value, and dredging without locks was almost a waste of time, they reported. Actually Crosby and Heuer had considered seven different plans to improve navigation on Bayou Lafourche before concluding that installing locks at Donaldsonville was the most practical solution to the problem.

Their sixth option called for the Corps of Engineers to purchase and complete the Company Canal. For the B & L No. 2 to function effectively, its locks on Bayou Lafourche and on the Mississippi River would both have to be in good condition. Crosby and Heuer found the brick locks on the river in good condition, but the locks in Lockport were in ruins. They stated, "As a convenience, replacement of the small lock at Lockport might be a paying investment, while to purchase and enlarge would be entirely too expensive."

The Corps seemed to change its mind again about closing the Lafourche a few years later, because it found the Company Canal "unnavigable." The Corps's annual report for 1894 sharply criticized the B & L No. 2. The Company Canal was "so unsatisfactory and uncertain that no vessels can run with profit; therefore the people of Terrebonne have to depend entirely upon a railroad for means of transportation to market." Planters bypassed the B & L No. 2 and shipped coal for use in their sugar mills down the Mississippi River and through Bayou Lafourche to Thibodaux, where it was transshipped by rail to Houma. Whether the tropical storm that struck the Louisiana coast near Grand Isle in 1893 had caused problems for the Company Canal or whether general neglect had left it in bad shape is not indicated by the report. The Corps's report was correct; the western portion of the Company Canal served Terrebonne Parish poorly, but shippers used the eastern section of the canal and its locks on the Mississippi River extensively, as financial records of the B & L No. 2 indicated. Robert Jr. earned a profit; shippers would not have continued to use an unprofitable means of transportation.

By 1895 conditions on Bayou Lafourche had not improved. The Corps spent $25,000 annually to keep a channel open while awaiting a decision on the locks. Sentiment in favor of building the locks was strongest during low water, as in 1893, when steamboats could travel on Bayou Lafourche only 123 days out of the entire year and freight rates rose. Fifty-five flatboats carried freight from the Southern Pacific station at Lafourche Crossing to the Texas and Pacific station at Donaldsonville during low water.

Bayou Lafourche experienced extensive flooding in March 1903, when the Waverly crevasse just north of Thibodaux sent floodwaters cascading across rich agricultural lands. Local political leaders took advantage of the Rivers and Harbors Act of June 13, 1902, which permitted the Atchafalaya Basin and Lafourche Basin Levee District to build a temporary dam on Bayou Lafourche, provided the district eventually constructed locks. Until the locks were completed, the district was to maintain an open channel behind the dam. The district began work on the earthen dam on December 17, 1902, at its own expense and according to plans finally approved by the secretary of war on November 20, 1903. Congress extended until December 1907 the deadline for removing the temporary dam.

Annual reports indicate that tonnage on Bayou Lafourche dropped considerably after the dam was built, but the Corps did not know if freight rates had been adversely affected. Only two small gasoline boats made regular runs through the Company Canal between New Orleans and Bayou Lafourche. In 1908 the Corps concluded: "It is believed that navigation or commerce would not be benefitted by opening and improving the bayou proper." In 1909 the levee district met without discussing the locks. Approximately one-third of the levees on the upper Lafourche had been flattened. The deadline for removing the temporary dam, which was completed in December 1903, was extended again to 1910. The levee district never constructed locks on Bayou Lafourche despite abortive attempts to do so in 1915 and 1917.[26]

At the beginning of the twentieth century, Robert Jr. was struggling to improve the Company Canal between Lockport and Westwego. President V. Moran of the levee district authorized him to dig a cut connecting Bayou Segnette and Bayou Bardeaux to shorten his route. Barrow was to retain rights for ninety-nine years. He contracted with Charles Coulon and Thomas A. Badeaux to dredge the Company Canal from Gheens plantation to Bayou Lafourche at Lockport for $1,000. This portion of the canal between Lake Salvador and Bayou Lafourche had been neglected for years. Barrow agreed to provide coal to run the steam dragline and to pay $500 to Coulon and Badeaux when the dredging reached Gayoso plantation, halfway between Gheens and Lockport. The balance was due when the contractors completed the job.

26. AR, 1874, Pt. 1, pp. 766–69 (Corps of Engineers library, New Orleans); AR, 1875, Pt. 1, p. 544; AR, 1880, Pt. 2, p. 1161; AR, 1886, Pt. 2, pp. 1267–72; AR, 1894, Pt. 3, pp. 1359–60; AR, 1895, Pt. 1, p. 249, Pt. 3, p. 1751; AR, 1897, Pt. 1, p. 281, Pt. 3, p. 1752; AR, 1903, Pt. 1, p. 641; AR, 1904, Pt. 1, p. 709; AR, 1906, Pt. 1, p. 388; AR, 1908, Pt. 1, p. 428; AR, 1909, Pt. 2, pp. 1482–83; AR, 1918, Pt. 1, p. 938.

The damming of Bayou Lafourche at its source near Donaldsonville in 1903 permitted Barrow to proceed westward in his canal renovation work without having to construct expensive locks. The Lafourche country traditionally had been susceptible to flooding when the water level of the Mississippi River rose. Levees along the bayou were not as high as on bigger streams; consequently, crevasses were common. After Bayou Lafourche was dammed at Donaldsonville, the annual flood dangers disappeared, at least from breaks in the levees on Bayou Lafourche itself. Floodwater from backlands could make its way to the plantations, but water from the Mississippi River no longer flowed directly into the Lafourche.

Taylor Beattie, a faithful observer of the weather, had recorded water levels in the bayou during low stages when steamboats could not navigate and during high water when crevasses flooded the land. In 1884 the Davis crevasse, on the Mississippi River above New Orleans, brought high water to plantations on the east bank of Bayou Lafourche and closed the Southern Pacific route from Raceland to the river opposite New Orleans. After 1903 Beattie noted no crevasses on Bayou Lafourche; however, flooding from backwaters fed by other streams caused damage.

Robert Jr. now saw a simple, inexpensive way to circumvent the problem of broken locks on Bayou Lafourche, which had troubled the B & L No. 2 since before the Civil War. During Reconstruction the B & L No. 2 had solved the problem temporarily by constructing an earthen dam across the canal where it met Bayou Lafourche at Lockport. Earthen dams stopped the flow of water but could not open and close, as locks did. Noting that waterways intersecting Bayou Lafourche no longer required locks since Bayou Lafourche had been dammed at its source on the Mississippi, Robert Jr. hoped to remove the earthen structure, which was a barrier to navigation.[27]

Potential customers pressed Robert Jr. for details regarding use of the B & L No. 2 as he cleared the Company Canal of barriers. Lumber operators eager to ship cypress logs to New Orleans, provided their

---

27. Lafourche Parish Conveyance Book, Thibodaux, La. (hereinafter cited as LCB), 33, fol. 27. The Taylor Beattie Diaries, 1883–1917 (Southern Historical Collection, University of North Carolina at Chapel Hill), microfilm copies of which were used here, contain countless entries on water conditions on Bayou Lafourche.

rafts would not have to be broken up to get over dams or through locks, asked Barrow about removing the earthen dam on Bayou Lafourche at Lockport.

The damming of Bayou Lafourche, Robert Jr. realized, would be a boon to the B & L No. 2 for a number of reasons. Mississippi River traffic could no longer enter Bayou Lafourche, thereby eliminating competitors to the Company Canal. To Robert Jr., the main advantage was not having to build and maintain locks in Lockport, but he was being challenged on that point. The Lafourche Parish Police Jury and the Atchafalaya Basin and Lafourche Basin Levee District, which had jurisdiction over flood control in the region, refused to allow Barrow to remove the earthen structure and reopen his canal unless he met certain conditions, even after Bayou Lafourche had been dammed.

Robert Jr. refused to comply. In a provocative writing style that was characteristic of his father, he asserted his rights in a ten-page diatribe to the levee district. He started off by explaining that there was no need for a dam where his canal intersected Bayou Lafourche, since waters from the Mississippi River no longer surged through the stream. He mentioned other cuts through the levees of Bayou Lafourche that were unprotected by dams—at Harang's canal below Lockport, at the Theriot Canal connecting Bayou Lafourche to Lake Boeuf, and at the Cancienne Canal leading to Lake Verret. Not content with charges of discrimination against him, Robert Jr. went further; he challenged the very authority of the public bodies to interfere in any way with his canal. He feared that they might usurp authority not specifically delegated and make undue demands on him. Their assertion of a right to close his canal at will was particularly distasteful to Robert Jr. He cited rights of charter and contract to challenge the authority of any public body to regulate his canal. He demonstrated knowledge of constitutional principles established by the Interstate Commerce Act, citing cases that limited state and local control of interstate commerce in favor of federal control. He cited Supreme Court cases that upheld his point of view.

Barrow wrote the Lafourche Parish Police Jury in 1904, "The right of the Canal to cross Bayou Lafourche at Lockport is not a new right just acquired, but is a right which has long been possessed and exercised." He went on relentlessly: "The right of the Canal to connect with Bayou Lafourche is a right of property and not a right of servitude, it is a right which has never been surrendered but the exercise of which has been interrupted." Also typical was Robert Jr.'s attempt to sound righteous. "With the closing of Bayou Lafourche at Donaldsonville has come the opportunity to secure to our people the advantages of the common carrier competition," he wrote, "and to fail now to embrace the opportunity presented becomes almost criminal in its neglect."[28]

Robert Jr. eventually won his battle with the police jury and the levee district; the Company Canal crossed Bayou Lafourche at Lockport without benefit of dams or locks. Since none of the other canals cutting across the bayou had locks, denying Barrow equal access would have been difficult to justify. Among the significant canals bisecting Bayou Lafourche was the Southwestern Louisiana Canal, which was owned by the rival Harvey Canal interests and crossed the bayou near Leeville.

Robert Jr.'s libertarian stance on eminent domain was based on expediency rather than on an articulated philosophy. When he served on public bodies, he sometimes acted differently from what one might expect. As chairman of the Terrebonne Parish Drainage Commission, he ruled in 1897 that Oscar Daspit, the proprietor of Honduras plantation, was not entitled to compensation for trees cut down by the drainage commission along Bayou Sale. Daspit asked for fair play, but Robert Jr. classified the trees a nuisance and of no monetary worth. Although Robert Jr. had challenged the right of public bodies to regulate the Company Canal, as chairman of the drainage commission he wielded power arbitrarily and capriciously against Daspit.

When he was not protecting his private interests or his reputation from local opponents, Robert Jr. somehow found time to serve the state. In 1898 he was a delegate to the state constitutional convention. He did not play a significant role in drafting the new document,

28. Robert Barrow, Jr., to Atchafalaya Basin and Lafourche Basin Levee District, August 29, 1904, in box "1904," RRBP; "Past History & Present Status of the Barataria & Lafourche Canal," 1903 (Box 1, RRBP); Robert Barrow, Jr., to Police Jury, n.d., in box 6, RRBP.

which disfranchised the vast majority of black voters and a smaller percentage of poor white voters, but as a member of the transportation committee he protected the B & L No. 2 from constitutional restrictions.[29]

After opening the long-neglected section of the Company Canal from Lake Salvador westward to Bayou Lafourche in 1903, Robert Jr. was eager to reopen his canal between Lockport and Houma. He realized the need to dredge much of the canal because of silting after years of abandonment. For dredging west of Bayou Lafourche from Lockport to Lake Field, Robert Jr. received help from commercial interests and from the village of Lockport. Townspeople subscribed $500 in 1904 to help defray the cost of dredging in exchange for free use of the Company Canal for five years. J. M. Dressner, president of the Louisiana Rice, Prairie and Canal Co. Ltd., also subsidized the venture, which called for digging the canal 6 feet deep and 35 feet wide. Dressner, who owned a store near Lockport, was a member of the Lafourche Parish Police Jury and a stockholder in the Bank of Lockport. His agricultural holdings on the Raceland prairie depended on the Company Canal route for transporting produce to market.[30]

In Terrebonne, too, Robert Jr. sought ways to achieve his long-sought goal without having to spend a great deal of money. In 1902 he and J. Wilfred Gaidry of Houma formed the Inland Transportation Line, a company to ship produce to market on the Company Canal. Robert Jr. provided a small push boat, the *Jennie B*, and a barge; Gaidry operated the freight line. Before long Robert Jr. was writing long letters to Gaidry complaining about certain aspects of their business arrangement.

Many of Robert Jr.'s financial deals soured and wound up in lengthy court battles. In 1905 he arranged for the Lower Terrebonne

---

29. Oscar Daspit to Robert Barrow, Jr., March 6, 1897, Harry Cage to Robert Barrow, Jr., March 9, 1897, both in box 23, folder 9, BFP; Official Role of the Constitutional Convention of the State of Louisiana, 1898 (Box 23, folder 9, BFP); *Official Journal of the Proceedings of the Constitutional Convention of the State of Louisiana, and Calendar* (New Orleans, 1898), *passim*.

30. LCB 33, fol. 27; "Agreement between Barrow and J. M. Dressner of Louisiana, Rice, Prairie and Canal Co. Ltd." (Box "1904," RRBP); *Southern Manufacturer; A Sketch of the Louisiana Inter-Coastal Canal Route from Morgan City to New Orleans via Houma and Lockport* (Spec. ed.; New Orleans, 1910), 37.

Refining and Manufacturing Company to dredge a feeder canal connecting to the Company Canal, estimated to cost $3,500, in exchange for special toll concessions to Lower Terrebonne and its subsidiary, Ashland plantation. According to the arrangement worked out with H. G. Bush, secretary-treasurer of the company, Robert Jr. would reimburse the dredging costs if Lower Terrebonne did not pay the Company Canal $3,500 in tolls within three years. When Lower Terrebonne's final dredging costs reached $3,949, Robert Jr. reimbursed the company $449, the amount in excess of $3,500. Later the sugarcane company became disenchanted with the arrangement because of disputes over locking fees at the Company Canal locks at Westwego and a shortage of sugar barges in which to ship its product. Robert Jr. permitted Lower Terrebonne to use the facilities of the Bradford Towing Company at his expense in order to retain the company's business. Nonetheless, the company sued Barrow but lost in a case that went to the Louisiana Supreme Court.[31]

A number of land reclamation projects between Lockport and Houma benefited from the revitalized Company Canal. Although none were as successful as Dressner's Raceland prairie, some operated for a number of years, mostly with out-of-state settlers. Land reclamation in Louisiana's bayou country was relatively simple, but it required periodic upkeep. To reclaim a swampy area, one had to dig a canal around the entire area, using the scooped soil to form a levee on the inside bank of the circular canal. Then water inside the retainer wall was pumped over the levee, creating an agricultural island in the midst of the marsh. Tropical storms, heavy rains, and breaks in the levees sometimes caused flooding of the reclaimed area, which in many cases was below sea level.

Several land reclamation projects bordered on the B & L No. 2 and were at least indirectly tied to the canal. Smithport, a 647-acre reclamation project near Lockport, was begun in 1907 by A. V. Smith, a native of Michigan. It was successful for a number of years. Tropical storms flooded the area in 1909 and 1913, but the project was completed in 1913. Smith noted that soil acidity reduced yields after

31. Agreement between Robert Barrow, Jr., and J. Wilfred Gaidry, May 3, 1902, and *passim*, in box 4, RRBP; *Lower Terrebonne Refining & Manufacturing Co. v. Barrow* (1910), 52 So 487.

several years of production. Edward Wisner, also from Michigan, headed the Louisiana Meadows Company, which had a number of subsidiaries engaged in land reclamation. One of the branches, the Terrebonne Land Company, had drained part of the Raceland prairie. Wisner brought in experienced people to perform drainage jobs. One of them was W. R. Pennington, who had worked for the U.S. government building dams and locks on the Tennessee River in Alabama. He came to Louisiana and formed the Pennington Dredging Company, of which Wisner was a vice-president. The company, whose office was in the Maison Blanche in New Orleans, had two big dredges and several barges and towboats. Pennington was a director of the Lockport Central Sugar Factory and the Louisiana Meadows Company; at one time the latter owned over 1.5 million acres in south Louisiana.[32] Although Robert Jr. had close dealings with land reclamation projects contiguous to the Company Canal and engaged in dredging and drainage work on his canal and plantations, there is no evidence that he invested in land reclamation schemes.

In 1905 Robert Jr. had redredged the Company Canal westward nearly to Bourg, located on the banks of Bayou Terrebonne 10 miles below Houma. Joseph LeCompte, a landowner in the area, authorized Robert Jr. to throw dirt dredged from the canal onto his property. In 1904 the Corps of Engineers had considered redredging Barrow's canal across Houma, connecting Bayou Black and Bayou Terrebonne, to induce a tidal flow in the bayous and reduce the buildup of vegetation. The section in Houma between Bayou Terrebonne and Bayou Black had not been dredged by 1909, but when the Corps of Engineers inquired about buying parts of the Company Canal, Robert Jr. sprang into action. Robert Jr. made hasty plans to redredge his old canal after Lieutenant Colonel Lansing H. Beach of the Corps of Engineers asked about buying the right-of-way "for a canal which existed between Bayou Black and Bayou Terrebonne at the town of Houma, La." Realizing that a fully operational canal would be more valuable to the U.S. government than a partly completed

32. Robert W. Harrison and Walter Kollmorgen, "Drainage Reclamation in the Coastal Marshland of the Mississippi River Delta," *Louisiana Historical Quarterly*, XXX (April, 1947), 675–704; Donald Davis, "Louisiana Canals and Their Influence on Wetland Development" (Ph. D. dissertation, Louisiana State University, 1973), 27; *Southern Manufacturer; Sketch of Inter-Coastal Canal Route*, 35.

one, Barrow signed a contract with E. F. Morgan to dredge the canal across town for $1 per running foot. Morgan was to dredge 6 feet deep and 40 feet wide and throw the dirt as far from the banks as possible. Robert Jr. soon became entangled in legal battles with the Terrebonne Parish Police Jury over dirt removed from his canal in Houma.[33]

As he proceeded with work on his canal, Robert Jr. attempted to win public support for his ambitious transportation project. In 1901 he joined a group of local businessmen dedicated to having Bayou Terrebonne dredged from Houma to its mouth. The group, promoting a deep-water channel to Houma, bragged that Houma would one day outrank Baltimore as the leading oyster-producing city in the United States. All the while, Barrow conferred frequently with the Corps of Engineers and the Mississippi River Commission, which planned work on improving navigation on the lower Mississippi with the approval of the chief engineer. In 1911 Robert Jr. asked Colonel W. L. Fish to repair the Mississippi River levee near the Company Canal locks at Westwego. He told Fish that he had nearly completed all repair on his canal, which would soon be open from the Mississippi to Morgan City.[34]

Robert Jr. came to realize in the first decade of the twentieth century the growing influence of the federal government in interstate transportation. This idea is consistent with a theme advanced by Robert Wiebe, whose *Search for Order* describes sweeping changes in the role of the national government, especially immediately after World War I. Like antebellum planters who had turned to the state legislature to subsidize their canal-building ventures, Robert Jr. turned to Washington, D.C., for aid rather than to the statehouse in Baton Rouge.

Thus by the end of the first decade of the twentieth century, the

33. Edward Slattery to Robert Barrow, Jr., September 18, 1903, in box "1903," RRBP; Joseph LeCompte to Robert Barrow, Jr., May 22, 1905, in box "1925," RRBP; Contract between Robert Barrow, Jr., and E. F. Morgan, April 27, 1911, in box "1911," RRBP; Defendant's brief, appeal from 20th Judicial District Court, Terrebonne Parish, n.d., in box 43, RRBP.

34. *Southern Manufacturer*, V (April, 1901), 19, 43 (Box 43, RRBP). Joining Barrow in the movement to improve waterways were Ernest Ellender, Jack Bisland, J. C. Dupont, and L. F. Suthon. Robert Barrow, Jr., to Joseph Ransdell, November 6, 1911, in box "1911," RRBP.

Barataria and Lafourche Canal Company No. 2 was in operation along its entire length. Undoubtedly Robert Barrow, Jr., was the first to accomplish the task of opening the entire route from New Orleans to the Attakapas country. He had turned the B & L No. 2 into a profitable venture, but in the new century he faced serious competition, both external and internal. The greatest danger to his operation came from changing public concepts of public rights vis-à-vis toll canals. The expanding automobile traffic placed heavy burdens on building and maintaining adequate bridges over canals. The problems of Robert Barrow, Jr., did not end with the completion of the Company Canal; they were just beginning. To pressing financial problems he could now add his own marital, physical, and mental woes.

5

Uncle Sam Buys the Company Canal

Early in the twentieth century, Robert Barrow, Jr., accomplished what had eluded his father; he opened the Company Canal, in its entirety, he liked to say, from New Orleans to the Attakapas country. Long after the heyday of toll canals, Robert Jr. turned the B & L No. 2 into a profitable venture. In fact, the canal was more important to his financial success than his agricultural holdings were.

Despite the success of the Company Canal, Robert Jr. had tried from time to time to sell the company. His agents, Houma attorneys Harris Gagné and Hugh Suthon (brother of Lucius Fane Suthon), had at various times since 1902 negotiated purchase agreements with buyers. Usually the asking price was $350,000, a figure that seemed excessive, considering the earning record of the B & L No. 2. Although Robert Jr. reminisced nostalgically about times in his youth when he transported sugar on the canal, and although he yearned to fulfill his late father's dream of linking New Orleans to the agricultural markets of the Attakapas country, he did not rule out selling the canal for the right price. Indeed, he became enthusiastic about selling the canal, especially when the figures tossed about were in the vicinity of a quarter of a million dollars.

Robert Jr.'s standing in the business community rose as his financial situation improved. Like his father, he was considered a wealthy man. The Barrows kept their home at Myrtle Grove plantation after they moved to New Orleans in 1890. As their economic status improved, they moved into larger homes in better neighborhoods, settling in 1909 at 4938 St. Charles Avenue, on the corner of Robert Street. The five-bedroom structure on prestigious St. Charles Avenue had the usual assortment of dining, music, and recreation rooms, along with two additional bedrooms on the third floor for domestic servants.

In the first two decades of the twentieth century, Robert Jr.'s agricultural and canal ventures prospered. Financial records of the B & L No. 2 for portions of 1902 and 1903 reveal that the Company Canal collected $13,500 in tolls and spent only $4,490 in operating expenses, for a clear $9,010 profit. In 1907 the figures were even more impressive: $25,192 in receipts, and operating expenses of $11,040, which produced a net profit of $14,152. For administrative purposes, Robert Jr. divided the Company Canal into three regional departments. At the Westwego headquarters, Harry Ogborn served as collecting agent from the Mississippi River to Lake Salvador. In the Lockport region, Clifton J. Masse, the agent, received $50 per month for collecting tolls and maintaining locks and bridges. Masse also served as general manager of the N. Lerille Fish and Oyster Company shucking and shipping plant. A. J. Falgout managed the canal near Bourg, on Bayou Terrebonne.[1]

Robert Jr.'s income tax returns reveal how his canal and agricultural operations fared. In 1913, the first year that returns were required by the recently ratified Sixteenth Amendment, his total income was $83,717: Myrtle Grove brought in $47,000; the canal, $22,000; rents, about $10,000; and interest income, about $2,000. However, Robert Jr.'s tax deductions totaled $65,372: $15,000 for the canal and $49,000 for his half-interest in Myrtle Grove. These figures show that he lost $2,000 on the plantation and earned $7,000 from the canal. His returns for 1914 varied only slightly from 1913. In 1916 he paid $768 in federal taxes on a taxable income of $35,000. His gross

---

1. B & L Ledger Sheets (Boxes "1903," "1907," Robert Ruffin Barrow, Jr., Papers, Division of Archives, Nicholls State University Library, hereinafter cited as RRBP); *Southern Manufacturer; A Sketch of the Louisiana Inter-Coastal Canal Route from Morgan City to New Orleans via Houma and Lockport* (Spec. ed.; New Orleans, 1910), 35.

income that year was $55,000, and his general deductions came to $20,000.

In 1917 Robert Jr. claimed a big loss on the Company Canal, because erosion on the banks of the Mississippi River threatened to undermine his locks. Fearing flood damage, the state engineer condemned the locks, which Barrow valued at $25,000. To this amount Robert Jr. added $11,000 in operating expenses. Then he subtracted the canal's gross receipts, $14,000, thereby calculating his total loss to be $22,000.[2]

Why would Robert Jr., who had worked so hard to acquire the B & L No. 2, consider selling the financially successful canal? A number of signs hinted that his financial empire was not entirely sound and that prospects for the future were not bright. As Robert Jr. viewed the possibility of selling the B & L No. 2 to the U.S. Corps of Engineers, he noted two obstacles that threatened to weaken his bargaining position: railroad links to Houma and competition from the Harvey Canal.

Robert Jr. made critical statements in 1902 about a proposed Texas and Pacific Railroad spur to Houma. As usual, anyone opposing his view was considered an enemy and a target for his broadsides. A railroad commission composed of local citizens interested in the line to Houma studied rail rates, steamboat rates, and toll figures from canals serving the area. The group concluded that rail rates would be considerably cheaper than water transportation costs, possibly saving the area $70,000 in shipping charges per year. Robert Jr. claimed that the members of the commission were appointed by the New Orleans, Opelousas, and Great Western Railroad. He labeled them puppets and published a fifteen-page pamphlet expressing his opposition to a railroad tax they supported.

The railway committee struck back. It accused Robert Jr. of deliberately misinforming the public about links to the interstate rail network. To refute him, a number of Houma citizens wrote an open letter that claimed that the canal tycoon, who was motivated by greed, did not want competition for his canal. They published a car-

2. Copies of Robert R. Barrow, Jr., income tax returns, in boxes "1913," "1914," "1916," "1917," RRBP.

toon showing Barrow blocking the railroad as he encouraged wider use of his own toll canal.[3] When the voters of Terrebonne Parish rejected the railroad tax in November 1902, Robert Jr. playfully enclosed the cartoon in a letter to his daughter Irene. He rejoiced that the election had gone his way and then talked about the new cook he had hired and the two new rooms he had added to the house.[4]

The railroad cut across the bayou country parallel to the Company Canal. Robert Jr. realized that this rail route bypassed many thriving population areas and that building additional roadbeds across marsh and swamps was even harder than digging canals across "trembling prairies." The Company Canal offered a viable alternative to transportation by rail. It served as a supplemental carrier for the local trade in sugarcane, fur, lumber, and seafood. From the train ferry near Avondale, on the west bank of the Mississippi River opposite New Orleans, tracks stretched westward across the marshland to Bayou Lafourche at Raceland. The main route proceeded up the left descending bank of Bayou Lafourche for approximately 10 miles to the rail bridge at Lafourche Crossing, approximately 5 miles below Thibodaux. The route continued to Schriever and then westward to Morgan City on the Atchafalaya River. Houma, 20 miles south of Thibodaux, was not on the original rail line, but eventually a spur line connected it to Schriever.

Eventually the New Orleans, Opelousas, and Great Western became a part of the Southern Pacific Railroad. The Southern Pacific and the Texas and Pacific railroads were a threat to the Company Canal mainly because of their shipping arrangements with Barrow's competitors. The Southern Pacific ran through Raceland, Lafourche Crossing, Schriever, and Morgan City. Spur lines branched off from the main line: One ran from Raceland southward to Lockport; another ran through Thibodaux northward on the west bank of Bayou

3. Lansing Beach to Robert Barrow, Jr., July 20, 1909, in box "1909," RRBP; Open Letter to R. R. Barrow, Jr., n.d. [1902], in box "1902," RRBP.
4. "Address of the Rail Road Committee to the People of Terrebonne," n.d. (Box 26, folder 2, Robert R. Barrow Family Papers, Manuscripts Section, Howard-Tilton Memorial Library, Tulane University, hereinafter cited as BFP); Open Letter to R. R. Barrow, Jr., n.d. [1902], in box "1902," RRBP; Robert Barrow, Jr., to his daughter Irene, November 11, 1902, in box 7, folder 5, BFP. Serving on the committee were F. Gagné, Henry Thibodaux, and A. Lirette.

Lafourche to Napoleonville. Still another ran from Schriever to Houma, paralleling Bayou Black. The Texas and Pacific ran spur lines southward from Donaldsonville on both sides of Bayou Lafourche. The spur on the west bank went to Napoleonville; the one on the east bank reached Thibodaux.

By working with small steamboat companies plying the numerous waterways, the railroads had developed an effective way of bypassing the Company Canal. They signed through-rate contracts with water shippers who reached plantations deep in the bayou country and transported goods to railheads for reloading and shipment by rail to market. This system of giving farmers a rate comparable to that paid to a single shipper was a way of nullifying the advantages Robert Jr. realized when Bayous Lafourche and Plaquemine were dammed at the Mississippi River. Quite naturally, Robert Jr. criticized the system, which required the reloading of goods from boat to boxcar at railheads. He did not want to lose his virtual monopoly in the east-west transportation link across the sugar country. When Barrow opened the Company Canal to the Lafourche around 1904, he became an important carrier.

Robert Jr.'s railroad problems were an ongoing source of irritation to him. In 1912 he threatened to sue A. J. Bonvillain, who managed the Marmande sugar estate, for violation of an agreement to ship via the Company Canal. Bonvillain had reneged on the agreement and shipped his cane by the Southern Pacific Railroad to mills in Houma. Robert Jr. sometimes made special concessions or granted rights-of-way to customers who agreed to use B & L No. 2 facilities. He gave Andrew Price, owner of Acadia plantation, near Thibodaux, the right-of-way to construct a narrow-gage railroad across the old Beattie plantation near Schriever.[5]

In addition to competition from major outside forces, Robert Jr. faced a number of nagging smaller problems. These included maintaining bridges, repairing flood damage, removing water hyacinths that clogged the canal, battling local governing authorities, and settling disputes over toll charges. One shipper complained that the B & L No. 2's fees were excessive, that the water level in the Company

5. Robert Barrow, Jr., to A. J. Bonvillain, November 11, 1912, in box "1912," RRBP; Robert Barrow, Jr., to Andrew Price, May 28, 1901, in box 7, folder 4, BFP.

Canal was low, and that boats passing his log rafts in the canal broke them up.[6]

One of the most frustrating problems for Robert Jr. and other users of Louisiana waterways was the water hyacinth, or water lily, as it is called locally. Because it had pretty lavender blossoms, the plant was brought from South America via Asia to the World's Industrial and Cotton Centennial Exposition held in New Orleans in 1884. Unfortunately, the aquatic plant flourished in Louisiana. Its bulbous stems and large leaves floated on the surface of the water and congested bayous and streams from bank to bank. Transportation by steamboat—and even by the trusty pirogue—became virtually impossible when hyacinths were packed tightly together. Robert Jr. blamed his competitors for allowing hyacinths to enter his canal; others accused Barrow of spreading the pesky plant by allowing it to move from one bayou to the next along his canal route. In reality, neither Robert Jr. nor anyone else was to blame. The hyacinths flourished naturally in Louisiana and spread rapidly. Not until the mid-twentieth century did the Corps of Engineers bring the plant under control using pesticides that contained dioxin. Even in modern times hyacinths occasionally pose a hazard to navigation, especially since many effective poisons used to control the plant have been classified as environmentally unsafe for use and their use discontinued.

Like so many other navigational concerns, the hyacinth problem devolved into a Corps of Engineers project. Early reports from the chief engineer had mentioned the growing menace, and in time the Corps developed a plan for control and received a budget to accomplish its task. The Rivers and Harbors Act of 1899 appropriated $25,000 to build a boat that would remove hyacinths from streams in Louisiana, Texas, and Florida. Booms, or gates at the surface of the water, proved totally useless despite optimistic experiments with devices that purportedly allowed hyacinths to float downstream but not return. The expectation was that once the plant reached saltwater, it would die. However, booms often broke or were left open because they were an impediment to navigation. In inland areas the hyacinths were thrown on dry land, where they wilted and died. The

---

6. A. J. Higgins to Robert Barrow, Jr., March 5, 1924, in box "1924," RRBP.

prolific plant flourished despite these early efforts. By 1904 Congress had increased the Corps's budget for hyacinth control to $30,000 and called for chemical spraying in certain areas.

Soon the Corps of Engineers had its own vessels battling the pesky problem. The *Hyacinth* and the *Ramos* operated across south Louisiana in 1905. Hyacinths blocked many of the streams feeding into the Company Canal. At one time or another, Corps boats worked to clear Bayous Lafourche, Teche, Barataria, Segnette, Plaquemine, Boeuf, des Allemands, and many others. Over the years Congress gradually appropriated additional funds to control the hyacinth.[7]

In order to keep water hyacinths from floating into the Company Canal, Robert Jr. placed booms across feeder streams. However, this created navigational problems for those using the natural waterways, which by law Barrow was not permitted to block. The engineering firm of Grant Smith and Company threatened to sue Barrow in 1920 for blocking Bayou Folse near Lockport, where it intersected the Company Canal. The company claimed it could not reach its headquarters and fuel-storing facilities because of Robert Jr.'s barricades. Barrow claimed that the stream he blockaded was a man-made canal, not Bayou Folse. Besides, Robert Jr. complained, he was justified in blocking the streams because the Corps of Engineers was threatening to prosecute him for allowing the hyacinths to spread. Tim Glynn, Barrow's bridgetender in Lockport, tried to keep the booms down, but hyacinths were everywhere, he complained. The hyacinth problem remained unsolved long after Robert Jr.'s death.[8]

In 1903 Robert Jr. responded to feelers from a prospective buyer of the Company Canal with a counteroffer of his own, a package deal: $300,000 for the canal, which Robert Jr. would manage for five years at an annual salary of $10,000 per year. Unfortunately for Barrow, this deal never materialized. Houma attorney Harris Gagné acted as Barrow's agent in many negotiations involving the Company Canal. In 1909 Gagné was working on a purchase agreement with E. J.

7. Chief Engineer, U.S. Corps of Engineers, Annual Report, hereinafter cited as AR, 1899, Pt. 2, p. 1855 (Corps of Engineers library, New Orleans); AR, 1904, Pt. 1, p. 361; AR, 1905, Pt. 2, p. 1477; AR, 1906, Pt. 1, p. 1327; AR, 1908, Pt. 2, p. 1504; AR, 1909, Pt. 2, p. 1484; AR, 1910, Pt. 2, p. 1625.
8. C. S. Hammont to Robert Barrow, Jr., June 22, 1920, Robert Barrow, Jr., to Grant Smith, June 23, 1920, both in box 9, folder 1, BFP; *passim*, RRBP and BFP.

Larkin for $350,000. Robert Jr. promised Gagné and Hugh Suthon a commission of $30,000 if they could get $350,000 for the canal. However, in 1910, when Gagné dickered with Robert H. Dowman, the price considered had dropped to $250,000.[9]

When the U.S. government became interested in an intracoastal canal from Florida to the Rio Grande in Texas, negotiations involving toll canals, including the Company Canal, changed dramatically. Like wars and political struggles, economic deals sometimes produce new alliances and adjustments to positions once held and defended tenaciously. Prospects of having the U.S. government develop an intracoastal canal produced a number of attitude changes.

Even as early as 1875, before Reconstruction had ended in Louisiana, engineers from the U.S. Corps of Engineers had envisioned an intracoastal canal stretching from the Mississippi River into Texas. In 1880 Major Charles Howell of the Corps took the intracoastal concept past the dream stage when he laid out a feasible canal route: from Donaldsonville, through the Attakapas Canal to Lake Verret, through Flat Lake to Morgan City. Typically, ambitious projects took time to move from the planning stage to the building stage. The Rivers and Harbors Act of 1909 encouraged canal building and called for a balanced transportation system that de-emphasized railroads. It provided for building a coastal canal network from Boston to the Rio Grande. These early reports from the Corps attracted wide interest both from those eager to have the U.S. government construct and maintain a free canal system and from those who owned toll canals.[10]

Naturally, Robert Jr. wanted the government to buy his canal rather than the Harvey Canal. He did everything he could to convince government authorities that his canal was the shorter, more sensible route for the new intracoastal waterway. He did not rule out the possibility that the Corps of Engineers would build an entirely new canal that followed neither the Harvey Canal route nor the Company

---

9. Robert Barrow, Jr., to Stephen Demmon, January 3, 1902, in box "1903," RRBP; Purchase agreement between Robert Barrow, Jr., and E. J. Larkin, October 15, 1909, in box "1909," RRBP; Box "1910," *passim*, RRBP.

10. AR, 1875, Pt. 1, p. 879 (Corps of Engineers library, New Orleans); Albert Cowdrey, *Land's End: A History of the New Orleans District, U.S. Corps of Engineers* (N.p., 1977), 62–64.

Canal route. However, he tried to discourage serious consideration of such a proposal.

When the Corps of Engineers began studying intracoastal waterway routes, some of Robert Jr.'s old adversaries suddenly became allies. Envisioning a government-owned, toll-free canal, Alex Barker and other businessmen who had battled Barrow over tolls and other matters now found themselves agreeing with him. They wanted the intracoastal route to go through their hometowns, just as the Company Canal did. On that point, at least, they agreed with Robert Jr. Undoubtedly the idea of a canal constructed and maintained by the U.S. government appealed to the business community. Besides, a new canal would remove the unpopular Robert Jr. from exercising any influence on local transportation. It would also mean an end to the perennial feuds with the aggressive businessman.

In 1909 the Corps of Engineers and several congressional committees inspected prospective routes between Morgan City and New Orleans. Among those studying the Company Canal were Louisiana congressman Joseph E. Ransdell, whose committee considered rivers and harbors, and Colonel Lansing Beach of the Corps of Engineers. Robert Jr. and his business associates accompanied the inspection party. Representing Lafourche at the meeting were John Barker; Alex Barker; Charles Claudet, a B & L customer; C. S. Mathews; Edward Wisner, the land developer; and A. V. Smith, proprietor of Smithport, the reclaimed marshland farm contiguous to the Company Canal near Lockport. Houma mayor L. H. Jastremski and A. T. Dusanberry took the trip along the Company Canal. The party also traveled along the Harvey Canal route from Larose through the Harvey locks to the Mississippi River, noting many local items of commerce that would benefit from improved shipping: lumber, shingles, crossties, fuel oil, sugar, molasses, rice, oysters, fish, moss, furs, bricks, and other items.

According to promotional literature that Robert Jr. may have had a hand in publishing, the Company Canal route was shorter and cheaper to use than the more southerly Harvey Canal route. Robert Jr. and local business interests hoped the optimistic reports from the Corps of Engineers would prod Congress to appropriate monies to make the intracoastal canal a reality.

A number of Robert Jr.'s supporters and competitors attended a national inland waterway convention meeting in New Orleans in 1910. The Terrebonne Parish delegation to the convention included members of prominent families. From Terrebonne, in addition to Robert Jr., were Ernest Ellender, L. H. Jastremski, Edmond McCollam, B. S. Shaffer, Charles Krumbhaar, Calvin Wurzlow, A. F. Davidson, Robert Butler, and Harris Gagné. Joseph Price of the Thibodaux *Democrat* came up with the idea of, and played a major role in, organizing the Lafourche Intercoastal Club, a lobby group to encourage the Corps of Engineers to select the route from Morgan City via Houma, Lockport, and Lake Salvador. This must have pleased Robert Jr.; his canal covered this route, which the club liked to say was only 75 miles from Morgan City to New Orleans.

The Houma *Courier*, too, promoted the Company Canal route, for Houma was along the B & L No. 2 route. Naturally, Houma businessmen wanted to make sure that the canal would not bypass their town. Like other communities, Houma bragged about its economic advantages. According to promotional materials prepared in 1910, Houma had a population of 6,500, owned its own power plant, and had an excellent drainage system. Its oyster and shrimp industries were significant. And in addition, "large river steamboats ply between Houma and New Orleans, through the Barataria and Lafourche Canal." The Bank of Houma endorsed the Company Canal route and bragged of its $50,000 in capital. Robert Jr. served on the bank's board of directors.

Robert Jr. may have written some advertisements included in a special waterways booklet published in 1910. The Waubun sugar company's endorsement of the Company Canal route that appeared in the promotional piece sounded like a populist polemic denouncing the "grasping selfishness and greed" of railroad tycoons. Waubun executives suggested floating a bond issue of $1 million to proceed with the project "without waiting for government action."

In neighboring Lafourche Parish, Lockport, a village established originally on land donated to the Company Canal, boasted of its attributes. It claimed a population of twelve hundred, one bank, seven stores, two hotels, a Catholic church, two livery stables, two drugstores, and other establishments. "This is a splendid locality for an oyster canning factory," the report indicated. Bayou Lafourche was navigable for flatboats and small craft the year round and by big riverboats for six months of the year. The town was on the Southern Pacific Railroad and was tied to the Mississippi River via the Company Canal.[11]

Late in 1911 Robert Jr. wrote to Congressman Joseph Ransdell to say that he had completed the final link in his dredging of the entire Company Canal. Undoubtedly, the shrewd businessman was thinking about selling his entire canal to the U.S. government rather than just a part of it. As he bragged to Ransdell about having completed his canal work, he dickered with E. F. Morgan about redredging the canal in Houma in time to haul sugarcane in 1911. Morgan pressed for payment, claiming he had lived up to his contract; Robert Jr. refused to pay him, insisting that Morgan had not done the required work. Barrow complained about losing tolls on the canal because of Morgan's negligence.[12] Eventually Morgan compromised with the obstreperous Barrow.

An even greater threat to the B & L No. 2 was posed by the Harvey Canal, which paralleled the Company Canal approximately 13 miles to the south. A part of the old canal begun by Nicholas Noël Destrehan in 1835, the Harvey Canal had stretched westward to Bayou Lafourche since the purchase of Harang's canal, which connected Lake Salvador to Bayou Lafourche at Larose. Improved dredging equipment in the 1850s made enlarging the canal relatively simple, but the Harvey Canal did not have locks on the Mississippi River until 1881. Prior to this time, mule-drawn railcars hauled boats on movable ways the 200 yards from the canal to the river. Even without locks on the Mississippi River, the Harvey Canal functioned effectively with its "sub-marine railway." Engineer H. S. Douglas of the Corps reported in 1881 that the Harvey locks were under construction. "Heretofore boats have been hauled over from the canal into the Mississippi by a marine railway," he wrote. Joseph Hale Harvey charged a fee to haul passengers and vessels, as well as storage fees on

11. *Southern Manufacturer; Sketch of Inter-Coastal Canal Route,* 5, 11, 17, 18, 27, 32, 39, 44.
12. Robert Barrow, Jr., to Joseph Ransdell, November 6, 1911, in box "1911," RRBP; Edward Slattery to Robert Barrow, Jr., September 18, 1903, in box "1903," RRBP; Joseph LeCompte to Robert Barrow, Jr., May 22, 1905, in box "1925," RRBP; Contract between Robert Barrow, Jr., and E. F. Morgan, April 27, 1911, in box "1911," RRBP.

his wharf along the canal. A skiff was assessed a fee of 25 cents each way; a pirogue paid 35 cents; and a hunter on horseback, 15 cents.

Joseph Hale Harvey died in 1882. Two years later his widow sold out to the Harvey Canal, Land and Improvement Company, which grew rapidly in the late 1880s and 1890s, transporting cypress logs in rafts for Joseph Rathborne. A native of Ireland, Rathborne started his cypress operations in 1889; by 1891 he owned 50,000 acres of cypress swamp and hired five hundred men in his mills. Before the turn of the century, Rathborne was operating the biggest cypress lumber mill in the world from his yards near the Harvey Canal.[13] The Harvey interests chartered a subsidiary, the South Louisiana Canal and Navigation Company, in 1878 or 1879. Like the Lafourche and Terrebonne Navigation Company, associated with the old B & L, the South Louisiana Canal and Navigation Company built feeder canals (or laterals, as Robert Jr. was fond of calling them) that tied into the main canal. The South Louisiana Canal and Navigation Company dug a canal across Bayou Lafourche connecting Barataria Bay to Timbalier Bay, two significant sources of oysters, fish, and shrimp.

In a pamphlet Robert Jr. wrote for the B & L No. 2, he exaggerated negative aspects of the Harvey Canal and celebrated the advantages of his own canal. Strong Mississippi River currents in 1881 had undermined the foundation of the Harvey Canal locks and threatened to create a huge crevasse. Authorities enjoined Harvey from using the locks because they were considered dangerous, according to Barrow. In 1904 Harvey built new locks, which were also threatened by floodwaters until the gates were reinforced with steel plates and concrete. The B & L No. 2 never experienced these problems, Robert Jr. claimed, since its locks were built on hard clay. Before Barrow sold out to the Corps of Engineers in 1925, his locks, too, were undermined by floodwaters on the Mississippi River.

Owners of the Harvey Canal also published promotional literature asserting the advantages of their canal route over the Company Canal. Henry Dart, a New Orleans attorney and historian, was part owner of the canal and president of the canal company. He may have written promotional tracts for the company.

13. Betsy Swanson, *Historic Jefferson Parish: From Shore to Shore* (Gretna, La., 1975), 89–90, 122, 125.

Defenders of the Harvey route were especially sensitive about crevasses caused by leaks in their locks. They provided in-depth explanations of their construction problems. In February 1881 a leak developed under a lower wing wall, a Harvey Canal publication stated, "causing some uneasiness among the more timorous in the neighborhood, a double bulk-head of sheet piling and earth-filled sacks was built in front, and after some days of effort and experiment, the leak was finally stopped."

That did not end flooding problems at the Harvey locks. When a company working on a dam across the Harvey Canal to prevent flooding and damage to the locks heard that the Harvey Canal, Land and Improvement Company intended to enjoin them from building the dam, they took out an injunction to prevent "any interference with them in finishing it or any such work as might be necessary to prevent a crevasse at the spot." Undoubtedly, the construction company feared being held liable for flood damage to property. The Harvey company promotional literature closed with its main point: "The Harvey Canal is the terminus, and now the only possible terminus, of this great inland route." Despite Robert Jr.'s critical comments, the Harvey Canal had become a flourishing reality.[14]

Even more vexing to Robert Jr. than competition from the Harvey interests was the possibility that the U.S. government would construct a rival inland waterway system from Florida to Texas and put him out of business. He worried, too, that the United States would buy the Harvey Canal and leave him with an antiquated toll canal facing competition from a free public canal run by the government. No one who knew Robert Jr. suspected that he would simply let matters run their course. Undoubtedly, he would become emotionally and politically involved in any efforts to construct an inland canal system.

Official government studies and reports provided details about both the Company Canal and the Harvey Canal, the two principal rivals. Each company had for years used economic and political

14. *The Intercoastal Canal from Its Incipiency to Date and the Logical and Proper Location for Same Between New Orleans and Morgan City* (N.p., n.d.), in box "1833–1912," RRBP; *The Harvey Canal and Locks as the Natural and Necessary Terminus of the Inland, Slack-Water Route of South and South-West Louisiana* (New Orleans, 1881), in box 43, RRBP; AR, 1881 (Box 43, RRBP).

propaganda to promote its own interests. Both companies published pamphlets and booklets (with photographs) extolling the virtues of their route over the other. Not surprisingly, both companies exaggerated and distorted the truth. Official reports were more objective and descriptive.

A detailed report prepared in 1914 by the Corps of Engineers dispelled myths about both canals. The study, prepared for the secretary of war and sent to the Committee on Rivers and Harbors of the U.S. House of Representatives, corrected a number of errors and distortions. It pointed out, for instance, that geographic problems that hindered railroad construction in the early days had not disappeared: "The land is of such character and so cut up by bayous and lakes that railroad construction is impossible, and no other method of communication than by water is practicable." Two private canals traversed the area from the Mississippi River to Bayou Teche: the Company Canal and the Harvey Canal. Cutting a third canal across the region would cost approximately $1.7 million, while buying either of the two existing canals would cost approximately $1.1 million, the report stated.

The study indicated that both canal owners had been contacted about selling their canals to the U.S. government. Both had agreed to sell to the government at cost, but the secretary of war did not necessarily see this as a great bargain: "This proposition is not exactly advantageous to the United States, for, as these canals were originally excavated prior to 1860 and before the existence of modern dredging machinery, their costs must have been considerably higher than the same amount of excavation would be to-day by modern dredges."

There were other problems with both the Company Canal and the Harvey Canal. Both had locks that would be too narrow for boats likely to use the canal today, the report showed. The Harvey locks were 29 feet, 11 inches wide and 150 feet long; the Company Canal locks were 25 feet wide and 160 feet long. Both canals were supposed to be 6 feet deep, but often the depth was only 4 feet, and the Company Canal "proprietor is constantly engaged in work of maintenance," the report stated. If the U.S. government bought either canal, it would probably have to maintain bridges over it. The free locks on the Mississippi River at Plaquemine reopened the old route to the Attakapas country, but it was considerably longer than either the Harvey Canal or the Company Canal.

The report contained some disturbing news for Robert Jr. about his major competitor. First, the Harvey Canal, Land and Improvement Company owned a 300-foot-wide right-of-way from the Mississippi River to Bayou Lafourche. Also, the company was in the process of extending the Harvey Canal from Bayou Lafourche to Bayou Terrebonne, from Larose to Bourg. "A survey party was in the field marking the location, but was withdrawn when the act of Congress directing this report was passed," the report stated. The Harvey Canal company, an effective competitor, apparently had decided to give the B & L No. 2 competition west of Bayou Lafourche. Its new cut would have provided an alternate route to the Company Canal. Only from Houma westward would the B & L No. 2 have had an advantage over the Harvey interests. More often than not, the Company Canal west of Houma had been clogged and unusable.

The B & L No. 2 received considerable critical attention in the report. The canal was old and had a number of problems. Its Mississippi River locks connected to Bayou Segnette, which "is very crooked and several cut-offs have been made to relieve navigation." Bayou Black, the westward leg of the Company Canal, was navigable to about 10 miles west of Houma. Several years earlier, the report continued, Robert Jr. tried to redredge the canal across Houma but later abandoned the idea. U.S. engineers thought that a cut connecting Bayous Black and Terrebonne should be made south of Houma, but they noted local preferences. "The people of Houma are anxious that the waterway should pass through that place," the report stated. The Corps of Engineers wanted the more southerly route, because excavation there would be easy. Also, there were many buildings along Bayou Terrebonne in Houma; obtaining rights-of-way there would be difficult and expensive. Lower Bayou Black was navigable and provided good access to Bayou Teche and the Atchafalaya through Bayous Boeuf and Chêne.

Engineers noted advantages and disadvantages of both the Company Canal and the Harvey Canal routes. The Harvey route entered the Mississippi River nearer to the business center of New Orleans than did the Company Canal. The B & L No. 2 route was slightly shorter overall than the Harvey Canal and provided easy access to boats heading up the Mississippi River from New Orleans. The Corps conducted cost studies based on several canal depths: Nine feet was considered necessary to ship coal; 7 feet would suffice for sugar, cotton, rice, and general cargo. Again, estimates for dredging the two canals were quite close. To dredge the Company Canal to a depth of 9 feet through Houma to the Atchafalaya River would cost approximately $2.35 million. The Harvey route would cost $2.24 million to dredge to the Lafourche and then up Bayou Lafourche to Lockport and the juncture with the Company Canal. Significantly, all proposals seemed to favor using parts of both canals to complete the inland canal route. As the intracoastal canal system came closer to becoming a reality, political leaders gravitated toward using both the B & L No. 2 and the Harvey Canal.

The Corps noted that both routes provided a link between New Orleans and Morgan City of less than 100 miles—about half the distance of the Bayou Plaquemine route to the Teche country, which had reduced freight rates significantly. If neither the B & L No. 2 nor the Harvey Canal were available, the Corps suggested cutting a canal between the two existing routes that would have been shorter than either one. This proposed route would have used part of Bayou Segnette to reach Lake Salvador. Then it would have cut from the western end of the lake in a straight line across Bayou Lafourche below Lockport, reaching Bayou Terrebonne just above the fork at Presque Isle, where Bayou Petit Caillou begins. From there the route would proceed up Bayou Terrebonne to a proposed new cut to Bayou Black below Houma, rather than using Robert Jr.'s old canal across town. Then it would follow Bayou Black via Bayou Boeuf to the Atchafalaya. This route would have been 88 miles long, but it would have required extensive excavation and the construction of several railroad bridges.[15]

In 1916 Major Edward Schulz of the Corps of Engineers inquired about buying a portion of the Company Canal from Robert Jr. Specifically, he wanted a price for the B & L No. 2 locks on the Mississippi

15. *House Documents,* 63rd Cong., 2nd Sess., No. 610, January 17, 1914, pp. 15, 33–40.

River at Westwego. Robert Jr. explained that selling just a portion of the Company Canal would "make the rest of the canal useless by cutting off the head." Refusing to name a price, he summarized the history of the canal in his reply to Schulz. He hoped that the government would not build a parallel route and put him out of business. The following year virtually the same discussion ensued, and Robert Jr. finally came up with a sale price for the B & L No. 2—$300,000, which he said was fair.[16]

The title of Robert Jr.'s pamphlet promoting the Company Canal as the only feasible route makes clear its message: *The Intercoastal Canal from Its Incipiency to Date and the Logical and Proper Location for Same Between New Orleans and Morgan City.* The eighty-page publication contained clear black-and-white photographs and two maps. Barrow did not overlook an opportunity to denigrate the Harvey Canal, whose office personnel, he said, conspired against the B & L No. 2 by insisting that the new canal route have a 300-foot right-of-way, knowing that in many places the Company Canal had only 192 feet. According to Robert Jr., the Harvey Canal locks were not as wide as the B & L No. 2 locks.[17]

Robert Jr. distributed his tendentious brochure widely to politicians and others interested in the proposed new canal route. Not surprisingly, he haggled with the man he hired to photograph and publicize the Company Canal. Perhaps Robert Jr. assumed that entertaining him with rides in his motor launch *Brer Rabbit* and taking him on swimming trips to Independence Island, the little Barrow hideaway in Barataria Bay just a few miles north of Grand Isle, would make him forget to send a bill for his service. He did send a bill, and Robert Jr., typically, questioned the itemized request for payment.[18]

Robert Jr. became concerned about the location of the intracoastal canal in 1919. He denounced a proposed cut through Houma connecting Bayous Terrebonne and Black a mile below his canal. The new cut was recommended by the Corps and endorsed by some Terrebonne Parish businessmen who wanted Robert Jr. to donate his

16. Maj. Edward Schulz to Robert Barrow, Jr., June 7, 1916, January 9, 1917, Barrow to Schulz, June 20, 1916, January 31, 1917, all in boxes "1916," "1917," RRBP.
17. *The Intercoastal Canal* (Box "1833–1912," RRBP).
18. Box 18, *passim*, RRBP.

Houma canal to the U.S. government. Robert Jr. considered this idea preposterous.

Robert Jr. tried to assure Houma residents that he was not motivated by greed, for the new cut would actually work to his advantage. Why, then, was he opposing a plan that would have helped him? He disliked the plan, he said, simply because it would have delayed the intracoastal project. He was thinking of the community. The new plan would save him money by reducing the number of bridgetenders and toll collectors on the Company Canal, he said. Besides, he could easily fill in the old canal and sell lots on the right-of-way running through the center of Houma. (Eventually this came to pass: The Corps made a new cut, and Robert Jr. sold the valuable strip in town.) Other factors had to be considered, Robert Jr. contended. Eventually the people from Grand Caillou would demand a bridge across the new canal that would block their overland access to Houma. Building and maintaining a new bridge would be a further tax burden on the people, he knew.[19]

Eventually Robert Jr. retained a prestigious law firm to negotiate with the United States for sale of the Company Canal. Robert Jr. agreed to pay 10 percent of the sale price of $300,000 to the firm of Milling, Godchaux, Saal, and Milling, and he authorized the firm to incur expenses, not to exceed $3,000, in promoting the sale. The firm, which was authorized to negotiate with private interests as well, was to receive half of any part of the sale price in excess of $300,000.

Like so many Barrow business arrangements, this one ended in court. When the law firm failed to close a deal, Robert Jr. considered their agreement canceled, even though the document he signed on September 11, 1919, contained no such stipulation. In a fiery note to Robert Milling, Robert Jr. accused the firm of neglecting his interests, but he acknowledged that there had been no legal cancellation: "I called on you to release me from the agreement, this you refused to do." Robert E. Milling, who represented the firm in communications with Robert Jr., soon grew weary of dealing with the stubborn and relentless owner of the Company Canal, but he did not acquiesce. In a letter to Robert Jr., Milling said that Robert Jr. would

19. Robert Barrow, Jr., to J. L. Caillouet, September 11, 1919, in box 18, RRBP; Barrow to Caillouet, March 20, 1920, in box 20, RRBP.

have to pay fees to the law firm when he sold his canal. Meanwhile, Harris Gagné was trying to work out a compromise with Milling. When Barrow learned of this, he claimed that Gagné had acted without his knowledge. What really galled Robert Jr. was paying 10 percent commission to Milling for a sale he had not negotiated. He wrote to Milling, "You would sneak in and gobble a share even in face of the fact you had nothing to do with it." He labeled Milling's letter blackmail and charged that Milling should be barred from practicing law in Louisiana. The matter remained unsettled until Robert Jr. died in 1926. The firm then tried to collect its fee from Jennie Barrow.[20]

Interrupted by World War I, negotiations over the intracoastal canal route continued into the 1920s without firm plans of operation. The war had demonstrated a need for an inland canal along the Gulf Coast, but it also had curtailed consumer spending in favor of war materials. Robert Jr. and his associates persisted in their efforts to encourage the government to become the prime mover in the canal project at war's end. In 1922 Barrow told his congressman, Whitmell Martin from Thibodaux, that he hoped the government would buy his canal rather than the Harvey Canal. Martin had told Robert Jr. earlier that the government planned to use parts of both the Company Canal and the Harvey Canal for the intracoastal canal. Early the next year Martin informed Barrow that Congress had appropriated $56 million for canals.[21]

Meanwhile Robert Jr. was trying to sell portions of the Company Canal the government did not need. An agent representing lumber dealer A. J. Higgins offered $65,000 for the Company Canal from the Mississippi River to Lake Salvador. This portion of the canal, which would have been expendable had the government purchased the Harvey route, Robert Jr. refused to sell because he considered the price insufficient.

In the spring of 1921, negotiations between Barrow and the Corps of Engineers began in earnest. Once again the Corps offered to purchase only a portion of the Company Canal, which Robert Jr. had

20. Robert E. Milling to Robert Barrow, Jr., August 16, 1919, and *passim*, Barrow to Milling, n.d. [1923], all in box 8, folder 11, BFP.
21. Robert Barrow, Jr., to Whitmell Martin, December 6, 1922, in box "1922," RRBP; Martin to Barrow, March 3, 1923, in box "1923," RRBP.

refused to sell piecemeal in 1916. Lieutenant Colonel E. J. Dent offered him $84,000 for the section between Bayous Lafourche and Terrebonne and $47,000 for the part between Bayous Lafourche and des Allemands. With both offers came the stipulation that Robert Jr. furnish abstracts proving clear title to rights-of-way 300 feet wide. Robert Jr. wrote back saying that he did not have 300 feet in some places. He further questioned why the government was offering a smaller figure for the long section of the canal east of Bayou Lafourche than for the short section connecting Bayous Lafourche and Terrebonne. Robert Jr. may have suspected foul play, but the Corps offered to pay exactly what he had asked for in 1917.

By early summer Dent indicated to Robert Jr. that if he wanted to sell his canal to the U.S. government, he would have to acquire the additional land necessary to "complete the 300-foot width throughout the entire length." Harris Gagné told Dent that Robert Jr. was negotiating for additional land.[22]

Meanwhile Robert Jr. had been applying political pressure to Congressman Martin, who soon resented his abrasive tactics. While indicating a desire to help in whatever manner he could, Martin advised Barrow to be sensible about the whole matter or his greed would get him nothing. Under no circumstances, Martin advised Gagné, could Robert Jr. expect compensation from the government if the Corps purchased the Harvey Canal. He told Gagné that the Harvey interests had dealt more openly and honestly with Dent than Robert Jr., who had not resolved the matter of the 300-foot clearance.

Late in 1922 Robert Jr. told Martin that he opposed the idea of the Corps's buying out the Harvey interests and making the Harvey Canal a part of the intracoastal route. He wanted Martin to use his influence and have the Corps buy out the Company Canal instead. In time Martin replied. He thought Robert Jr. fortunate that the Corps, which had $56 million to purchase existing canal rights-of-way, was willing to buy even a portion of the B & L No. 2.

Martin told Gagné that General Lansing Beach of the Corps

22. Lt. Col. E. J. Dent to Robert Barrow, Jr., March 7, 1921, Robert Barrow, Jr., to T. E. Lipsey, March 17, 1921, Dent to Barrow, June 25, 1921, Harris Gagné to E. J. Dent, July 21, 1921, all in box 22, RRBP; Robert Barrow, Jr., to Whitmell Martin, December 6, 1922, in box "1922," RRBP; Martin to Barrow, March 3, 1923, in box "1923," RRBP.

favored the Harvey route from the Mississippi River to Lake Salvador because "the Harvey locks are very much better situated and in better condition than the locks on Mr. Barrow's canal." Martin indicated that the Corps had not closed the deal with the Harvey interests yet. He advised Robert Jr. to contact Colonel Dent immediately, since the Corps seemed eager to purchase the Company Canal route west of Bayou Lafourche. Martin told Gagné that time was a factor, since Congress would consider budgetary allotments in December.

Gagné thanked Martin for his frank advice, but he disagreed on a number of points. Undoubtedly expressing Robert Jr.'s sentiments, Gagné barged ahead in the style of his client. First of all, the Harvey locks were not bigger and better than the B & L No. 2 locks. In questioning the 300-foot right-of-way, Gagné resorted to a favorite Barrow theme—the conspiracy theory. He claimed that the right-of-way question was put in by the Harvey interests "for the express purpose of putting his [Barrow's] canal out of competition." Gagné closed with a Barrowlike observation, wondering why the government wanted "to pay Harvey $300,000 for a canal running *away* from Morgan City in preference to paying Barrow '*any thing*' for a canal running *towards* Morgan City."[23]

Robert Jr. blamed the people of Terrebonne Parish for his problems. Indirectly, at least, they were encouraging the Corps to choose the Harvey route over his, he told the editor of the Houma *Courier*. He saw conspiracies everywhere. Robert Jr. obtained a list of stockholders in the South Louisiana Canal and Navigation Company, the Harvey Canal subsidiary partly owned by prominent people from Terrebonne Parish: Shaffers, Minors, McCollams, Cages, and others. He blamed D. S. Cage, president of the company, and other local investors for influencing the Corps to choose the Harvey route. They chose another route, he added bitterly, "fearing that they might be of some benefit to me."

Robert Jr. also thought that engineers from the Corps had conspired against him because they had been offended by his promotional brochure. Yet he wondered what had offended them. He told Congressman Martin that the Harvey company was lucky that some-

23. Whitmell Martin to Harris Gagné, July 16, 1921, Gagné to Martin, July 18, 1921, both in box 22, RRBP.

one had convinced the Corps that a canal route had to be 300 feet wide. He told Houma newspaper editor Tris Easton that he had no confidence in the whole procedure, "judgeing from the experience I have had with the engineers and there determination to ruin me if possible." Robert Jr. became infuriated when someone in Terrebonne Parish suggested that he donate his canal through Houma to the police jury in exchange for help from the jury in obtaining additional rights-of-way along the Company Canal. He finally asked Easton rhetorically, "Does the Parish want the Intracoastal Canal or not?" If the engineers really were looking out for the interests of the people, Robert Jr. continued, they should choose the Company Canal route to Bayou Lafourche; then let the route continue upstream to the old Attakapas Canal, which provided access to the Atchafalaya River and Bayou Teche.[24]

Through the summer of 1921, Robert Jr. and Gagné continued their verbal assault, this time directing their fire against the Corps of Engineers. In July Robert Jr. told General Beach that even if the government bought the Harvey Canal, it should compensate the B & L No. 2, for he had spent "little short of a million dollars and a life time of work and energy" building up the Company Canal. Gagné, too, corresponded with the Corps, but in a more conciliatory tone. He told Colonel Dent that Robert Jr. was an old man and that the Company Canal was his life's work, undertaken at considerable expense and effort. Gagné wondered, in closing, just who had decided that 300 feet was the magic figure for the width of the inland route. Dent neither backed down nor minced words. There certainly was no precedent, he said, for reimbursing Barrow, since there was "inevitable risk associated with any commercial venture." The 300-foot right-of-way simply would allow for future growth, Dent felt.[25]

Congressman Martin, too, thought the Corps was trying to be fair to Barrow. He encouraged Robert Jr. to deal with Colonel Dent and to either accept his offer to buy the Company Canal or reject it, rather than claim to be at the mercy of the government. "I believe General

24. Robert Barrow, Jr., to Tris Easton, July 18, 1921, Robert Barrow, Jr., to Whitmell Martin, July 22, 1921, both in box 22, RRBP; Barrow to Easton, August 20, 1923, in box 26, RRBP.
25. Robert Barrow, Jr., to Gen. Lansing Beach, July 20, 1921, Harris Gagné to E. J. Dent, July 21, 1921, Dent to Gagné, July 22, 1921, all in box 22, RRBP.

Beach is most anxious to purchase at least a part of your canal, so as to save you from financial loss," Martin told Robert Jr. He considered ridiculous Robert Jr.'s political request to replace officers in the New Orleans district of the Corps of Engineers. Instead, Robert Jr. should face reality and stop stalling. Martin warned, "This matter may be cleared up within a short time and your opportunity may be lost."

Finally, in August 1921 Robert Jr. wrote the War Department citing a figure he would accept for the Company Canal. His total amount was $300,000, the same as in 1917. For the locks and canal connecting the Mississippi River to Bayou Segnette he wanted $169,000; for the section from Lake Salvador to Bayou Lafourche he wanted $47,000; and for the section between Bayous Lafourche and Terrebonne he wanted $84,000. He sent copies of his letter to Martin and Beach.

Robert Jr. tried to flex his political muscle, but often he had to sidestep conspiracies against him, real or imaginary. Early in 1923 he wrote Martin requesting that he consult Beach about some particulars regarding the sale of the Company Canal. With typical conspiratorial caution, he warned Martin not to let other members of the Louisiana House delegation know that he and Martin communicated. He told Martin that Congressmen Ransdell and Dupré "are friends of Harvey and antognistic to me."[26]

By late summer of 1923, Robert Jr. was again unhappy with canal developments, which he suspected were plots against him. He feared the government would build an entirely new canal rather than acquire parts of already functioning canals. He complained that any canal built by the government parallel to the Company Canal would undermine his life's work to make the B & L No. 2 a functioning reality. When the Corps of Engineers suggested that he would have to widen his canal before selling it to the government, he used *sneak, skunk, blackmail, cur,* and *coward* to express his feelings for those who suggested such ideas to the Corps.[27]

On March 10, 1924, the Corps of Engineers purchased the Harvey Canal for $500,000. This must have been unnerving to Robert Jr., for

26. Whitmell Martin to Robert Barrow, Jr., July 26, 1921, Robert Barrow, Jr., to War Department, August 1, 1921, both in box 22, RRBP; Barrow to Martin, February 28, 1923, in box 26, RRBP.

27. Benjamin Waldo to Robert Barrow, Jr., July 23, 1923, Barrow to Waldo, August 12, 1923, both in box "1923," RRBP.

the price was considerably more than he stood to get for the Company Canal. New Orleans newspapers carried the story on page one and included pictures of the Harvey Canal locks. The lead article, which did not mention the Company Canal, explained that the Harvey Canal would become a part of the intracoastal canal system stretching from the Mississippi River to Bayou Lafourche at Larose. Henry Dart was president of the new Harvey Canal and Land Development Company, and Horace Harvey was secretary.[28]

Robert Jr. had reason to fear that the Corps of Engineers would take action and bypass the Company Canal altogether unless he cooperated and did what was necessary to sell his canal interests. On August 30, 1924, the Corps completed a 1.8-mile cut across Houma connecting Bayous Black and Terrebonne just a half-mile south of Robert Jr.'s old canal. The new canal ran in a straight line from Bayou Terrebonne to the lower loop of the great bend that Bayou Black formed in Houma. Now that his canal in town was not needed, Robert Jr. searched for ways to turn it into needed cash.

In 1925 Robert Jr. sold the narrow tract of land on either side of the canal across Houma. No longer usable as a canal after the Corps of Engineers completed the new cut across town, the shallow ditch eventually was filled with dirt that the U.S. dredge *Delatour* scooped from Bayou Terrebonne in 1932. Allen J. Ellender, acting as trustee for convenience only for his partners Charles A. Ledet and Lee P. Lottinger, paid Barrow $5,500 for the old canal right-of-way. The purchase was a successful one for Ellender and his partners, who in turn sold sections of the land to oil companies, retail stores, and a railroad.[29]

Meanwhile, Robert Jr. tried to settle complicated boundary disputes on parts of his canal the government was interested in buying. In time he compromised boundaries with the village of Lockport, the

---

28. AR, 1925, Pt. 1, p. 854 (Corps of Engineers library, New Orleans); New Orleans *Times-Picayune*, March 11, 1924.
29. The entire transaction can be traced in the Terrebonne Parish conveyance records, starting with Terrebonne Parish Conveyance Book, Houma, La. (hereinafter cited as TCB), 83, fol. 137 (July 3, 1925), and ending with TCB 123, fol. 592 (September 11, 1939), when the three partners partitioned the property among themselves. Randolph A. Bazet, "Houma—An Historical Sketch," in *Centennial Celebration, Houma, Louisiana, May 10–13, 1934* (Morgan City, La., 1934), 30–31.

Smithport Planting Company, and the Fayport Planting Company. To old friends he complained that the government should have bought his canal, since it was shorter than the Harvey Canal. Often he talked of the long struggle to build the canal and of his father's efforts in the days before the Civil War. All the while he encouraged local interests to speed up the surveys required by the U.S. government. He told C. J. Bourg of Lockport that the government would buy more of the Harvey route and bypass Lockport altogether unless he completed the survey.

Naturally Robert Jr. wanted the surveys conducted at no expense to the Company Canal. He asked Joseph Price to use his influence with the police jury to get the Lafourche Parish engineer, J. A. Lovell, to conduct the survey. Playing on Price's sympathy, Robert Jr. referred to himself as Price's "life long friend who is now in distress." As the next chapter will show, Robert Jr. was not exaggerating; he had fallen on hard economic times by 1924. Apparently Price came to the aid of his old friend, for in June, Bourg reported that Lovell was surveying in the vicinity of Eagle Island, just southwest of Lockport.[30]

In Terrebonne Parish, too, Robert Jr. turned to the local governing body and to business interests for help in acquiring the 300-foot right-of-way that the Corps of Engineers required along the Company Canal. Without spending his limited resources, he worked out a sensible arrangement with the police jury and the Bourg State Bank. He acquired from local landowners additional rights-of-way along the Company Canal; he paid for the land with certificates of indebtedness guaranteed by the police jury and held by the Bourg State Bank. When the U.S. government paid him for the Company Canal, he was to reimburse the police jury. Madison L. Funderburk, first vice-president of the bank, assisted in the negotiations conducted with the blessing of the Ellender brothers, local planters who were the largest depositors in the bank. Technically the landowners sold the additional rights-of-way to the police jury, which guaranteed payment.

30. Lafourche Parish Conveyance Book, Thibodaux, La. (hereinafter cited as LCB), 56, fol. 113, 323; Robert Barrow, Jr., to Tris Easton, August 20, 1923, in box "1923," RRBP; Robert Barrow, Jr., to C. J. Bourg, March 12, June 3, 1924, Robert Barrow, Jr., to W. H. Price, April 3, 7, 1924, Robert Barrow, Jr., to Calvin Wurzlow, April 19, 1924, all in box "1924," RRBP.

Among those who received money from the sale of the Company Canal were Joseph Bascle ($400), Wallis Whipple ($120), Mrs. S. Hornsby ($110), S. Domangue ($200), François Roger ($300), James Champagne ($100), and Charles Whipple ($170). Undoubtedly Robert Jr. would not have been able to complete these negotiations without the help of the bank and the police jury. He owned property but had little cash, and he had not been on friendly terms with local landowners.[31]

Robert Jr.'s problems, however, were far from over. The U.S. government required clear titles before buying the canal; in many instances Robert Jr. could produce only phantom claims to property along the Company Canal. One attorney working for the government informed Harris Gagné that Robert Jr.'s canal ran "through lands evidently belonging to other persons." Besides requiring more detailed property descriptions and chains of titles, the government was also concerned about bridges and authorization to collect tolls on the B & L No. 2. U.S. attorney Louis H. Burns told Gagné that confusion with the Lafourche Parish titles could hold up the government's purchase of the Company Canal.

The most troublesome of all titles was in Jefferson Parish, where the elder Barrow had acquired the B & L No. 2 in the mysterious sheriff's sale in 1862 as Yankee forces advanced toward New Orleans. A lawyer conducting a title search informed Gagné that the titles were not nearly as clear as Robert Jr. thought. The sheriff's sale, he said, was made without clear references to earlier owners and titles. Perhaps it was Robert Jr.'s problems with land titles between Bayou Lafourche and the Mississippi River that prompted the government to buy the Harvey Canal even though it was several miles south of the Company Canal and not in a straight line with the rest of the proposed canal route.[32]

Sale of the Company Canal to the government came none too soon for Robert Jr., who was experiencing extreme financial problems in 1925. He told longtime friend Joseph H. Humphreys that he would

---

31. See box "1924," *passim*, RRBP, for details of the transaction involving the bank and the police jury.
32. Louis H. Burns to Harris Gagné, February 7, 1925, in box "1925," RRBP; Ulisse Marinoni, Jr., to Harris Gagné, May 25, 26, 30, 1925, all in box 9, folder 7, BFP.

have to let his insurance policy lapse because he simply did not have any money to pay premiums. In a tone that suggested he was depressed over his personal finances, he added, "I have few friends left in Terrebonne but I count Joe Humphrys as one of them."[33]

Before selling the Company Canal to the U.S. government, Robert Jr. had only to clear up a few questions regarding bridges and bridgetenders. His attorney informed the Corps of Engineers that he had constructed a bridge across his canal in Lockport, where Tim Glynn served as bridgetender and toll collector. A. J. Falgout performed a similar duty in Bourg. According to Barrow, the police jury in Terrebonne Parish would not only assist in obtaining the 300-foot right-of-way required by the Corps; it would assume responsibility for maintaining bridges and paying the salaries of bridgetenders. Robert Jr. had requested that the Louisiana Highway Department assume responsibility for maintaining bridges in Houma until he could fill in the old canal. Robert Jr. also received complaints from District Attorney J. A. Coignet, who requested that he make badly needed repairs on the bridge in Lockport.[34]

On June 18, 1925, Robert Jr. sold the Company Canal to the U.S. government for $84,000. The sale was passed in the District Court of the United States, Eastern District of Louisiana, New Orleans Division. The detailed property description—seven pages noting the location of each metal stake along the route—was also recorded in conveyance records of Lafourche and Terrebonne parishes.[35] Louisiana's private canal era had ended.

Why had Robert Jr. received only $84,000 for his canal and the Harvey Canal Company, $500,000? This was due in part to Barrow's own confusion. As the next chapter will explain, he was ill and so beset by marital and financial problems in 1925 that he lost his usual sharp eye for business. To be sure, he haggled over price, but it was he who had set the selling price for the western portion of the B & L No. 2, expecting that the Corps of Engineers would buy the entire canal for $300,000. Instead the Corps bought Harvey's locks for

33. Robert Barrow, Jr., to Joseph H. Humphreys, February 8, 1925, in box "1925," RRBP.
34. Attorney to U.S. Army Engineers, February 3, 1925, J. A. Coignet to Robert Barrow, Jr., May 22, 1925, both in box "1925," RRBP.
35. LCB 56, fol. 513.

$500,000 and tacked on the inexpensive western part of the Company Canal. In time even this section became expendable as the Gulf Intracoastal Waterway was straightened, enlarged, and improved. Thus the long Barrow association with the Company Canal ended. Today all that remains of the canal are a few remnants of old locks and shallow, partly filled ditches.

6

The End of the Barrow Era

The success of the B & L No. 2 in the twentieth century undoubtedly attests to the business acumen of Robert Barrow, Jr., who realized the potential of the Company Canal and capitalized on the unique geography of Louisiana's bayou country. Only in a limited way did railroads, which enjoyed several economic advantages over water transportation, solve the east-west transportation problems encountered by early south Louisiana settlers. Louisiana railroads that traversed the marshy terrain from New Orleans to Morgan City reached only a portion of the region served by the Company Canal.

One can estimate Robert Jr.'s total worth by extrapolating between his conservative income tax records and his exaggerated credit-rating statements. In 1924 his property included the Company Canal, twenty-one town lots in Houma, his St. Charles Avenue home, land in Terrebonne Parish, and the offer of $84,000 from the U.S. government for a portion of the B & L No. 2 between Lafourche and Terrebonne. He usually valued the house at $50,000 and estimated his total worth between $700,000 and $800,000. Robert Jr. had come a long way since the 1870s, when he had struggled to reopen the canal. His rebuilding seemed doomed to fail, but the B & L No. 2 had become a good investment. Before he sold it to the U.S. government in 1925, it had become the basis of his modest fortune.[1]

1. Robert Barrow, Jr., to L. M. Pool, April 14, 1924, Robert Barrow, Jr., to American

Robert Jr. did not come by his wealth easily. Controversial like his father, and equally as unpopular, he struggled against a number of business adversaries eager to have a rail link to Houma to compete against the Company Canal. Like his father, Robert Jr. viewed economic and political challenges as personal affronts, and he responded accordingly. His moods ebbed and flowed with the economy. In April 1914 he told a son-in-law that sugar farmers faced ruin. He predicted that next year "there will be no more sugar raised in Louisiana." The outbreak of World War I four months later changed his outlook considerably. "We in the Sugar belt will be in clover if the war keeps up," he wrote his daughter Zoe. "Sugar should go to 6 or 7¢ per lb.," he predicted. Also helping the situation was an increase in domestic sugar production when foreign sources of sugar seemed likely to be cut or severely restricted. He did not show any compassion for the lumber and cotton industries, which did not fare as well as sugar: "I am not feeling any sorrow for them in their misery they acted so contemtable in wishing us all the horror possible. Things certainly look brighter at present for us, but let us not spend money until we get it," he added, with typical pecuniary caution.

Even though he was tight-fisted and cautious, Robert Jr. left room in his world for entertainment and even charity. When the Barrow family visited Terrebonne Parish, they sometimes attended the boat races below Houma at Sea Breeze in the motor launch *Brer Rabbit*. From time to time Robert Jr. loaned money to his children, but the tone of their requests indicates that he lectured them on the virtue of saving. In 1914 daughter Jennie, who was married to Dr. Harris P. Dawson of Montgomery, Alabama, asked to borrow $2,000 for some emergency. She assured her father that she would try to practice frugality. In 1907 Robert Jr. transferred to St. Matthew's Episcopal Church title to land in Houma that his father had given to the church without signing the proper legal forms.[2]

Bank, November, 1924, both in box "1924," Robert Ruffin Barrow, Jr., Papers, Division of Archives, Nicholls State University Library, hereinafter cited as RRBP.

2. Robert Barrow, Jr., to Zoe Topping, August 7, 1914, in box 8, folder 3, Robert R. Barrow Family Papers, Manuscripts Section, Howard-Tilton Memorial Library, Tulane University, hereinafter cited as BFP; Robert Barrow, Jr., to Jennie Dawson, January 14, 1914, in box 8, folder 1, BFP; Gardner Tucker to Robert Barrow, Jr.,

Before selling the Company Canal to the U.S. government, Robert Jr. grappled with problems brought on by a changing public attitude toward twentieth-century transportation. The damming of Bayou Lafourche in 1903 and the opening of the Plaquemine locks by the Corps of Engineers in 1909 afforded Robert Jr. an opportunity to capitalize on the ancient east-west transportation problem in the bayou country and expand B & L No. 2 operations. The locks at Plaquemine provided an effective route to the Attakapas country, but the Bayou Plaquemine route was nearly twice as long as the Company Canal. The damming of Bayou Lafourche clearly reduced traffic and tonnage on that stream and allowed Robert Jr. to pick up the bayou trade that once flowed directly into the Mississippi River. But this opportunity was soon challenged by local steamboat companies that transported goods to railheads under through-rate arrangements with the railroads. Robert Jr. tried to prevent railroads from negotiating additional shipping deals that would bring more spur lines into his territory.

By the end of World War I, a number of through-rate shipping arrangements between steamboat lines and railroads flourished on Bayou Lafourche, the geographic center of the sugar country and the heart of Company Canal operations. Private warehouses at Lockport, Raceland, Lafourche Crossing, Thibodaux, and Donaldsonville utilized mechanized equipment to load and unload at their docks. The Lower Lafourche Barge Line, which had a shipping arrangement with the Southern Pacific Railroad, used machinery to unload corn at its facilities in Lockport. At Lafourche Crossing the Southern Pacific owned unloading equipment, which it leased to the Williams Barge Line. In Thibodaux the Percy Lobdell Company also had corn-loading equipment at its dock. Derricks along Bayou Lafourche loaded and unloaded sugarcane barges running up and down the bayou. In Houma, the Daigle Barge Line had a similar working arrangement with Southern Pacific. A 1919 report by the U.S. Corps of Engineers noted a significant point that Robert Jr. somehow did not

---

January 3, 1907, in box 7, folder 8, BFP; Copies of Robert R. Barrow, Jr., income tax returns, in boxes "1913," "1914," "1916," "1917," RRBP.

exploit: Rail rates had increased appreciably since the damming of Bayou Lafourche.[3]

Alex Barker, of Lockport, became a serious economic and political threat and the very embodiment of the new competition Barrow faced. A man of wealth and prestige, Barker owned the Lower Lafourche Barge Line, which transported freight between New Orleans and the bayou country on his two steamboats, the *Lockport* and the *Climax*. He also owned freight barges and a boat building and repair yard. His vessels steamed from New Orleans to Bayou Lafourche on Mondays and Thursdays, making stops at Lockport, Raceland, Lafourche Crossing, and Thibodaux. Barker regularly used both the Company Canal and the Harvey Canal. A member of the state legislature, he attended a waterways congress that met in Washington, D.C., in December 1910.

What greatly upset Robert Jr. was Barker's business arrangement with the Southern Pacific Railroad. Since steamers could no longer enter Bayou Lafourche via the Mississippi River, Barker profited from his rail-water shipping contract. The Southern Pacific spur extended only a short distance below Lockport; Barker's boats transported goods from the railhead to the watery fringes of the Lafourche country, often bypassing the Company Canal altogether.

The Barker-Barrow confrontation exposed a sensitive B & L No. 2 nerve during the automobile age: its vulnerability to public scrutiny and regulation as the masses became more accustomed to free public transportation. At first Barker and Robert Jr. haggled over minor issues such as toll charges, the prompt payment of bills, or the accuracy of Barrow's agents in recording how many boats and barges passed through Company Canal locks. Their extended exchanges over these issues became far more vituperative than circumstances warranted. Each was headstrong and confident, and neither was likely to walk away from a fight. Robert Jr. once asked Barker to reimburse him for piles that Barker's boat had knocked down; Barker considered the piles a hazard to navigation that should have been removed by Barrow for safety reasons.

3. Chief Engineer, U.S. Corps of Engineers, Annual Report, 1919, Pt. 1, pp. 990–1012 (Corps of Engineers library, New Orleans).

Robert Jr. became especially riled when Barker introduced bills in the state legislature to regulate canals. Any law to regulate tolls, Barrow claimed, would ruin his business. He accused Barker of legislating for personal gain, of trying to force out the B & L No. 2 so as to maintain a monopoly over freight trade in the area that he had enjoyed since Bayou Lafourche was dammed in 1903. Barker called Robert Jr. from Baton Rouge on June 18, 1908, to say he would introduce a bill the next day to amend the original 1829 B & L charter. Barker had promised to show Barrow any bill relating to canals at least ten days before he introduced it.

Most attempts to regulate the B & L No. 2 failed, but Robert Jr. worried anyway. His close friend in the legislature, Frank Whitehead, promised to vote against bills to regulate locks. Barrow rushed to Baton Rouge to round up opposition to Barker's bill, which was faulty because the 1829 charter had long since expired. He called Barker names and accused him of greed and of trying to put the B & L No. 2 out of business. Barrow published his version of the dispute in a rambling discourse titled *History of the Attempt of Aleck Barker, Representative from Lafourche Parish, to Injure Me and Ruin the Canal Business, By a Bill Supposed to Amend the Charter of the Barataria & Lafourche Canal, Which Resulted in a Failure and His Withdrawing the Bill.*

Robert Jr.'s simplistic conspiratorial view of Barker's position sheds some light on the controversy but hardly qualifies as impartial. He claimed that the B & L No. 2 made rail shipment unnecessary and that Barker did not like that. He said that Barker had forced out of business the defunct Bradford Towing Company, which operated in Lockport around 1910 in competition with Barker. Robert Jr. did not say how Barker had achieved his objective, but he was convinced that Barker was trying to close the B & L No. 2 for the same reason—to eliminate competition. All the while, Robert Jr. claimed that when Barker used the Company Canal as a customer, he received the same impartial consideration extended to all shippers.

As an elected official and businessman dealing with the public, Barker could ill afford to reply in language as forceful as that used by the pugnacious Barrow. Instead he usually struck back with blows to the Company Canal's pocketbook. Occasionally, however, Barker let

Robert Jr. have a sample of his venomous pen. He once described the Company Canal as "a narrow muddy ditch," which he compared to "its owner's mind." He characterized Robert Jr.'s writing in 1908 as "a weak Barrow-like attempt to belittle me."

In 1910 Barker provided information on navigation for a special study on Louisiana waterways, using economic arguments to show the advantages of the Harvey Canal over the Company Canal. Perhaps Henry Dart, the New Orleans attorney and historian who was president of the Harvey Canal, Land and Improvement Company, wrote some of the copy for the eighty-page booklet. At any rate, the editor described Barker as an impartial expert on shipping in the area: "He pays tollage through both canals, which is the same rate, and he is not interested financially in either route." Barker soundly criticized the Company Canal and warmly endorsed the Harvey Canal. This conclusion, he said, came after his using the Barrow route for six months and the Harvey route for nine months. The Harvey route was faster, he said. The locks on the Harvey Canal, Barker contended, were 30 feet wide and could accommodate a boat 145 feet long; the Company Canal locks were only 23 feet wide. Nor was the Company Canal as deep as the Harvey Canal. Robert Jr. warned his customers not to load to a depth over 3 feet, Barker said. In a final parting comment, he stated that the pilings on the Mississippi River at the Company Canal were hazardous to navigation, especially during rough weather.[4] Barker had shown that he was not objective in his judgments about the Company Canal. His description of the two canals was slanted in favor of the Harvey Canal, whose locks he made a bit wider than they actually were. He made the B & L No. 2 locks a few feet narrower than they were.

In 1912 Robert Jr. became embroiled in a heated dispute with the Whipple brothers of Bayou Blue over toll charges. The Whipples lived on the banks of the Company Canal, where they earned a living close

---

4. *Southern Manufacturer; A Sketch of the Louisiana Inter-Coastal Canal Route from Morgan City to New Orleans via Houma and Lockport* (Spec. ed.; New Orleans, 1910), 34, 41, 43, 46, 63; Various exchanges between Alex Barker and Robert Barrow, Jr., in boxes "1908," "1916," *passim*, RRBP. The Henry Dart Papers, housed in the Manuscript Division, Earl K. Long Library, University of New Orleans, indicate that at one time the files of the Dart law firm contained documents relating to the Harvey Canal. Unfortunately, the firm discarded some old documents for lack of storage space.

to nature. The numerous members of the family planted garden crops and were professional hunters and decoy carvers. For $5 per day, they took hunters in pirogues on duck hunts in Lake Field and Lake Long in nearby Lafourche Parish. In March, Whitmell P. Martin, then a judge of the Twentieth Judicial District Court (Terrebonne and Lafourche parishes), enjoined Thomas Whipple from using the Company Canal. According to a report prepared by Robert Jr., at Bayou Blue the Whipples refused to pay toll charges assessed by Barrow's agent A. J. Falgout. Later Robert Jr. and Thomas Whipple met face to face. Barrow was standing on a bridge over Bayou Terrebonne when he encountered Whipple heading upstream in his boat. He asked Whipple to confer with him. According to Barrow, Whipple called Falgout a liar and a son of a bitch. Then Whipple threatened Robert Jr.: "You have been a king around here long enough," he said. "You may have money but you havent but one life and I will put you where you wont give me or any body else any trouble." Robert Jr. claimed that Whipple had a shotgun in his possession when he made the threat.[5]

Less dangerous to Robert Jr.'s health but more burdensome to his pocketbook were his disputes with the police jury, the governing body of Lafourche Parish. When backwaters from the Kilona crevasse on the Mississippi River threatened to inundate the bayou country by sending floodwaters through the Company Canal into Bayou Lafourche, the police jury ordered Robert Jr. to dam his canal. Local residents had vivid memories of the Hymelia crevasse of 1903, a levee break in the same area as the Kilona rupture, which flooded farms on the east bank of Bayou Lafourche from Thibodaux to below Raceland. Robert Jr. claimed that he had the materials necessary for building the dam on his canal near Bayou Lafourche, but sugar growers on the Vacherie and Gayoso ridges east of Lockport then obtained an injunction that would have forced Robert Jr. to dam his canal east of their holdings, thereby protecting them also from approaching floodwaters. In the confusion, W. R. Pennington and his associates built a dam across the Company Canal near Bayou

5. Barrow's report, March 3, 1912, and Judge Martin's injunction can be found in box "1912," RRBP; Floryde Hebert and Lavis Hebert, interview, Oral History of Terrebonne (Terrebonne Parish Library, Houma, La.), reel 144.

Lafourche at their own expense. They requested reimbursement from the police jury, which then sought subrogation from Robert Jr. In 1912 the jury passed a resolution requiring the closing of canals flowing into Bayou Lafourche in the event of high water. In March 1913 jury president J. L. Basset sent Robert Jr. a bill for $547.29, the cost of constructing the earthen dam across the Company Canal east of Lockport. The whole matter infuriated Barrow, who only reluctantly paid the costs requested by the jury.

Robert Jr. became accustomed to bad news from Basset, who reported that the bridge over the Company Canal in Lockport was in need of repairs. Parish enginer J. A. Lovell thought the bridge, which rested on the foundation of the old locks, was in danger of collapsing. In fact, the whole structure could topple over. The walls were out of plumb, and the bridge approaches were excessively steep. Robert Jr. denied these reports and complained that the jury maintained a double standard: It built wooden bridges at public expense, but it demanded that he construct steel bridges.[6]

In Terrebonne Parish, Robert Jr. sometimes resorted to legal technicalities to save himself the costs of building bridges across the Company Canal. In 1914 and again in 1916 he wrote to his son-in-law Harris P. Dawson, who lived in Montgomery, Alabama, to explain his plan for transferring B & L No. 2 stock to someone residing outside Louisiana. Litigation among diverse owners in several states, Robert Jr. explained, came under federal jurisdiction. Robert Jr. felt he stood a better chance in federal court than in a local one. The people of Houma, he suspected with some justification, bore ill will against him. Actually he hoped that local governing officials would compromise with him rather than pursue an expensive and lengthy federal suit.[7]

Never one to admit his shortcomings, Robert Jr. often blamed his problems on conspiracies. He accused J. M. Dressner of stirring up prejudice against him in Lafourche Parish. As a result, inadequacies

6. J. L. Basset to Robert Barrow, Jr., May 9, 1912, in box "1912," RRBP; Basset to Barrow, March 4, 1913, in box "1913," RRBP; Barrow to Basset, March 26, 1913, in box "1913," RRBP; Robert Barrow, Jr., to J. A. Lovell, November 11, 1916, in box "1916," RRBP; Philip Uzee, Thibodaux *Daily Comet*, May 1, 1985.
7. Robert Barrow, Jr., to Harris P. Dawson, April 26, 1914, in box 8, folder 3, BFP; Barrow to Dawson, September 20, 1916, in box "1916," RRBP.

on public bridges in the parish were overlooked, whereas Company Canal bridges were subjected to rigorous inspection. In 1914 officials in Houma not only demanded that Robert Jr. repair the bridge across his canal, but also obtained an injunction to force him to remove dirt dredged from his canal and dumped on Canal Street.[8]

The flu epidemic of 1918, which affected many Americans, touched Robert Jr. personally and professionally. His son-in-law Robert Topping, who was married to Zoe, succumbed to the flu that year. The epidemic reached workers on the Company Canal. In the Westwego office a number of men were absent from work because of the flu. In the bayou country one of Barrow's bridgetenders, a young fellow named Babin, died from the flu. Terrebonne, too, suffered extensively from the epidemic, according to a correspondent.[9]

Robert Jr. hoped the sale of the Company Canal to the U.S. government early in the 1920s would solve his growing financial problems. His agricultural fortunes had declined greatly after the death of Henry Clay Duplantis in 1919. For twenty-nine years Duplantis had run Myrtle Grove plantation smoothly and effectively. Profits were good in 1903 and even better during World War I. With Duplantis gone, Robert Jr. discovered just how reliable his trusty partner had been. He complained how time-consuming plantation operations could be. He also discovered that replacing Duplantis would not be easy. Caliste Duplantis, Henry Clay's son and the administrator of his father's estate, maintained friendly relations with Robert Jr. for some time, but soon the two disagreed over a number of points. Barrow wanted Caliste to hire Josh Dillard to run Myrtle Grove; Caliste did not think Dillard was the right man, but he hired him anyway. Before long Robert Jr. and Dillard haggled over money and other matters. Another source of friction with Caliste was the overseer's house at Myrtle Grove, where Henry Clay's numerous descendants continued to live after his death. Robert Jr. told Caliste that any new overseer he would hire would expect to reside in the large overseer's house occupied by the Duplantis clan. The status of the overseer was a big

---

8. The injunction, dated March 16, 1914, is in box "1914," RRBP.
9. Robert Barrow, Jr., to C. C. Krumbhaar, November 7, 1918, in box "1918," RRBP.

factor in plantation life, he told Caliste. Nonetheless, the Duplantises remained for some years in the big house.[10]

Occasionally there were signs that all was not well in the Barrow household. Robert Jr.'s response to his daughter Jennie's Father's Day poem in 1919 hinted at serious family problems. In thanking Jennie for her poem, he wrote apologetically, "I have tried to be kind, considerate and just to my children, if I have failed in any way it was largely due to weakness of the flesh and not intentional, we are none of us perfect and I have never claimed to be."[11] He would repeat this refrain in the next decade as his financial and personal world came tumbling down about him. Like his father, Robert Jr. could not keep his house in order in the waning years of his life. He, too, would leave a tangled web of property complicated by mortgages and rigged sales, conducted in most cases to elude an equally large number of creditors clamoring to collect money owed them. His affairs, like his father's, would not be settled until many years after his death.

Robert Jr.'s marital and economic fortunes deteriorated rapidly in the 1920s. His financial difficulties came not only from his agricultural endeavors; unwise investments also contributed to his financial woes. Strained relations with his wife, Jennie, became apparent in the mid-1920s. This may have resulted from Robert Jr.'s mental strain brought on by diabetes and Bright's disease (a kidney ailment). Eventually Robert Jr. left his wife and sought the company of another woman. The family engaged in heated disputes over both her and money matters. His children became involved in the controversy, just as he and his sister, Roberta, had waged legal battles against their father in order to obtain their inheritance.

The Barrows' marital friction is a complicated story that may never be fully understood, but a number of possible explanations are feasible. Undoubtedly Robert Jr.'s monetary, medical, and marital problems were interrelated. To be certain, he had to grapple with all three. Whether one had greater impact than another is problematic; eventually they meant disaster—financial ruin and family disruption for Robert Jr. Like his father, he became distrustful of his chil-

10. See box 18, *passim*, RRBP, for details regarding the Duplantises.
11. Robert Barrow, Jr., to Jennie Dawson, June 23, 1919, in box 18, RRBP.

dren and his longtime and faithful employees. Like his father, he saw conspiracies against him everywhere. Some may have been real; many were obviously the product of a troubled mind.

Depression in the sugar industry was the catalyst of Robert Jr.'s financial problems, for he was a sugar planter and a canal tycoon who shipped sugarcane via the Company Canal. The boom times for sugar before World War I gave way in 1920 and 1921 to low sugar prices, high operating costs, and a general malaise in the industry brought on by cane blight and other diseases. The industry experienced an especially bad year in 1922. Robert Jr. rented land to tenants and engaged the services of day laborers as well. As agricultural problems grew, tenants on his lands in Terrebonne Parish asked for extensions in meeting their financial commitments to him. He raised funds with which to operate by selling some of his small landholdings.

No longer able to juggle accounts and avoid creditors, Robert Jr. suffered a major economic setback in 1922. At first the financial crunch did not change his way of living, but gradually he was forced to make big adjustments. He continued to live like a gentleman, however. He paid dues to his social clubs—the Boston Club, the Crescent Club, and the Juanita Club—but he had to make many short-term loans to meet these and other obligations. Usually he borrowed $3,000 or $4,000 and signed ninety-day notes. He bought twenty mules from the Mattingly firm of Thibodaux in April, putting down $3,219 and agreeing to pay off the balance in monthly installments. Soon, however, he was unable to meet his monthly commitments.

Robert Jr. learned to evade creditors who hounded him. He received many letters requesting payment for equipment purchased and for services rendered. Meanwhile he relentlessly pressed his debtors to pay money owed to him. In the last five years of his life, approximately 90 percent of his correspondence dealt with debts he owed or tried to collect. About the only encouraging news for Barrow was that the U.S. government was planning to purchase the Company Canal or the Harvey Canal and make it a part of an intracoastal canal system.[12]

12. See boxes "1921," "1922," *passim*, RRBP, and box 17, *passim*, BFP.

Even though receipts from the Company Canal averaged just below $20,000 from 1921 to 1923, Robert Jr. was becoming discouraged about his economic plight. Writing to the attorney Harris Gagné in January 1923 about the bleak prospects at Myrtle Grove plantation, Robert Jr. feared seeing the annual report: "Burdened as I am with obligations, I can not see the light ahead." Later in the year he was even more despondent: "I am getting desperate. I am at the end of my resources and can go no further." Other developments added to his distress. The B & L No. 2 shipping arrangement with A. J. Bonvillain, which had been successful for years, ended in 1924. The announcement in the Houma *Courier* stated simply that at the consent of both parties, their agreement was over. Robert Jr. managed to hang on to Myrtle Grove plantation, but it required maneuvering that would have made his old father proud. First he sold the plantation to Myrtle Grove, Inc., which in turn sold it back to him and his daughter Zoe Barrow Topping for $50,000 each. To pay for the plantation, he and Zoe borrowed from the Federal Land Bank.[13]

In 1923 Robert Jr. conferred with Houma attorney Allen J. Ellender about selling property for him. One parcel of land Robert Jr. wanted to sell was the small tract in Lafourche Parish he had acquired from Ludy Jones, the black mistress of his late cousin John Pittman. Pittman's will ceded the tract to Ludy, who in turn sold it to Robert Jr. He told Ellender he wanted $1,500 for the property, but he would take $1,200 if necessary.[14]

In order to remain solvent, Robert Jr. relentlessly pressed those who owed him money; at the same time, he performed a tightwire act to evade creditors. Here, too, he acted in the manner of his father, who had used similar tactics in his declining years. When users of the Company Canal near Lockport requested a 21-cent reduction in the toll for using the canal, he refused, claiming that he could not afford to reduce tolls that were already low. When canal users fell behind in toll payments during the hard times for sugar farmers in the early twenties, he instructed toll collectors to demand cash before allowing

13. Robert Barrow, Jr., to Harris Gagné, January 7, June 16, 1923, both in box "1923," RRBP; Barrow to Gagné, January 1, 1924, in box "1924," RRBP. Information on the Myrtle Grove business maneuverings can be found in box 17, folder 3, BFP.
14. Robert Barrow, Jr., to Allen J. Ellender, February 24, 1923, in box "1923," RRBP.

them to pass. For example, boats owned by Charles Wyat of Fayport Planting Company near Lockport were not allowed to pass through the canal in January 1923 unless they paid cash.[15]

When pressed unduly by his creditors, Robert Jr. sometimes postured dramatically and disingenuously as a southern gentleman. After agreeing to pay $105 to M. M. Mallary, president of the Louisiana Delta Farms Company, for damaging his boat, Robert Jr. stalled for four years. Mallary finally said that if Robert Jr. would not pay like a gentleman, he might have to resort to other means. His pride wounded, Barrow wrote back and included his check for $105. "Gentlemen of the old South, of which I claim to be one," he wrote, "do things for which they feel obliged through a sense of justice and fairness." Then, in a face-saving attempt to justify his delay, he carped about some portions of Mallary's itemized bill. Equally as sensitive, Mallary wrote back, offering to return Barrow's check if he really wanted to renege on a promise made to settle a just account like a gentleman. Mallary was determined not to let Robert Jr. have the last word. He wanted it known that Robert Jr. was not being magnanimous; he was merely settling a just debt.[16]

By 1925 Robert Jr.'s world was falling apart. According to legal documents filed by his wife, he suffered from diabetes and from Bright's disease, which may have caused mental disorders. Possibly Robert Jr., who was now sixty-seven, suffered a loss of mental acuity associated with aging. At any rate, he seemed different. He became amorously associated with Stella Leathers, the widow of his former classmate Captain B. S. Leathers, who had died in 1919. Stella worked in the B & L No. 2 office at the locks in Westwego. People close to the family knew of Robert Jr.'s paramour, but few knew many details of their illicit affair. Eventually his wife and children took legal steps to prevent him from squandering what was left of the family property. They feared that he would sell some of the land in Terrebonne Parish in order to obtain funds to court Stella.

Letters from his daughters provide some information about Stella.

15. Robert Barrow, Jr., to Lockport Central Refining and Manufacturing Company, October 6, 1921, H. R. Claudet to Robert Barrow, Jr., October 3, 1921, both in box 22, RRBP; Robert Barrow, Jr., to canal collectors, January 30, 1923, in box 26, RRBP.
16. Robert Barrow, Jr., to M. M. Mallary, October 16, 1921, Mallary to Barrow, October 4, 18, 1921, all in box 22, RRBP.

Discussing her father's amorous escapades, Zoe referred to him as "Hot Papa" in a letter to her sister Hallette. "We are enjoying his absence and mother is feeling much better," she wrote on another occasion. Later she understood why he dallied in Houma longer than usual: "Mr. Harris [Gagné] thinks Stella is crowding him and that is why he is hiding out in Houma." In a tone bristling with hostility toward her father, Zoe added, "We all hope she runs him into the Gulf." When her father removed a Lockport bridgetender from the B & L No. 2 payroll, Zoe surmised, "He is trying in any way to get all the small cash he can lay his hands on." Zoe knew that her stubborn father would explore other sources of money. "Mr. H[arris Gagné] says he promised mother he wouldn't let him have any money & cant go back on his word," she said. "So he [Robert Jr.] may try elsewhere."

Jennie and her daughters feared that Robert Jr. would try to sell Roberta Grove and Myrtle Grove plantations. They realized that he was acting strange and displaying signs of paranoia. Zoe observed that her father refused to take a tonic prescribed by his doctor after he noticed Jennie's strychnine tablets on a table next to his medicine. She surmised that her father feared being poisoned.[17]

All the while, Robert Jr. continued to see Stella. With the help of Harris Gagné, Jennie and her daughters prevented him from making any hasty or foolish business transactions while he was in a confused mental state. In 1925 Jennie Tennent Barrow became president of R. R. Barrow, Inc., the recently formed family agricultural corporation. Robert Jr. was furious, but Jennie had the support and votes of her daughters. His hands were tied; he could not conduct plantation business on his own. In fact, he soon found himself without funds to maintain his usual living standards. Official records of the legal transactions that took place are silent on personal and marital tension. Conveyance records in Terrebonne Parish indicate simply that the old family plantation was now an agricultural corporation. It contained 1,800 acres of prime sugarcane land.

17. Madison L. Funderburk and Elton Darsey, interviews with author, February 18, 1985, Houma, La.; Zoe Topping to Hallette Cole, n.d., Topping to Cole, August 12, 1925, both in box 9, folder 5, BFP; Robert Barrow, Jr., to B. S. Leathers, January 15, 1919, Robert Barrow, Jr., to "My Dear Mrs. Leathers," April 28, 1919, both in box 18, RRBP.

Soon Robert Jr. was forced to grapple with the realities of change that left him powerless and destitute. Attorney Hugh Suthon requested a family financial conference. He wanted Jennie to give Robert Jr. $200 per month so that he could live like a "gentleman." Meanwhile Harris Gagné advised the daughters to dissuade their mother from meeting with Suthon or Robert Jr. Gagné suggested that Jennie say nothing, but Zoe told her sister Hallette that it "will be hard to shut her up." Zoe was furious at Suthon for suggesting to her father that he flee to Cuba with Stella. At about this time, Stella, realizing that Robert Jr. no longer controlled his own affairs, called Harris Gagné and demanded that the family return pictures and letters that she had given to Robert Jr.

Jennie and her daughters made life miserable for Robert Jr. They frustrated his efforts to borrow money by informing banks that they would not honor his debts. Without legal authorization to administer Myrtle Grove, he was powerless. He did not even realize that his family was negotiating for the sale of portions of the Company Canal that the U.S. government had not bought. The Barrow women had received offers from several parties, but they did not inform him of recent developments. Selling the rest of the Company Canal was a real possibility, but the matter was more complicated than Jennie and her daughters ever realized. Zoe complained that she had to help her mother attend to the many details of running the family empire. The Barrow women later became embroiled in lawsuits stemming from decisions made while Robert Jr. was in a state of mental confusion.

On October 10, 1925, Robert Jr. filed suit in the Seventeenth Judicial District Court of Terrebonne Parish for a legal separation from Jennie. This act served two purposes: It severed the bonds of community property between Jennie and him and set the stage for divorce by separation from bed and board. The document contained over one hundred pages of property description, responses to interrogatories, and Robert Jr.'s confused account of how he had been badly treated by Jennie and his children. The law firm of Ellender and Ellender represented Robert Jr., who sought control of property that he owned jointly with Jennie. His attorneys proposed to Jennie's counselor, Robert E. Milling, that Robert Jr. be made head of the family again and placed in charge of the property. They proposed an equal division of all community property owned by the Barrows. They also considered the possibility of placing the property under a trust management system.

Robert Jr.'s suit against Jennie sheds light on the confused state of affairs in the Barrow household. According to Robert Jr., Jennie and her daughters conspired against him, beginning in June 1925. Jennie was guilty of "cruelty, excesses, and ill treatment," he said, and she and Zoe "attempted to eject him from his New Orleans residence." They forced him, he contended, to endorse the $84,000 check from the U.S. government for the Company Canal, promising that they would deposit the money in his account.

Jennie, who did not deposit the check in her husband's account, had a different version of what had transpired. She denied that Robert Jr. was a resident of Terrebonne Parish and rejected overtures from his attorneys. She claimed that for the past twenty-five years Robert Jr. had been a legal resident of Orleans Parish. She was equally adamant on other points stipulated by Robert Jr.'s attorneys. She claimed that her husband left their New Orleans home in mid-August, and six weeks later he filed for a separation in Terrebonne Parish, where he maintained only a business residence. The court agreed with Jennie and ruled that Robert Jr. was a resident of Orleans Parish. Robert Jr. appealed to the Louisiana Supreme Court, but the high court confirmed the ruling of the district court on November 30, 1925, and denied him a rehearing.

Robert Jr. seemed to blame his daughters Hallette and Jennie for most of his marital difficulties. In a rambling five-page letter to Hallette's husband, Dr. Christian Cole, he explained his version of the involved family feud. He urged Cole to stay out of the family dispute and to dissuade Hallette from any further action that would impoverish her father and possibly cause the loss of the entire sugarcane crop in Houma. Robert Jr. told Cole that "these women trying to make use of you to obtain further money is an outrage." He referred to daughters Jennie and Hallette as "these vindictive women." Although he blamed Hallette for his problems, he absolved Cole of wrongdoing: "You have little or no control over her feeling or action." He concluded with the observation that "they have made me suffer as punishment all human flesh should be called on to suffer in this world. What more should they require." His letters were similar to those written by his father before he died in 1875.

Barrow made improbable statements in the suit he filed against his wife. He charged that she and her daughters beat him when he was helpless to defend himself and conspired to make him a pauper. He asserted that he was a resident of Terrebonne Parish, where he always voted, even though he owned property in other parishes. He charged that Jennie had kept large sums of community property funds from him: $36,000 from a land sale at Grand Caillou, $40,000 from the sale of a portion of the Company Canal to Donelson Caffery, and $84,000 from the sale of the Company Canal to the U.S. government. Unable to manipulate deals as he had done for years, Robert Jr. found himself strapped for funds. Eventually he was unable to obtain pocket money.

Robert Jr.'s suit filed in the Seventeenth Judicial District Court of Terrebonne Parish against R. R. Barrow, Inc., is more revealing for personal information about the family than for fine points of law. Like his separation suit against Jennie, this action, too, included Robert Jr.'s conspiratorial version of family intrigue against him. Simply put, he considered "the whole scheme" to form R. R. Barrow, Inc., "fraudulent," and he wanted his property back. He asked the court "to set aside the shams and devices by which he has been misled and tricked and stripped of all his property." He acknowledged that he had been forced "to submit to the demands of his persecutors and to yield to force" because he was "too sick and feeble to exercise an independent judgment." At one point he referred to his daughter Zoe as "Mrs. Topping, one (1) of the co-conspirators."

Robert Jr. explained his legal position in the suit, which was filed by attorney Allen J. Ellender. Robert Jr. contended that Myrtle Grove and other Barrow lands in Terrebonne were inherited from his family and were never alienated by him. The formation of Myrtle Grove, Inc., in 1923, the document went on to explain, was done for convenience only. Part interest was sold to Zoe Topping in order to obtain a loan from the Federal Land Bank; no money changed hands. Then, in 1925, his suit continued, when he was desperately ill, his wife and children conspired against him and formed R. R. Barrow, Inc., an agricultural corporation and land company. He signed the document on June 11 because he "was sick in body and had lost all power of resistance." The document was signed in New Orleans because Robert Jr. was "too ill and feeble to be moved to the Parish of Terrebonne."

The charter of R. R. Barrow, Inc., spelled out its structure. Robert Jr. owned 400 shares of stock valued at $100 each; Jennie owned 110 shares; and each of the four daughters, 60 shares. It provided for the election of officers at the annual meeting. Even though Robert Jr.'s 400 shares (compared with the 350 shares owned by Jennie and the daughters) gave him controlling interest, he had to be present to vote at the meeting—and three stockholders present constituted a quorum to conduct business. When Robert Jr. was too ill to attend a meeting, Jennie became president of R. R. Barrow, Inc. Robert Jr.'s suit dragged on for many months in arguments over sequestered property and the sugarcane crop at Myrtle Grove, and he died before it was settled.

Robert Jr. wrote his will in 1925, the year before he died. In it he attempted to set the record straight, at least as he saw matters from his twisted perspective. In reality the will only added to the farrago. The long, rambling document reflected his confused state; it is laced with contradictions and filled with invective directed against family and former friends. He poured out the animosity he felt toward his wife, and especially toward daughters Jennie and Hallette, "who I consider the most vindictive humans I have ever known and largely responsible for the trouble and bitterness of my wife to me, believing as I do had it not been for these two women a reconciliation with my wife could and would have been possible." He accused his wife and daughters not only of robbing him of his funds but of conspiring "to bring about my death which they desire and therefore being both robers and murderers."

Robert Jr. accused daughters Hallette and Jennie of striking him as he lay dying: "These two women came into my sick room and pounded me with their fists while I was powerless to defend myself and for this and other torture given me, I desire if it is possible to do so to disinherit Mrs. Cole & Mrs. Dawson." He wanted to leave the least part possible of his estate to daughters Hallette and Jennie and the largest part possible to daughters Irene and Zoe. He left his wife a share of his property with a wish that "the almighty place in her heart regret for the injustice she has done to me."

To Houma attorney Harris Gagné, Barrow left mostly confusion. In one part of the will, he gave Gagné his motor launch the *Brer Rabbit*, as well as Independence Island, his little island in Barataria Bay. Later in the same document he renounced his gift to Gagné, whom he now labeled a double-crosser. Longtime worker and friend Harry Ogborn received nothing but scorn. Robert Jr. called Ogborn a scoundrel and one of the most ungrateful humans alive. He accused Ogborn of trying to drive him to suicide, "going so far as to furnish the drug to do so with."

Before he died, Robert Jr. also filed suit in Jefferson Parish to recover from Jennie gifts he now wished to renounce. A Jefferson Parish court ruled against him. The court said that since August 1925 his affliction with diabetes and Bright's disease "produced mental delusions and hallucinations, which resulted in his filing suit, revoking the manual gifts to his wife and seeking their restitution to himself, which suit has been dismissed by final judgment because of the want of jurisdiction of this court, *ratione personne*."[18]

Attorney Donelson Caffery represented Jennie and her daughters in negotiations for the sale of the eastern portion of the Company Canal to private interests. The sale, which was conducted without the knowledge of Robert Jr., was far more complicated than the sale to the U.S. government. For $75,000, of which only $35,000 was in cash, Caffery became trustee for the unnamed owners. He agreed to dredge the canal from the railroad bridge in Westwego to the locks on the Mississippi River, as well as the basin between the gates, to a depth of 6 feet. In the meantime Caffery advised the Barrows to run the B & L No. 2 properly, since he was accountable to the owners. Eventually

18. Zoe Topping to Hallette Cole, n.d., Topping to Cole, August 12, 1925, both in box 9, folder 5, BFP; Robert Barrow, Jr., to Christian Cole, October 30, 1925, in box 9, folder 6, BFP; Robert Barrow, Jr., to Robert E. Milling, January 16, 1926, in box 9, folder 8, BFP; Terrebonne Parish Conveyance Book, Houma, La. (hereinafter cited as TCB), 83, fol. 134; Terrebonne Parish Wills Book, Houma, La., 1A, fol. 327; Box "1925," *passim*, RRBP; *Barrow* v. *Barrow* (1925), 106 So 705; *R. R. Barrow* v. *Jennie Tennant Barrow* (1925), Suit No. 8921, *R. R. Barrow* v. *R. R. Barrow, Inc.* (1925), Suit No. 8922 (Houma, La.), 17th Judicial District Court, Terrebonne Parish.

Caffery sold the canal and locks at Westwego to William T. Nolan, who in turn sold out to the Westwego Canal and Terminal Company, Inc. The $40,000 balance due the Barrow family was to be the subject of friction and legal struggles for many years to come. Jennie Barrow sued Caffery to recover the $40,000, but he claimed that he was not personally responsible, because the debt was not a personal debt.[19]

Robert Ruffin Barrow, Jr., died on March 24, 1926, at 6:30 in the morning and was buried quietly at 5:30 that afternoon in Magnolia Cemetery in Houma. His burial expenses came to $389: His lot in Magnolia Cemetery cost $15, his tomb cost $100, and the undertaker charged $274. The second Robert Barrow had departed this world without a great deal of ceremony, the family barely lingering to mourn his passing. In view of the vicious family controversies that had been brewing for so long, it was not surprising. Like his father, Robert Jr. departed with creditors clamoring to salvage remnants of his estate, which was deeply in debt. But also like his father, he sheltered choice pieces of property from these creditors. His disgruntled heirs benefited from his belligerence.[20]

Before he died, Robert Jr. had completed the ambitious canal project envisioned by his father before the Civil War. Like his father, he had left a record of financial achievement, but its path was littered with human casualties. Jennie and his four daughters inherited considerable property, but they also acquired many obligations and legal headaches. Jennie's legal bills alone totaled $16,000. Corporate income taxes filed by the B & L No. 2 and family agricultural records from 1926 through 1934 indicate that the financial downslide continued after Robert's death. In 1926 Jennie had to request an extension of ninety days from the collector of internal revenue because she did not have money to pay her taxes. The corporation had shown considerable losses lately, she said. It was in litigation, and its finances were tied up in legal battles. In 1927 the family tried to sell the home at 4938 St. Charles Avenue in New Orleans, but realtor Harold

19. See box "1925," *passim*, RRBP, for details of the bargain with Caffery; Jefferson Parish Conveyance Book, Gretna, La., 66, fol. 396.
20. Jefferson Parish Succession, Gretna, La., No. 1720 (Box 17, folder 6, BFP); Hallette Cole Scrapbook (Box "1833–1912," RRBP).

Stream apparently found no buyer. In 1929 Myrtle Grove showed a loss of more than $1,800, according to accounts Zoe Barrow Topping kept.[21]

Jennie's hopes of collecting $40,000 from Donelson Caffery were dashed by the Louisiana Supreme Court in May 1926, when the case of *Jennie Tennant Barrow* v. *Donelson Caffery* was decided in favor of Caffery. Jennie's contention that her husband had made a manual gift to her of Caffery's $40,000 note was not the major sticking point. Instead the court ruled that Robert Jr.'s arrangement with Caffery did not call for Caffery to bear personal liability.

Even this decision did not end all dealings with Caffery over Company Canal business, for in June 1927 Caffery wrote to Harris Gagné about a canal compromise that might save trial expenses for both parties. As late as 1931 Jennie still entertained hopes of collecting from Caffery. However, her legal action against him, like earlier suits, was not decided in her favor.[22]

Despite the confused and complicated state of Robert Jr.'s affairs at his death in 1926, he left considerable property in Lafourche, Terrebonne, Jefferson, and Orleans parishes. In Terrebonne the family owned R. R. Barrow, Inc., and Myrtle Grove, Inc., the family agricultural corporations. The few remnants of B & L No. 2 property in Terrebonne Parish were valued at only $883.31. The dredge boat tied up in Bayou Terrebonne 5 miles below Houma, and described as being in bad shape, was appraised at only $500. Other vessels were apparently in an advanced state of disrepair. The *Contrary*, a sternwheel boat, was appraised at only $500. The *Brer Rabbit* was valued at only $50 and the *Zoe*, also a small launch, at only $25.

In Jefferson Parish Robert Jr. left a few small pieces of real estate. Independence Island, his little vacation hideaway in Barataria Bay that he bought in 1915, was appraised at $400. He also owned several lots on Grand Isle that were worth a total of $500; he had bought these in 1884. In Orleans Parish he owned the family house on St. Charles Avenue. In Lafourche his holdings amounted to $13,220,

21. Jennie Barrow to Collector of Internal Revenue, March 5, 1926, in box "1926," RRBP. See box 9, folder 10, box 17, folders 4, 6, BFP, for details of the family finances. *Milling* v. *Succession of Barrow* (1930), 129 So 134.
22. See box 9, folder 10, box 14, folder 10, BFP, for details of the legal struggle with Caffery.

mostly for portions of the Company Canal east of Bayou Lafourche that the U.S. government had not bought. He also owned land contiguous to the Company Canal east of Bayou Lafourche. Zoe Topping and Hallette Cole had bills outstanding against the estate in the amount of $9,080, mostly for legal fees, burial expenses, and ordinary debts that had not been paid. On July 22, 1926, Zoe Topping bought six pieces of Company Canal property in Lafourche Parish at a sheriff's sale for $9,150.[23]

Jennie Barrow's financial woes continued. In 1926 the Lower Terrebonne Refining and Manufacturing Company, which bought cane from the Barrows, was experiencing financial difficulties. Eventually the mill failed, and its holdings became a part of South Coast Corporation, a large sugar corporation. Lower Terrebonne offered Jennie a compromise price of $4,500 for her cane crop, but on the advice of her lawyer, Robert Milling, she turned down the offer as insufficient. Anticipating further legal action against the refining company, Milling asked Jennie to send him a copy of the contract she had negotiated with the refinery.[24]

Elton Darsey, a Houma attorney who represented the Barrow heirs for many years, credited Hallette Barrow Cole for salvaging the remnants of the Barrow estate. She was a good businesswoman, Darsey felt, who held on to the family property despite mortgage foreclosures and tax sales. Once, when offered a compromise settlement in federal court over income taxes, Hallette told Darsey to refuse the government offer. In a style indicating that she had inherited some Barrow traits, she told Darsey to tell them, "Hell no." She no longer had the problem of running the Company Canal; Uncle Sam had taken over that role. The Barrow canal era had ended.[25] Since Robert Barrow, Jr., left no male heirs, the family name, too, soon faded into oblivion except for a few place-names to remind local residents of the once proud Barrow agricultural and canal ventures.

23. Jefferson Parish Succession, Gretna, La., No. 1720 (Copy in box 17, folder 6, BFP); Lafourche Parish Conveyance Book, Thibodaux, La., 58, fol. 175.
24. Robert E. Milling to Jennie Barrow, February 17, 27, 1926, both in box 9, folder 8, BFP.
25. Elton Darsey, interview with author, Houma, La., February 18, 1985.

Epilogue: The Intracoastal Canal System Today

The long Barrow association with canals ended with the sale of the Company Canal to the U.S. government in 1925. Robert Barrow, Jr., died in 1926. Even though he left no male heirs to carry on the family name, his daughters displayed the pugnacity and tenacity of their father and their grandfather, who first acquired the Barataria and Lafourche Canal Company No. 2 before the Civil War. Robert Jr.'s widow and four daughters no longer owned the canal, but they held on to plantations in Terrebonne Parish purchased by Robert Ruffin Barrow over a hundred years earlier.

The Company Canal was different from most U.S. canals. Chartered originally in 1829, the B & L failed to turn a profit during the heyday of canals in this country. Yet it continued to operate, mainly because of the tenacity of two generations of stubborn Barrows. When canals were falling into disuse during the 1850s, the B & L was receiving construction grants from the state of Louisiana. Financial losses eventually forced the state to withdraw support from the venture. Even the Civil War and Reconstruction, however, did not cause Robert Barrow to give up his hope of making the Company Canal a profitable business. His dream did not come true; his canal generally had fallen into disuse or had been sold piecemeal at tax sales in Lafourche, Terrebonne, and Jefferson parishes before he died. During the difficult years of the 1880s, Robert Jr. reacquired rights to the canal and struggled to put it back into operation. By the turn of the century, Robert Jr. had not only revamped the canal once considered an anachronism but also made it profitable.

During the heyday of steamboats in the 1840s and 1850s, shippers came to realize a painful fact about Louisiana's natural waterways and canals: They were not navigable the year round. Streams always accessible to pirogues or flatboats could not necessarily accommodate large river steamboats during low water. A variety of obstacles impeded water transportation: sandbars, shoals, snags, water hyacinths, crevasses, and wrecks. Even in an age of states' rights, many southern politicians wanted the U.S. Corps of Engineers to perform the difficult and expensive task of improving navigation on Louisiana streams.

The astute sweeping generalizations in Robert Wiebe's *The Search for Order, 1877–1920* about the ever-increasing role of the federal government in the lives of citizens applied to the Company Canal from the 1890s to the 1920s. Gone by then were the remote island communities isolated from other settlements that the elder Barrow and his associates attempted to link through the Company Canal during the transportation revolution. By and large they failed to achieve their goal, even though they received considerable financial assistance from the state of Louisiana. Shortly before the Civil War, the Company Canal became a private toll canal, which Robert Barrow acquired and somehow held on to even through the Civil War and Reconstruction.

Robert Barrow, Jr., pieced together the B & L No. 2 in the 1880s and made it a profitable venture. Like his father, he capitalized on government aid—in this case, from the U.S. Corps of Engineers. Ironically, canal building, long past its zenith in the United States, had declined as early as 1840, when railroads threatened to make canals extinct. No major canals were built from 1840 to 1860; during the 1850s there were more abandonments than initiations of new projects. Nationwide approximately 3,326 miles of canals had been constructed prior to 1840. Some failed because they could not compete with railroads, which provided fast, cheap transportation to many remote sections of the country. Others declined because of poor management or poor planning that made them obsolete before they were even completed.

As Wiebe's study confirms, the Corps of Engineers played an expanding role in improving navigation after Reconstruction. After the great Mississippi River flood of 1927, the Corps assumed overall supervision of the entire Mississippi Valley levee protection system as well. The Corps also built and maintained a modern intracoastal canal waterway.[1]

By the 1920s privately owned toll canals were viewed generally as a vestige of the past that had no place in twentieth-century America. The idea of paying tolls to use waterways conflicted with the concept of the general welfare and seemed incongruous in an age of comprehensive tax programs for roads, bridges, and other public means of transportation. It became increasingly difficult for owners of toll canals to maintain exclusive control over antiquated, but strategically located, waterways. These private waterways eventually became free public canals, maintained and improved by the U.S. government.

The automobile age accentuated new problems for private canals. Albert Fishlow's study of internal transportation in the United States is an important complement to George Taylor and Robert Wiebe. Fishlow's work updated transportation studies and explained what befell the Company Canal and other toll canals after the turn of the century. The problem was money. Fishlow discovered that a large percentage of all capital invested in the United States in the nineteenth century went into transportation, but that only 15 percent or less of total capital investment went into transportation facilities during the heyday of trucks and busses in the twentieth century. This was true in part because canals and railroads built before the turn of the century remained in use. Significantly, Fishlow noted that taxes and license fees levied on trucks have helped to maintain modern highways, but canals had no broadly based consumption component to tax.[2]

Almost immediately after buying the Harvey Canal in 1924, the Corps of Engineers made significant changes. It spent $11,614 that first year for surveying, improving locks, and dredging. It removed

1. Robert Wiebe, *The Search for Order, 1877–1920* (New York, 1962).
2. Albert Fishlow, "Internal Transportation," in Lance Davis *et al.*, *American Economic Growth: An Economist's History of the United States* (New York, 1972), 531, 546.

some tenants from the old Harvey Canal property and demolished some old buildings. Most of the 1,116 boats that used the locks that year transported shrimp, oysters, vegetables, sugar, crossties, and logs. Commerce between New Orleans and Bayou Teche in 1925 was 166,501 tons, valued at nearly $13 million.

The modern Gulf Intracoastal Waterway system came into existence after the Barrow and Harvey interests sold out to the U.S. government. At first it included parts of both old toll canals. It followed the Harvey route from New Orleans to Bayou Lafourche at Larose. Then it coursed upstream to Lockport, where it followed the Company Canal route to Bayou Terrebonne near Bourg via Lake Field, Lake Long, and the old Belanger canal. It proceeded up Bayou Terrebonne to Houma and followed the new cut connecting Bayou Terrebonne to Bayou Black at the lower end of the great loop that stream makes in Houma about a half-mile below Barrow's old canal.

The intracoastal canal grew and improved. The Corps's 1925 annual report explained, "The elimination of tolls, the removal of an obstructive bridge, and the repairs to the locks have noticeably increased commerce." (The obstruction was a steel girder bridge just below the Harvey Canal locks.) During the second year of operation, 3,892 boats used the locks and 5,890 used the canal but did not go through the locks.[3] In 1929 the canal carried 2,435 passengers and 34,213 tons of commerce, valued at $14.3 million.

Before long the Corps was making annual improvements. It widened and improved the locks on the Mississippi River and deepened the canal to accommodate large diesel tugs used to push oil barges and drilling barges. The Corps later completed the shortcut contemplated by the Harvey Canal company at the time of the sale to the government: a cut from Larose across the marsh to Bayou Terrebonne near Bourg, eliminating the detour on Bayou Lafourche to Lockport. Eventually the Corps abandoned the route through Lockport, which caused navigational hazards because of sharp bends and traffic jams on Louisiana Highway 1 when pontoon bridges opened for boats. West of Houma the Corps dug the canal south of Bayou Black, which it bypassed altogether. However, the Corps acquiesced

3. Chief Engineer, U.S. Corps of Engineers, Annual Report, 1925, Pt. 1, pp. 856, 858.

to local demands and routed the intracoastal canal through Houma. This proved to be a costly mistake that has not been rectified totally even today. The Corps also tied Baton Rouge to the intracoastal canal by making a dry-land cut from the Mississippi River at Port Allen to Bayou Plaquemine, which connects to the Atchafalaya River.

Political factors figured prominently in the Corps's purchasing the Company Canal and the Harvey Canal, as well as in its improving and maintaining the route after acquiring it. Local political leaders pressured the Corps to choose an impractical route. Their motive was a genuine, but nonetheless unrealistic, fear that if their communities were bypassed by the intracoastal canal, they were doomed to suffer economic ruin and become ghost towns.

Special interest groups banded together in Lake Charles, Louisiana, and formed the Intracoastal Waterway Association, an articulate lobby dedicated to influencing the Corps of Engineers on inland waterway matters. The association hired René Clerc, a Washington, D.C., lobbyist. Clerc wanted to run the canal through Houma, but he faced formidable opposition from W. B. Smith, chief of the operations division of the Corps, who favored locating the intracoastal canal south of Houma. The offer of a free access route across Presquille plantation, below Houma, strengthened Smith's recommendation: The southern route had the advantage of being economically feasible and geographically sound.

However, the Corps rejected this route. Elton Darsey, the Houma attorney who for years represented the Barrow heirs, contends that the Dupont family had convinced political leaders to follow René Clerc's advice to route the canal through town. Albert Dupont and later his son Julius, wealthy businessmen and landowners, were prime movers in the drive to keep the canal in town. Darsey believed that they and local political interests were misinformed; indeed, their persistence eventually cost taxpayers and the U.S. government millions of dollars for a transportation system that inconvenienced townspeople and caused irreparable damage to the ecology of Terrebonne Parish.

Darsey, who worked for the Corps of Engineers as a file clerk before graduating from law school, had access to correspondence concerning the location of the canal in Terrebonne Parish. Those who favored the route through town, he felt, underestimated the number of families living along the proposed route that would have to be relocated at government expense. Nor had they considered the costs of constructing bridges; of placing sewer, gas, and water pipes under the canal; or of running power lines high above the canal. Most assuredly, they de-emphasized navigational and traffic problems created by the waterway coursing through town. An expensive tunnel under the canal in Houma has only partially solved traffic congestion created by the waterway.

Later the Corps constructed a ship canal connecting the Gulf of Mexico to the intracoastal canal. The ship canal, built at the behest of local businessmen, has served the interests of the modern seafood and oil industries well, but it has caused ecological problems by facilitating the flow of salt water into the fragile brackish coastal marsh. The intrusion of salt water into formerly freshwater marsh has contributed to the destruction of Louisiana's delicate coastline. Wetlands in Terrebonne have deteriorated rapidly. Tropical storms send tidal surges, walls of water sometimes 15 feet high, far into the interior of the parish via man-made channels. Thus the problem remains of balancing public good versus short-range economic expediency. How legislators resolve the dilemma remains to be seen. Local political leaders have asked the U.S. Corps of Engineers to study the problem.

In the 1980s the Gulf Intracoastal Waterway continues to be a viable means of transportation. It is a flourishing route used principally by the modern oil and seafood industries of the Gulf Coast states. Neither the modern railroad nor diesel-powered trucks have made canals obsolete. They still perform an important function by carrying freight across Louisiana's marshy terrain. The volume of traffic, both in number and in tonnage, is impressive.

The Barrows were truly the founders of the inland waterway system. Their determination helped make the canal a reality. Darsey considered Robert Barrow, Jr., "a man of foresight." For years Robert Jr.'s Company Canal had been a more viable transportation system than the railroad, which sometimes could not prevent people from tampering with merchandise. According to Darsey, the Bradford Towing Company and the Daigle Barge Line provided reliable shipping service to New Orleans through the Company Canal. Robert Jr. used political clout to protect his interests. Like his father, he benefited by championing the cause of better public transportation in the name of the general welfare.

The two generations of Barrow men were remarkably similar. Both enjoyed normal married family life and gloated over their children for a number of years, but each ruled his family with an iron fist. Neither divorced, but both father and son were legally separated from their spouses late in life, and both became embroiled in heated family disputes over community property, place of residence, and inheritance. Both argued emotionally with children over property and successions. Both were heavily in debt, but each managed to leave disgruntled heirs at least a portion of the financial empire he had acquired.

Both father and son were quick to express opinions, even unpopular ones, which they defended rambunctiously. They wrote lengthy diatribes, usually directed against those they suspected had done them wrong. Neither was erudite, but each was quick to voice his beliefs in a forceful, ungrammatical style that clearly stated his position. The Barrows wrote letters to editors and published book-length treatises, at times, simply to show their neighbors they were right.

In money matters they were ruthless. They speculated in land and made risky investments, usually on credit, and they became masters at avoiding creditors. They hounded those who owed them money, posturing frequently on the ethics of paying one's just debts. Both engaged in complicated rigged sales with relatives to evade creditors. Mortgages, notes, and complicated business arrangements were normal features of their existence. Obfuscation often was their goal, for it was another device to thwart creditors. They sold and resold property, formed partnerships, mortgaged property and cancelled mortgages, signed notes, and kept all but close associates confused about their true intentions. They became embroiled in many disputes that ended in lawsuits. At different times and under different circumstances, each was threatened by irate Terrebonne Parish citizens with firearms. No rugged individualists when it came to accepting subsidies from state or national governments, the Barrows always proclaimed an interest in the general welfare, even though they considered the Company Canal their private sanctuary.

The Barrows were never popular, but they considered themselves gentlemen and claimed to live by a rather vaguely defined gentleman's code. For them this code was malleable and flexible, but for their adversaries, real or imaginary, the rigid rules were etched in stone and not to be violated. The Barrows always saw conspiracies about them; their problems were never the result of their own ignorance or greed, but of the viciousness of those who were jealous of their success. Both enjoyed the finer things of life: travel, fine homes, nice clothing, and opportunities for leisurely relaxation.

Today Louisiana industries ship products to market on a canal system that owes its start to the tenacity of two generations of Barrows. Robert Ruffin and his son, Robert Jr., were among the first investors to realize the viability of water transportation during the railroad era and afterward. They were steadfast on the idea of completing the Company Canal from the Mississippi River to Bayou Teche. Aggressive to a fault, both father and son displayed a ruthless business sense. They were strident, energetic, bellicose, irascible, truculent, stubborn, petulant, and not surprisingly, unpopular, but their foresight and determination paved the way for the Gulf Intracoastal Waterway traversing Louisiana today.

Bibliographical Essay

Only the most significant works that contributed directly to this study are mentioned here. Readers should also refer to the footnotes for a listing of all materials consulted. The principal materials for this study are primary manuscript sources: two sets of Barrow papers and also public records of the U.S. Congress; the U.S. Supreme Court; the U.S. Corps of Engineers; the Supreme Court of Louisiana; various state agencies and boards; and the parishes of Terrebonne, Lafourche, St. Mary, Orleans, and Jefferson. Often the writings of the Barrows themselves provided invaluable insights and perspectives. Even though the Barrows were biased observers, they kept voluminous records of their economic and personal lives. They did not hesitate to state a position, bluntly and usually ungrammatically.

Manuscripts

A major source of information was the Robert Ruffin Barrow, Jr., Papers, owned by the Terrebonne Museum, which is administered by the Terrebonne Historical and Cultural Society, Inc. The collection is on indefinite loan to the Division of Archives, Nicholls State University Library, Thibodaux, Louisiana. It contains valuable material about the family, the Company Canal, agriculture over a long time span, and Louisiana politics.

Another important collection is the Robert R. Barrow Family Papers, housed in the Manuscripts Section, Howard-Tilton Memorial Library, Tulane University, New Orleans. This collection complements the Terrebonne Museum holdings and contains correspondence, photographs, copies of laws, contracts, and many other personal and business papers.

The Allen J. Ellender Papers, housed at Nicholls State University, contain some information on the Barrows. Ellender was Robert Jr.'s attorney, transacting sales for him and representing him in legal action against his wife in the mid-1920s.

The Taylor Beattie Diaries provide information about agriculture and navigation and indicate a business partner's attitude toward the Barrows. As a judge, Beattie rendered decisions affecting the Barrows.

Smaller manuscript collections add bits and pieces of information about remote associates and business partners. The Louisiana Collection of the Howard-Tilton Memorial Library, Tulane University, contains the pamphlet that Robert Barrow published during the secession controversy in 1861. The Historic New Orleans Collection, 533 Royal Street, New Orleans, has some information on early investors in the Barataria and Lafourche Canal Company, as does the Brashear Collection in the Morgan City Archives, housed in the Morgan City Public Library. The Henry Dart Papers in the Manuscript Division of the Earl K. Long Library at the University of New Orleans provides some information on the Harvey Canal, the main rival of the B & L.

Public Documents

Public records in the parishes of Terrebonne, Lafourche, St. Mary, Jefferson, and Orleans provide considerable information about the family and the Company Canal. Conveyance records are particularly useful on financial matters; civil suits, marriage records, and probate records reveal information about marriages, separations, children, successions, and the like.

Federal documents are most useful on navigational matters pertaining to rivers, bayous, canals, locks, and the like. The annual reports of the chief engineer of the U.S. Corps of Engineers are a gold mine of information on remote streams and waterways. House and Senate documents describe legislation and appropriations affecting these streams.

Records of state agencies in Louisiana are important for the antebellum period. The annual reports of the state engineer, the board of public works, and various levee boards and drainage districts all provide useful information about navigational problems. Legal decisions rendered by the Louisiana Supreme Court frequently dealt with the Barrows, who were involved not only in many suits but also in countless appeals. The official records of the Constitutional Convention of 1898, of which Robert Barrow, Jr., was a member, shed some light on his thinking.

Interviews

Interviews with acquaintances of Robert Barrow, Jr., provide information about his personality but only hint at his marital problems late in life. A series of tape-recorded interviews conducted by the Terrebonne Parish Library in conjunction with the Terrebonne Historical and Cultural Society is a valuable source of information on life in the early days of settlement. Called the Oral History of Terrebonne (OHT), it is a part of the Terrebonne Parish Public Library, Houma, Louisiana, and is available to researchers and students. Its index and cross-reference guide make it invaluable for local history.

Elton Darsey participated in the OHT and granted personal interviews to the author. Darsey served as attorney for the Barrows for many years and worked for the Corps of Engineers.

Some citizens of Terrebonne Parish who did not participate in the OHT granted interviews to the author. Madison L. Funderburk, a prominent Terrebonne banker, knew Robert Barrow, Jr., and the principals in the intracoastal canal controversy in Houma. Randolph A. Bazet served as clerk of court for Terrebonne Parish for many years. A man of many talents, Bazet knew history, politics, and geography, as well as much about science.

Books, Articles, and Dissertations

Even though the Barrows were wealthy and well known in their days, surprisingly little has been written about them. The most useful works are William Barrow Floyd, *The Barrow Family of Old Louisiana* (Lexington, Ky., 1963); Joseph K. Menn, *The Large Slaveholders of Louisiana, 1860* (New Orleans, 1964); P. A. Champomier, *Statement of the Sugar Crop in Louisiana* (New Orleans, 1844–62); and G. W. Pierce, "Historical and Statistical Collection of Louisiana—Terrebonne," *De Bow's Review*, XI (July, 1851–January, 1852).

Travel accounts during the colonial period bring to life the transportation problems of the age and explain the need for the B & L. Among the most useful are those published in *Louisiana History*, in *De Bow's Review*, and in various collections. James Cathcart, Daniel Dennett, Amos Stoddard, and Timothy Flint all described the miseries of early travel across Sugar Country. See, for example, Daniel Dennett, *Louisiana as It Is* (New Orleans, 1876); Amos Stoddard, *Sketches Historical and Descriptive, of Louisiana* (Philadelphia, 1812); and Timothy Flint, "Timothy Flint's Louisiana," in Glenn Conrad (ed.), *Readings in Louisiana History* (New Orleans, 1978).

Geographic studies, both scientific and amateur, add to our knowledge of canals cutting across the wetlands of south Louisiana. They include the following works: *Biographical and Historical Memoirs of Louisiana* (2 vols., Chicago, 1982); Malcolm Comeaux, *Atchafalaya Swamp Life: Settlement and Folk Occupations* (Baton Rouge, 1972); Albert Cowdrey, *Land's End: A History of the New Orleans District, U.S. Corps of Engineers* (N.p., 1977); Donald Davis, "Louisiana Canals and Their Influence on Wetland Development" (Ph.D. dissertation, Louisiana State University, 1973); Edwin Davis (ed.), *The Rivers and Bayous of Louisiana* (Baton Rouge, 1968), which contains, among other useful chapters, Robert M. Crisler, "Bayou Teche," and Philip Uzee, "Bayou Lafourche"; Fred B. Kniffen, *Louisiana: Its Land and People* (Baton Rouge, 1968); Barnes Lathrop, "The Pugh Plantations, 1860–1865: A Study of Life in Lower Louisiana" (Ph.D. dissertation, University of Texas, 1946); Donald J. Millet, "The Saga of Water Transportation into Southwest Louisiana to 1900," *Louisiana History*, XV (Fall, 1974), 339–56; Walter Pritchard *et al.* (eds.), "Southern Louisiana and Southern Alabama in 1819: The Journal of James Leander Cathcart," *Louisiana Historical Quarterly*, XXVIII (July, 1945), 735–921; Betsy Swanson, *Historic Jefferson Parish: From Shore to Shore* (Gretna, La., 1975); Philip Uzee (ed.), *The Lafourche Country: The People and the Land* (Lafayette, La., 1985), a particularly useful chapter of which is Richard Weinstein and Sherman Gagliano, "The Shifting Deltaic Coast of the Lafourche Country and Its Prehistoric Settlement."

Virtually no secondary works discuss the B & L. On the waterborne commerce of New Orleans and environs, the most helpful works are John G. Clark, *New Orleans 1718–1812: An Economic History* (Baton Rouge, 1970); Nancy M. Miller Surrey, *The Commerce of Louisiana During the French Regime, 1699–1763* (New York, 1916); and Allie Bayne W. Webb (ed.), *Mistress of Evergreen Plantation: Rachel O'Connor's Legacy of Letters, 1823–1845* (Albany, N.Y., 1983).

Important works on American economic history and life provide a framework into which this study falls. The most important of these works are discussed in the Prologue and Epilogue. Among the most stimulating are Albert Fishlow, "Internal Transportation," in Lance Davis *et al.*, *American Economic Growth: An Economist's History of the United States* (New York, 1972); Carter Goodrich, *Government Promotion of American Canals and Railroads, 1800–1890* (New York, 1960); George Taylor, *The Transportation Revolution, 1815–1860* (New York, 1962); and Robert Wiebe, *The Opening of American Society from the Adoption of the Constitution to the Eve of Disunion* (New York, 1984) and *The Search for Order, 1877–1920* (New York, 1967). In addition, John C. L. Andreason, "Internal Improvements in Louisiana, 1824–1837," *Louisiana Historical Quarterly*, XXX (January, 1947), and Merl E. Reed, *New Orleans and the Railroads* (Baton Rouge, 1966), provide a Louisiana perspective on the national movement. Robert Fogel, *Railroads and American Economic Growth: Essays in Economic History* (Baltimore, 1964), provides material against which to weigh the Louisiana situation. J. Carlyle Sitterson, *Sugar Country: The Cane Sugar Industry in the South, 1753–1950* (Lexington, Ky., 1953); Joe G. Taylor, *Louisiana Reconstructed, 1863–1877* (Baton Rouge, 1974) and *Negro Slavery in Louisiana* (Baton Rouge, 1963); and works cited in footnote 10, Chapter 3, explain the political and economic setting in Louisiana during various phases of this study.

Newspapers did not provide a great deal of material for this study, but occasionally they are the only source of information on remote incidents or people.

Index

Abolition of slavery, 71–72
Acadiana, 20
Acadians, 26, 32
Acts of Louisiana legislature: Act 41 (1829), 45; Act 22 (1831), 47; Act 3 (1833), 47; Act 58 (1835), 50; Act 172 (1843), 56; Act 78 (1846), 56; Acts 236 and 320 (1850), 57; Act 236 (1852), 61; Act 331 (1853), 62; Act 215 (1857), 65; Act 205 (1858), 65; Act 139 (1877), 86
Adams, John Quincy, 5
Afton Villa plantation, 13
Agrarian myth, 67–68
Agricultural expansion, 2, 11
American system, 5
Ames crevasse, 105
Andry, Louis, 32
Ashland plantation, 128
Atchafalaya Basin and Lafourche Basin Levee District, 122–23, 125
Atchafalaya River: history of, 19–20, 24–25, 34; and Old River route, 31, 42, 115; mentioned *passim*
Atchafalaya Swamp: problems of, 22; routes across, 31–36, 45, 119
Atchafalaya (vessel), 65
Attakapas Canal, 31, 33, 35, 39
Attakapas District: isolation of, 31; routes to, 31–36, 46
Attakapas Steamboat Company, 36
Avondale, 135

Badeaux, Thomas, 123
B & L. *See* Barataria and Lafourche Canal Company; Barataria and Lafourche Canal Company No. 2
Barataria, Bayou, 28
Barataria and Lafourche Canal Company: charter of, 41, 45; envisioned, 42; state support of, 45–46, 47, 50–52, 64; failure of, 62–65; sale of, 68–69
Barataria and Lafourche Canal Company No. 2: organized, 68–69; leased, 85–91; profits of, 116, 132–33; report on, 122; viability of, 124–25, 184; locks of, 125; completion of, 133; bridges of, 167, 168; characterized, 182–83
Barataria Bay, 28
Barker, Alex: feud with Robert Barrow, Jr., 163; and Southern Pacific Railroad, 163; and Barrow pamphlet, 164
Barker, Benjamin, 12
Barker, Charles, 112
Barrow, Ascension Slatter, 13
Barrow, Bartholomew, 13
Barrow, David Bennett, 13
Barrow, Hallette. *See* Cole, Hallette Barrow
Barrow, Irene, 104
Barrow, Jennie. *See* Dawson, Jennie Barrow

Index

Barrow, Jennie Tennent, 103–106, 173, 175, 176, 178, 180
Barrow, Roberta. *See* Slatter, Roberta Barrow
Barrow, Robert Ruffin: wealth of, 3, 15, 70, 94; as Whig, 7, 51, 70; to Louisiana, 13–14; wife of, 13; children of, 14; sketch of, 14; unpopularity of, 15, 17; on secession and Civil War, 16, 78–81; writings of, 71–72, 76; separation of, 77; on leasing the B & L No. 2, pp. 85–91; hid ownership of B & L No. 2, p. 88; decline of, 95; will of, 95; death of, 96
Barrow, Robert Ruffin, Jr.: and Robert Wiebe, 3, 7–8, 37, 130, 183–84, 194; birth of, 14; disputes with his father, 91–93, 94, 102; similarities to father, 93, 101, 108, 111, 161, 169–70, 171, 179, 183, 188–89; feuds with Roberta, 102–103; and Jennie Tennent, 103–106; children of, 104; and B & L No. 2, pp. 106–31, 183; writings of, 106, 125–26, 148, 164; wealth of, 116, 117, 132–33, 160, 180; worries of, 117–18, description of, 117; and Duplantis, 117, 168–69; social clubs, 117, 170, 197; and railroads, 119, 134–36; and Houma, 149; conspiracy theories of, 152, 167, 170; generosity of, 161; and Alex Barker, 163–65; feuds with Whipple brothers, 165–66; health of, 169–72; and financial setback, 170–72, 174; and Stella Leathers, 172; and R. R. Barrow, Inc., 173, 176–77; separation of, 174–75; will of, 177–78; death of, 179
Barrow, Ruffin C., 69, 78, 79, 80–81, 102
Barrow, Volumnia Hunley: sketch of, 15; defense of husband, 72–73; separation of, 77; death of, 78; on Confederacy, 81; will of, 92
Barrow, William Bennett, 13
Barrow, Zoe. *See* Topping, Zoe Barrow
Bascle, A. J., 111
Bassett, J. L., 167
Bazet, Randolph, 192
Beach, Lansing, 129, 140, 151
Bearce, Horace M., 87–89
Beattie, Taylor: and Lafourche and Terrebonne Navigation Company, 46, 56; and mortgage of B & L No. 2, pp. 85, 90; on weather, 124

Beauregard, P. G. T., 75
Belanger canal, 43
Bell, John, 72
Bergen, Peter, 93
Bienville, Jean-Baptiste LeMoyne, 22
Bisland, William, 17
Black, Bayou: and B & L, 43, 52, 83, 107–108; navigability of, 53–55, 119
Board, James W., 95, 95–98
Board of Public Works, 50
Boeuf, Bayou, 23, 52
Bond, Howard, 68
Bond, Joshua, 68
Bonnet Carré crevasse, 86
Bonvillain, A. J., 136, 171
Boston Club, 117, 170
Bouligny, Francisco, 32, 35, 47
Bourg, C. J., 156
Boykin & Lang v. *W. A. Shaffer*, 56–57
Bradford Towing Company, 128, 164, 187
Brashear, Dr. Walter, 35, 41
Brashear City. *See* Morgan City
Brer Rabbit (vessel), 161, 178, 180
Brown, John, 71
Buisson, Benjamin, 52, 53, 54
Bureau of Freedmen and Abandoned Lands, 77
Burnside, John, 14
Bush, H. G., 128
Butler, Benjamin, 87
Butte la Rose, 24, 33

Caffery, Donelson, 176, 178–79, 180
Cage, D. S., 109, 152
Caillou Grove plantation, 85
Calhoun, John C., 5
Canals: and east-to-west problems, 27, 160–61; problems of, 38–39; and the economy, 41–43; and railroads, 61
Cancienne Canal, 125
Carroll, Charles, 111
Cathcart, James Leander, 34–35, 47
Chamberlain, A. F., 87–89
Chawasha Indians, 26
Chêne, Bayou, 23
Chênière Caminada, 114
Chitimacha Indians, 22
Civil War: and B & L No. 2, pp. 73–76; financial problems of, 84–85
Clerc, René, 186
Climax (vessel), 163
Coignet, J. A., 158

Cole, Christian, 175–76
Cole, Hallette Barrow, 104, 173, 181
Company Canal. *See* Barataria and Lafourche Canal Company; Barataria and Lafourche Canal Company No. 2
Conner, C. R., 79
Connor, James, 14
Constitutions of 1845 and 1852, p. 61
Contrary (vessel), 180
Conway, Thomas, 77
Corps of Engineers: role of, 8, 53, 54, 64, 84, 87, 107–108, 118–23, 183; and intracoastal concept, 118; buying out old canals, 121; and hyacinths, 137–38; mentioned *passim*
Cotton, 11
Coulon, Charles, 123
Courtableau, Bayou, 30, 31, 36
Crescent Club, 117, 170
Crosby, O. T., 119, 121, 122

Daigle Barge Line, 162, 187
Darsey, Elton, 181n, 186, 187, 192
Dart, Henry, 143, 155, 165
Daspit, Oscar, 126
Davis, George, 68
Davis crevasse, 124
Dawson, Harris P., 14, 105, 161, 167
Dawson, Jennie Barrow, 161
Dawson, Sarah, 14
De Bow, James, 27
De Bow's Review, 15, 53, 60, 62
Delaporte, Alfred, 68
Deltas, 19–26
Dennett, Daniel, 33
Dent, E. J., 151, 153
Derbigny, Charles: sketch of, 41–42; and the B & L, 46, 48–49, 50; donation of, 48
Derbigny, Pierre, 41
Des Allemands, Bayou, 63
Destrehan, Nicholas Noël, 30, 142
Destrehan canal, 30
D'Hèmecourt, Allen, 49
Dillard, Josh, 168
Douglas, H. S., 109, 142
Dowman, Robert H., 139
Dressner, J. M., 127–28, 167–68
Dreux, J. G., 73, 74, 113
Dubreuil, Claude Joseph Villars, 28
Dubreuil's canal, 28, 45
Dunbar, George, 54
Duplantis, Caliste, 168

Duplantis, Henry Clay, 168–69
Dupont, Albert, 186
Dupont, Julius, 186

Easton, Tris, 152–53
Ellender, Allen J., 155, 171, 176
Ellender, Ernest, 141
Ellenders, 13, 156
Ellis, Richard, 48
Eminent domain, 126
Erie Canal, 5, 37–38
Experiment (vessel), 54

Falgout, A. J., 133, 158
Falgout, Marcelin, 111
Farragut, David, 73, 74, 113
Fayport Planting Company, 156
Fazend, F., 45
Fazend, John, 82
Field, William, 43, 49
Field, Lake, 43, 47, 49, 50, 59
Fish, W. L., 130
Fishlow, Albert, 8, 184
Fisk, J., 93
Flint, Timothy, 36
Flu epidemic, 104, 168
Fogel, Robert, 69–70
Foret, Michel, 115
Foucher, Antoine, 28
Franklin, La., 33, 36
Franklin *Planters' Banner*, 33
Frossard, Frederick, 116
Funderburk, Madison L., 156, 173n, 192

Gagné, Harris: attorney, 132; agent, 132, 139; sale of B & L No. 2, p. 150; and Robert Barrow, Jr., 174
Gaidry, J. Wilfred, 127
Gallatin, Albert, 5
Gardère, François, 28
Gardère Canal, 28
Gas Light and Banking Company of New Orleans, 50
Gayoso de Lemos, Don Manuel, 103
Gayoso plantation, 123
Gayoso ridge, 166
Gibbons v. *Ogden*, 57
Gibson, Randall L., 110
Glynn, Tim, 138, 158
Goode, F. S., 18, 67, 76, 93, 111
Goodrich, Carter, 4–5, 6–7, 51
Grand Isle, 114, 180
Grant Smith and Company, 138

Gulf Intracoastal Waterway. *See* Intracoastal canal

Hall, W. A., 91
Harang, Alexandre, 30
Harang's canal, 30, 125, 142
Harris, J. B., 54
Harvey, Horace, 155
Harvey, Joseph Hale, 30, 143
Harvey Canal: history of, 30, 120–21, 142–44; and B & L No. 2, pp. 139–40; report on, 144–48, 151, 165; sold, 154–55
Harvey Canal and Land Development Company, 155
Harvey Canal, Land and Improvement Company, 165
Hébert, Louis, 64
Hébert, Paul, 62
Hennessey, David, 105
Henry Tate (vessel), 120
Heuer, W. H., 119, 121, 122
Higgins, A. J., 150
H. L. Hunley (submarine), 73
Honduras plantation, 102, 126
Hornsby, James, 68
Hornsby, Sam, 68
Houma: history of, 13; canal across, 43, 53, 56, 109–10, 129–30, 145; population of, 43; bridges in, 168; intracoastal canal through, 186–87; mentioned *passim*
Houma *Ceres*, 73
Houma *Courier*, 141
Houma Indians, 26
Howard, Charles, 86
Humphreys, Joseph, 157–58
Hunley, Horace L., 14, 72, 73, 78
Hyacinth (vessel), 138
Hyacinth, water, 137–38
Hymelia crevasse, 166

Iberville Parish Police Jury, 83, 119
Independence Island, 23, 148, 178
Intracoastal canal: origins of, 114, 139–40; route of, 118; and other canals, 141; new route of, 147, 170–71; and the Harvey Canal, 184–85; today, 185, 187; through Houma, 186–87; mentioned *passim*
Intracoastal Waterway Association, 186
Isley, John, Jr., 97

Jeffersonian myth. *See* Agrarian myth
Jennie B (vessel), 127
Jennie Tennant Barrow v. *Donelson Caffery*, 180
Joe Webre (vessel), 114
Jones, Ludy, 79–80, 171
Juanita Club, 117, 170

Karstendiek, John A., 112
Kilona crevasse, 166
Knowlton, Ephrain: and B & L No. 2, p. 68; leasing canal, 84–85, 88–90; sketch of, 84–85
Krumbhaar, Charles, 141
Krumbhaars, 13

LaBranche, L., 45
LaCarpe, Bayou, 59
Laffite, Jean, 28
Lafourche, Bayou: history of, 22–24; navigability of, 63; damming of, 121, 123–24; locks on, 121
Lafourche and Terrebonne Navigation Company, 67, 84, 143
Lafourche Intercoastal Club, 141
Land reclamation, 128–29
Landridge, William, 113
Lapene, Jules, 95
Larkin, E. J., 138–39
Latham, F. W., 16
Laughland, G. L., 87, 90
Leathers, B. L., 172
Leathers, Stella, 172–74
LeBreton, Noël, 45, 48
LeCompte, Joseph, 129
Ledet, Charles A., 155
Lizzie Hopkins (vessel), 120
Locke, Samuel, 76
Lockport: founding of, 49; locks of, 54, 59–60, 83, 125; and B & L No. 2, pp. 127, 167; population of, 141–42; mentioned, 12, 63, 127
Lockport Central Sugar Factory, 129
Lockport (vessel), 163
Lodi (vessel), 18
Long, Lake, 43, 47
Longueville, 49
Lonn, Ella, 118
Lottinger, Lee P., 155
Louisiana Board of Public Works, 42
Louisiana Canal and Land Improvement Company, 85–91, 112

Louisiana Levee Company, 86
Louisiana lottery, 86
Louisiana Meadows Company, 129
Louisiana Rice, Prairie and Canal Co. Ltd., 127
Lovell, J. A., 156, 167
Lovell, Mansfield, 74
Lower Lafourche Barge Line, 163
Lower Terrebonne Refining and Manufacturing Company, 127–28, 181

Magnolia Cemetery, 179
McCollams, 13, 77, 152
McDonald, John, 17–18
Mallary, M. M., 172
Marshall, John, 57
Martin, François Xavier, 55, 56
Martin, Whitmell, 150–53, 166
Martin, Willie, 115
Masse, Clifton J., 133
May, George, 62
Maysville veto, 5
Merrick, C. J., 56
Meyer, Joseph, 61
Milling, Robert E., 149–50, 174, 181
Milling, Godchaux, Saal, and Milling, 149
Minor, William, 12, 68
Mississippi River: distributaries of, 19–25; deltas of, 19–20; locks on, 59, 74; mentioned *passim*
Mississippi River Commission, 130
Mississippi River–Old River–Atachafalaya River route, 31, 34, 42, 115
Moran, V., 123
Morgan, E. F., 130, 142
Morgan City, 24–25, 35, 41
Morris, John, 86
Morse, George, 59–60, 63–64
Mouton, Alexandre, 50
Myrtle Grove, Inc., 171, 176, 180
Myrtle Grove plantation: granted to Volumnia, 79, 85; purchased by John Pittman, 93–94; returned to Barrow children, 102; and broken mill, 106; profits from, 133; and Duplantis, 168–69; decline of, 176, 180

Nepotism, 51
Neville, Edmund, 13

New Orleans: trade center, 20, 22, 26, 27, 32, 36, 41, 50; flood in, 58; mentioned *passim*
New Orleans *Daily Picayune*, 71, 96
New Orleans Navigation Company, 55
New Orleans, Opelousas, and Great Western Railroad, 61, 75, 134–35
New Orleans *True Delta*, 71
Nicholls, Thomas Clark, 32–33
N. Lerille Fish and Oyster Company, 133
Nolan, William T., 179

Oak Grove plantation, 16, 81
O'Connor, Andrew, 18
Ogborn, Harry, 133, 178
Opelousas, 22, 25, 31
Opelousas Steamboat Company, 36

Panic of 1837, pp. 26, 50
Paynswick (vessel), 80
Pennington, W. R., 129, 166
Pennington Dredging Company, 146
Percy Lobdell Company, 162
Phelps, A. S., 63
Pichauff, Laurent, 48
Pierce, G. W., 15
Pioneer (submarine), 73
Pittman, John: arrived in Louisiana, 12; and Oak Grove plantation, 16, 81; and B & L No. 2, p. 68; and Civil War, 75, 84; and Barrow family business, 79, 93, 96–98; and will of, 79; and Ludy Jones, 79–80, 171
Plaquemine, Bayou: early use of, 31–32; damming of, 83, 119; locks on, 119–20
Population figures, 42–43, 108–109
Price, Joseph, 141, 156
Prince (slave), 14, 17
Pughs, 13

Raceland prairie, 128–29
Railroads: and Atchafalaya Swamp, 25; construction problems of, 39; competition with canals, 134; routes of, 135–36, 182; through-rate arrangements of, 136, 162; and east-west transportation, 160. *See also* specific lines
Ransdell, Joseph E., 140, 142, 154
Rathborne, Joseph, 143

Residence plantation, 14, 85, 102
Rights-of-way, 48, 64, 69, 115, 129, 137, 146, 151, 153, 156–57, 158
Roberta Grove plantation, 77, 93
Roman, Alexandre, 42
Rousseau, E., 52–53
Roxburgh, James L., 112
R. R. Barrow, Inc., 173, 176–177

Saint-Denis, Louis Juchereau de, 1
St. John, Bayou, 31
St. Matthew's Episcopal Church, 161
Salvador, Lake, 45, 147
Sampson (dredge), 109
Segnette, Bayou, 47, 123, 138, 146, 147, 154
Shaffer, William, 107
Shields, Thomas R., 16, 18, 49
Sidney, Henry, 98
Slatter, Roberta Barrow, 14, 77, 91–93
Slatter, William, 14, 88–89, 91, 97
Smith, A. V., 140
Smith, Benjamin, 68, 87–90
Smithport Planting Company, 128–29, 156
South Coast Corporation, 181
Southern Pacific Railroad, 124, 137, 142, 162
South Louisiana Canal and Navigation Company, 109, 143, 152
State of Louisiana v. *New Orleans Navigation Company*, 56
Stephens, Henry C., 82
Stoddard, Amos, 31–32
Sugar cultivation and production, 11, 170–71
Suthon, Hugh, 132, 139, 174
Suthon, Lucius Fane, 111, 132

Taney, Roger, 57
Tariff, 6, 70, 117
Taylor, George, 3, 184
Teche, Bayou, 20–22
Tennent, Charles, 102
Tennent, F. Gayoso, 111, 112, 113–14
Tennent, Jennie. *See* Barrow, Jennie Tennent
Terrebonne, Bayou, 56

Terrebonne Parish, 56
Texas and Pacific Railroad, 120
Thibodaux *Democrat*, 141
Thompson, P. H., 114–15
Topping, Robert, 104, 168
Topping, Zoe Barrow, 104, 161, 168, 171, 173, 176
Trainasses, 27
Transportation revolution, 2
"Trembling prairies," 39
Turtle, Thomas, 110

Vacherie ridge, 48
Verret, Lake, 31, 42
Villère, Jacques, 41–42
Voorhies, Albert, 111
Voorhies, C. A., 111

Walker, Joseph, 57
Wallace, J. E., 94
Washa Indians, 26
Washington, Henderson, 115
Waubun plantation, 141
Waverly crevasse, 122
Westwego, 47, 130
Westwego Canal and Terminal Company, Inc. 179
Whigs, 7, 51, 70
Whipple, Thomas, 166
Whipple brothers, 165–66
Whitehead, Frank, 164
Wickliffe, Robert, 65, 69
Wiebe, Robert, 3, 7–8, 37, 130, 183–84, 194
Winder, John, 113
Wisner, Edward, 129, 140
Witherspoon, William, 48
Wooldridge, Absalom D., 58–59
Wrotnowski, A. F., 86
Wurzlow, Calvin, 141
Wyat, Charles, 172

Yellow fever, 63

Zeringue, Camille, 45
Zeringue, Michel, 30
Zoe (vessel), 180